CLEAN ENERGY LAW AND REGULATION

Climate Change, Energy Union and International Governance

CLEAN ENERGY LAW AND REGULATION

Climate Change, Energy Union and International Governance

Edited by

Vicente López-Ibor Mayor

Wildy, Simmonds & Hill Publishing

Clean Energy Law and Regulation: Climate Change, Energy Union and International Governance

A catalogue record for this book is available from The British Library

ISBN 9780854902262

Wildy, Simmonds & Hill Publishing
58 Carey Street
London WC2A 2JF
England

www.wildy.com

Contents

II CLEAN ENERGY REGULATION AND
TECHNOLOGICAL CHANGE

CLEAN ENERGIES IN MÉXICO AFTER AND BEFORE THE LAST ENERGY REFORM

Francisco X. Salazar Diez de Sollano

RENEWABLE ENERGIES IN PERU

Alfredo Dammert L.

THE REGULATION OF RENEWABLE ENERGY IN LATIN AMERICA: THE EXPERIENCES OF BRAZIL AND MEXICO

Gabriel Cavazos Villanueva and Carolina Barros de Castro e Souza

Prologue

DANIEL CALLEJA

Director General for the Environment, European Commission

It is a great pleasure to present to you this new book "Green energy law".

The world needs to move towards green energy and Europe has a great role to play in this move. We need to switch to sustainable renewable energy - and energy efficiency - if we are to keep climate change within bearable limits, but we also need green energy to tackle other environmental challenges such as improving air quality. Moving to green energy will also bring us economic and social benefits.

Europe is at the forefront of this energy transition. Indeed, one of the ten priorities of European Commission President Juncker is to develop a resilient Energy Union with a forward-looking climate change policy. He has highlighted his determination to make Europe the world number one in renewable energies.

The EU's economy has a lot to gain from this energy transition. It opens up new markets, boosts innovation and gives EU companies first movers' advantages. Investing in renewables and energy efficiency now will also make the EU economy less exposed to future (fossil) energy price hikes and volatility. It will also help the European economy to achieve the recent climate goals, cutting its emissions to 40% below 1990 levels by 2030, 60% below by 2040 and 80% below by 2050. But for all this to happen, the regulatory environment has to adapt and Member States need to sustain supportive policies.

In addition to the environmental and economic side of the energy transition, there is also a social dimension: access to new energy services (e.g. smart metering, connected houses) and to the most energy efficient housing is still not widely enough spread in the EU. The energy transition must therefore be accompanied by a strong push towards a wider dissemination of these innovations, so that they also benefit society's most vulnerable groups.

So, in order to ensure a rapid and smooth development of sustainable renewable energy sources, a stable, clear and fair legal environment is necessary. It must provide investors with the right incentives, with energy pricing and subsidy mechanisms that reflect the externalities of diverse energy sources. It is therefore crucial to ensure that subsidies go to energy sources that really need it and that really provide benefits to the society:

- Subsidies to renewable energy sources should not be seen in isolation but in comparison with the subsidies received by other energy sources, such as fossil fuels and nuclear energy, for production, transmission and consumption.

- Renewable energy sources have different impacts on the environment and on the use of resources. Biomass is a well-known example where several sectors use the same limited resource and where environmental benefits are questioned. On the contrary, wind and solar energy do not face this type of challenge. They are the energy sources with the lowest environmental impacts even if they also use rare elements whose supply are limited.

The regulatory framework has to ensure that all these aspects are reflected in order to provide a clear and predictable setting for investments while maximising social benefits. This concerns primarily the energy-related regulatory framework, but not only. A case in point is the need to ensure that financial markets work in such a way that sufficient long-term private finance is mobilised in order to meet the huge investment needs associated with the energy transition.

This necessary move towards green energy is fully consistent with a wider move towards circular economy. Like the energy transition, switching towards a circular economy is not only an environmental necessity: it also makes full economic sense to use natural resources in a smarter way. It is estimated that eco-design, waste prevention, reuse and similar measures can bring savings of €600bn or 8% of the annual turnover for businesses in the EU, while reducing total annual greenhouse gas emissions by 2 to 4%.

Europe cannot compete with other parts of the world on wage costs or natural resources availability. So we have to use our resources in a smarter way: by designing products and services in a sustainable way so that they don't deplete the earth's natural resources; by using, re-using and recycling materials and products; by preventing and reducing waste; by developing the use of secondary raw materials, etc.

This mind change will allow our businesses to reduce their costs, innovate, introduce new business models and increase their competitiveness while reducing resource use, energy needs and other environmental pressures. Reflecting the increasing environmental challenges and resource scarcity, environmental technologies, products and services have grown in demand. This has facilitated the emergence of green industries, with

Europe proving a strong exporter and with a third of a global market, worth a trillion Euro and expected to double by 2020. The EU should use its green technologies for competitive advantage.

Within the Energy Union Strategy, the European Commission is committed to further establish synergies between energy policies and the circular economy, in particular through energy and resource efficiency.

The International Resource Panel, working under the auspices of the United Nations, and to which the EU is a major contributor, has articulated these synergies very clearly: "Decoupling economic growth from environmental and resource degradation, and creating a circular economy through reuse, recycling, and remanufacturing are key strategies for reducing both greenhouse gases emissions and other environmental and resource pressures".

This change will not happen by itself. The Commission recognises the need to reinforce circular economy-related innovation, enabling the emergence of new technologies and business models which will shape our future. This task cannot be left to the public sector alone. It is essential to direct private sector funding towards the new opportunities created by the circular economy and greener energy.

Consumers and citizens are at the centre of the equation for ensuring both the energy transition and the move towards a circular economy. Indeed, many energy *consumers* are today also energy *producers*, new energy services emerge, demand for resource efficient products is growing... The regulatory framework has to adapt to these changes and allow a stronger role for consumers (e.g. by allowing them to easily sell electricity produced from solar panels). Consumers and citizens need also to be well informed of the consequences of their choices. They need new tools to access the most complete and credible information about the characteristics of the products and services offered to them.

The transition does not happen in a static landscape. In order to maintain its leading position on green energy, the EU has to carefully assess recent developments in the rest of the world, in terms of legal, economic and technological changes. International commitments play an important role and cooperation within EU and between EU and neighbouring countries is also increasingly necessary. We need to learn from others.

For all these reasons, this book very usefully sheds light on these complex issues and provides a very valuable input to policy making.

Preface

PROFESSOR RAPHAEL J. HEFFRON

Jean Monnet Professor in Energy & Natural Resources Law & Policy
Energy & Natural Resources Law Institute
Queen Mary University of London, United Kingdom

There has been ongoing reflection on 'what actually energy law is' by the international energy law community over the last few decades. Early academic literature on this question is from Australia and the US and only more recently the EU. Although there are a few, the current definition of energy law being used in the field is: energy law is the area of law concerning the management of energy resources and the rights and duties over all energy activities over each stage of energy life-cycle (diagrammatically represented in Figure 1) and at the local, national and international level.

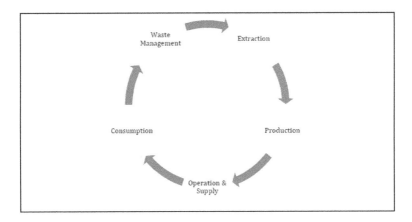

Figure 1: The Energy Life-Cycle

Source: Heffron, R. J. 2015. Energy Law: An Introduction. Springer: Heidelberg, Germany.

Indeed, this is a more holistic definition than was used in the past and it accommodates a more interdisciplinary perspective on the energy sector and one covers the energy sector (system) in its entirety. Indeed, in considering this energy system focus, clean energy sources (or low-carbon energy sources) are sources that have a more complete energy-life cycle than all other energy sources in that they factor in the waste issue. Managing the waste (which includes CO_2 emissions) of traditional energy sources is not something society has yet resolved. It is therefore welcome that there is another addition to the emerging literature on clean energy through this text entitled *Clean Energy Law and Regulation*.

Further, this book will be an exciting addition to the general energy law academic and practitioner literature. The study of energy law is under review and university institutions are adapting their curricula to accommodate the rise of clean energy infrastructure development. For example, in the United States there exists an *Energy Bar Association*[1] which is comprised of professionals and academics. This aims also to ensure that lawyers are equipped with the knowledge necessary to handle the legal challenges of the energy sector in the future. Significantly, the *US Energy Bar Association* has reviewed in 2015 energy law education across all institutions in the US in an article entitled *Energy Law Education in the U.S.: An Overview and Recommendations*.[2] Similarly in the UK, in 2015, academics and practitioners formed the *UK Energy Law and Policy Association*[3] and it aims to bridge the gap between energy law academics and practitioners. It also produced an article reviewing energy law education in the UK in 2016 entitled *A Review of Energy Law Education in the UK*.[4] Both these articles aim to address how energy law education should develop in the future, examine the energy law curricula offered by universities, and identify the gaps in current energy curricula.

Energy law as a discipline is entering an exciting phase of development. Exploring what energy law is, and in essence aiming to derive or formulate a theory of energy law is increasing. This move in academia is referred to as the '*Modern Energy Law Movement*'; and, it has the potential for a significant impact on the field.[5] In the past, energy law has been researched and practiced in a dysfunctional way and there has been and still is limited holistic thinking. Energy law traditionally has operated in silos, and principally around oil, gas and coal and with limited cross-border legislative initiatives. Energy law now interacts with many disciplines and currently it is in its third evolutionary stage of development where it is

---

[1] US Energy Bar Association. See the website, available at: http://www.eba-net.org/ (last accessed June 2016).
[2] US Energy Bar Association (Donna Attanasio, Committee Chair), 2015. Energy Law Education in the U.S.: An Overview and Recommendations. *Energy Law Journal*, 32, 217-260.
[3] UK Energy Law and Policy Association. See the website, available at: http://www.energylaw.org.uk/ (last accessed June 2016).
[4] Heffron, R. J., Roberts, P., Cameron, P. and Johnston, A. 2016. A Review of Energy Law Education in the UK. *Journal of World Energy Law and Business*, 9 (5), 346-356.
[5] See the following: (1) Heffron, R. J. and Talus. K. 2016. The development of energy law in the 21st century: a paradigm shift? *Journal of World Energy Law and Business*, 9 (3), 189-202.

emerging from predominantly been influenced by economics.[6] The aim of the *Modern Energy Law Movement* is to unite traditional energy law scholars with law and economic energy law scholars, low-carbon academics and even energy tax scholars. Cooperation is needed to further develop the discipline and establish similar theoretical concepts and principles. As there are many legislative challenges in the energy sector. A book in an under researched area such as clean energy law, like this book on *Clean Energy Law and Regulation* is therefore most welcome.

In thinking of the future of energy law, there is much uncertainty, as the world heads towards an unknown energy future and therefore it is important to consider the legal boundaries of the energy sector. More often than not energy law has been forgotten in the debate around the energy transition and climate change scenarios that list years such as 2020, 2030, 2040, and even 2050. Probably the biggest challenge to the energy sector is the recurrent issue of the challenge of energy law stimulating investment in the energy sector. It is clear that the incentivizing of investment is critical to where the energy sector will stand in 2040 and whether society can meet its aims of a 2°C future limit.

It is expected that the actual financial resources are there as wind and solar will account for only 60 *per cent* of the $11.4 trillion invested in the energy sector (based on Bloomberg 2016 data). Indeed, fossil fuels are expected to still account for $2.1 trillion in investment from now until 2040. To meet the 2°C future limit, an estimated $208 billion in investment in low-carbon energy sources will be needed annually over the next 25 years. In addition, one of the major problems is that while power sector emissions are scheduled to peak by 2027 there will be a problem in that India and South-East Asia will continue to increase their use of fossil fuels, and hence additional support for technology deployment of clean energy sources will need to be given to these countries.[7]

---

[6]   Heffron, R. J. and Talus. K. 2016. The Evolution of Energy Law and Energy Jurisprudence: Insights for Energy Analysts and Researchers. *Energy Research and Social Science*, 19, 1-10. There are a number of other energy law papers and texts that also look at the evolution of energy law, and these note similar influences but are not quite as direct as the Heffron and Talus (2016) article see: Zillman, D. N. 2012. Evolution of Modern Energy Law: a Personal Retrospective. *Journal of Energy & Natural Resources Law.* Vol. 30 (4), 485-496. Nevertheless, one US text states discusses 'eras of energy law', but similarly identifies economics as a key influence: Eisen, J. *et al.* 2015. (4th Ed.). Energy, Economics and the Environment. MN, US: Foundation Press. In contrast to the more international energy law perspective examining the stages of energy law: Heffron. R. J. 2015. Energy Law. Roundhall, Thomson Reuters: Dublin, Ireland.

[7]   For more on this see the analysis in: Heffron, R. J. 2016. The Global Future of Energy Law. International Energy Law Review, 7, 290- 295.

In this context with major investment in new clean energy infrastructure planned, there is a need for this book on Clean Energy Law and Regulation. And it is with great pleasure that I have been asked to write this *Preface* for this new informative text and a valuable addition to the emerging literature in Clean Energy Law. A particular highlight is that the chapter contributors represent a mix of academic and practitioners and several contributions from beyond law. Finally, while the primary focus is on the EU there is a range of chapters examining a number of other countries and this international and comparative focus is a key feature of this engaging book.

Introductory Note

DR. VICENTE LÓPEZ-IBOR MAYOR

Ph.D. in Law
President of Estudio Jurídico Internacional, Spain
Chairman of Lightsource Renewable Energy, United Kingom

The reasons for writing this book arose from a concern and a certain realization about developments in today's energy industry. This realization has allowed me to see what an extraordinary process of technical transformation the energy industry is currently undergoing. It is a technical transformation from within, spurred by the constant advancement in systems and processes, and the increasing development of new energy technologies, coupled with the furthering of those already in existence. However, it is also a transformation stimulated by the co-existence of energy-related factors and technologies at the same time as similar advancements flourish in other fields of activity, including telecommunications, transportation and the environmental sciences.

The concern I feel, which falls within a strictly legal and regulatory realm, results from the fact that Energy Law has not yet become fully settled and asserted as a recognizable system of its own, based on a set of general guidelines shared among all energy sources and technologies, or a series of similar techniques and instruments for regulation and interpretation to form one single coherent unit that does not fail to take into account the size of the energy value chain or the wealth of nuanced situations existing in the sub-disciplines which make up the field as a whole.

Without a doubt, one of the areas in which we are most notably witnessing the energy industry's unstoppable momentum and its value to society in terms of economic development and environmental protection is that of "clean energies," thereby helping to build the foundations of Energy Law, a field undergoing necessary construction and consolidation.

This book is meant to serve two purposes: on the one hand, the general task of drawing attention to the unquestionable establishment of Energy Law, while also suggesting what aspects are required to do so, using the best knowledge available on some of the most novel and necessary real-world situations which this involves, including clean energies, while on the other hand, the book also highlights a series of essential legal and regulatory factors surrounding these forms of energy.

The book is divided into three large sections. The first, titled "Energy and Climate Change," includes works on the energy transition, a phenomenon which, to sum it up briefly, has arisen in response to the basic facets of the aforementioned transformation within the industry and modern economies. It also provides an in-depth analysis of the efforts many countries will have to make to achieve essential objectives inherent to the energy industry transformation required to decrease coal use in the economy. On a worldwide scale, these efforts have been summarized in the conclusions of the agreements reached at the Paris Climate Change Summit. The "ambition mechanism" established at that international summit adds a requirement for signatory countries, which include the vast majority of the international community, to review and increase their emissions reduction obligations every five years in order to achieve "zero CO_2 emissions" during the second half of the twenty-first century, or in other words, by the middle of the century under way. This shift in energy goals linked to environmental objectives will entail a radical change in the energy model. This is an unprecedented historical change, because it involves not only the production, availability and use of new energy sources, but most importantly a change in the way their production is oriented and they are perceived and used by the people.

The second subject covered by the book is the regulation of a wide range of clean energy technologies. This book is not intended to discuss each and every technology defined as a clean form of energy with a specific analysis of them all, because doing so would require a highly detailed analysis of monumental length, delving into both the legal system governing the industry and its economic and technical regulation, matters which stretch beyond the scope of this work. However, I do wish to provide a proper analysis of some of the most important technologies, how they have changed over time, and their legal and regulatory characteristics, identifying the most exceptional aspects involved in each of the topics mentioned above. This analysis has been dealt with by examining specific themes involving clean energy technologies, such as the territorial question, thereby examining and explaining how the fast-paced penetration of clean energies is taking place and the environmental demands created by running the energy system in most regions of the world, and therefore in a large number of countries. The book deals with both legal and regulatory aspects, and even technical factors, because a further central feature of the new energy model is the intertwining of these factors and their ever cross-cutting nature with a presence of the environmental question in each variable. These aspects include the legal systems governing renewable energies in Latin America, from Mexico to Brazil and Argentina, with a look at countries such as Colombia, Peru and Ecuador along the way. Also covered is the significance of renewable energy regulation in several EU countries, to a great extent subsidiary to the EU definitions and programs for promoting, furthering and regulating green, renewable and clean forms of energy. In doing so, there are explanation and study of systems such as solar, wind, biomass and energy storage, with in-depth looks at the mechanisms which enable and justify efficiency models and demand-side response, as well as the way in which distributed generation is structured technically and in regulation, and the potential models for how it will change and get handled in the future. In this analysis, electricity plays a notable role, because the focal point of quite a significant portion of the energy transformation or transition revolves around "demand-side" reform or, in other words, change with a view to end consumers of the electricity supply. This trends towards drawing closer to consumers is an innovation in the sector and partially replicates some of the value mechanisms seen in added-value products and services now implemented in the worlds of telecommunications and information and communications processing systems. However, further innovations specific to the energy industry are being undertaken, as well, such as waste management and the "circular economy," the relationship between power and water, digitalized energy storage, multi-convergence and multi-functionality in power networks, and electric, non-polluting mobility. Ultimately, we are approaching a new paradigm or electricity ecosystem that will allow us to take a new qualitative leap forward into societal modernization from a technological perspective. In particular, it will have a clearly positive impact on advanced urban space management and building sectors.

The final subject covered by the book includes several works on international energy cooperation, the European Energy Union and governance. It is obvious that each of these topics, like many others throughout the book, are more than worthy of their own monographic works of great interest. However, the attempt herein is to outline at least some highlights of special importance regarding each of these subjects, allowing readers to get a closer, more accurate look at them. Most are discussed on the basis of their repercussions and material scope both within the energy industry itself and in terms of research, reflection and interpretation of a merely legal nature. Regarding this state of affairs, there is a series of highly interesting contributions on the Energy Charter Treaty, the first major global effort to achieve legal cooperation in the energy industry, though it first came about as a project to move towards an energy policy of a pan-European nature. Another of the topics studied is the geopolitical angle on energy or "energy geopolitics." It explains energy dynamics in the Atlantic Basin, currently the most prosperous in resources and energy activity worldwide, including the very powerful Eurasian "heartland." The energy factor is analyzed, as well, as a basic service of a universal nature in accordance with the postulates and objectives of the United Nations system.

Alongside all of these topics, you will find just as many other subjects of great interest. Some are specifically legal in nature, such as the EU's legislative reforms and those by other countries in different regions, the legal regulation of public purchase agreements and the modernization needed in energy and environment taxation, and even the relationship between the energy transition and the fight against climate change through sports and technology, as explained in the section on the "Formula-E" championship, with Formula racing for electric cars.

I would like to express my sincere gratitude to the publishing firm Wildy, Simmonds & Hill Publishing for having seen this book from the very outset as an appealing and useful work needed in the legal and regulatory world, thereby remaining at the cutting edge amongst publishers of materials which will surely soon become the subject of extensive study and attention in many arenas, including academia, public policy, business and the legal profession and practitioners.

I owe special thanks to Daniel Calleja for his auspicious and accurate words in this book's prologue, and to Professor Raphael Heffron for his magnificent viewpoints on the topic of energy law.

Last of all, I would like to express my gratitude for the support give by colleagues and contributors, in particular Jorge Vasconcelos, Ece Gürsoy, Ana María Salazar, Alexandre Díez, Christophe Schramm, María José Gómez Serrano, José María Martínez, Vicente López-Ibor Lobato and Paula Vázquez, in addition to the excellent organization and transcription work performed for the book by África García.

I
CLIMATE CHANGE AND ENERGY

The energy transition from the European perspective

JORGE VASCONCELOS

President
NEWES, New Energy Solutions, Portugal

1. ENERGY TRANSITION – HOW TO DESCRIBE IT

Worldwide, the energy industry is undergoing an extensive metamorphosis. The evolutionary stimuli have different origins, in different countries, and the direction and pace of change are not the same everywhere. However, some common trends can be easily identified as regards the major mutations currently taking place, such as:

- energy related sectors (transport, heating and cooling, electricity, gas, etc.) become more interconnected, old energy silos become increasingly obsolete;

- gone are the days of cheap energy and wasteful energy value chains, nowadays energy efficiency is a top priority, from single devices to buildings, vehicles and complex urban or industrial systems;

- green electricity takes a prominent place in the new energy landscape;

- the old top-down planning and control approach is being challenged by new bottom-up experiments performed by consumers (who can easily master their consumption through internet and very often become producers of thermal and electrical energy) and by new types of energy services offered by newcomers.

In the European Union (EU), the "energy transition" results from the combination of three major transition processes:

- the transition from national monopolies to the integrated European fully liberalized electricity (and natural gas) market, initiated more than twenty years ago and not yet fully accomplished;

- the transition from high-carbon energy systems to low-carbon energy systems, formally initiated at EU level in 2007 but with an earlier start in some Member States, now anchored in the Paris Agreement;

• the transition towards fully observable and fully controllable energy systems, triggered by the global digital revolution.

The energy transition is not a one-dimensional movement along one axis – be it digitisation, decarbonisation or supra-national market integration. The energy transition must be depicted as a trajectory in the three-dimensional space shaped by these three axis (see Figure 1). The energy transition means changing from the current state A (high carbon, low integration, low information) to a future state B (low carbon, high integration, high information).

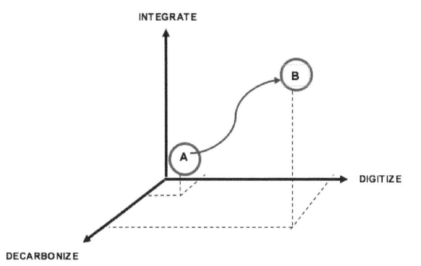

Fig. 1 The three dimensional EU energy transition

Although EU Member States share common goals and quantitative targets as regards decarbonisation and market integration, as well as the advancement of the single digital market, energy transition(s) may take place along several alternative paths. Each EU Member State may choose a different approach, a different energy mix, different timings. Different national paths may coexist – full harmonization is not a pre-condition for a well-functioning internal energy market. However, full consistency is essential: both consistency of the national paths among themselves and with EU goals and targets and internal consistency of each national path (across all energy related sectors and over time).

In the EU, liberalization abolished vertically integrated monopolies (in the 1990s), introduced full retail competition (2007) and imposed legal unbundling of transmission system operation (2009), thus introducing full competition within each energy sector (electricity and natural gas). However, these liberalized sectors are still mainly vertically organized, showing little horizontal interaction among them. Now, the virtual currencies of "CO_2" and "information", introduced respectively by decarbonisation and digitisation policies, enable new types of economic transactions across a large spectrum of sectors; these virtual currencies trigger significant financial flows across previously nearly isolated sectors.

Until now, the growing interaction among energy and energy related sectors (transport, waste management, etc.) has been based on *ad hoc* schemes focused on definite cases and more or less opportunistic behaviour. Enabling those interactions to grow in number, scale and complexity, requires a new approach where, by design, resource flows follow a comprehensive "technical metabolism" pattern aimed at optimizing efficiency and minimizing waste according to the "circular economy" model, inspired by the analysis of biological metabolism and large ecosystems.

In February 2011 the European Council described the challenges faced by the energy industry in the following terms: *"reducing greenhouse gas emissions by 80-95% by 2050 compared to 1990 as agreed in October 2009 will require a revolution in energy systems, which must start now"*.

2. ENERGY TRANSITION – HOW TO MANAGE IT

The energy transition is a disruptive, "revolutionary" process; it cannot be understood through the lenses of "quasi-stationary" system analysis and it cannot be managed through reluctant small steps and incremental thinking.

Whatever transition path is selected, it is necessary to ensure a dynamic balance between the "creative destruction" of market forces and technological innovation, on the one hand, and the intrinsic stringency of system reliability governance, on the other hand. This applies to all energy sectors, but particularly to electricity. Any lack of internal consistency will make energy transition unnecessarily costly and protracted, as shown by several examples. California is probably the best known and the most expensive failure due to lack of internal consistency – in order to please all constituencies, the 1996 electricity market model, unanimously approved by the California Legislature, was inconsistent by design and led to multiple large-scale blackouts and the ultimate market collapse in 2000.

5

Each path presents its own governance and regulatory challenges and it commands specific actions, in particular as regards infrastructure investments. Not only investments on wires and pipes are necessary - investment on new information and communication technologies (ICT) are crucial. Identifying and optimizing the benefits of ICT to energy systems and energy markets is a big challenge faced nowadays by energy industry and energy regulation alike.

The transition towards low carbon energy systems requires not only new rules, but also new roles. In particular, the role of networks and the role of network operators are changing and need to evolve even faster over the coming years due to increasing decentralization and diversification of energy sources. This transformation is facilitated by modern ICT. Given the different time-scales for investments in production and in networks, any successful energy transition wishing to preserve current security of supply and reliability standards requires timely and coherent adjustments of the role played by network operators. Therefore, the legal and regulatory frameworks must be adapted, namely in order to:

a) Clearly define and assign each operational function, indicating, for each, appropriate cost and liability sharing mechanisms.

b) Establish appropriate coordination mechanisms, for both normal and abnormal situations, including appropriate redundancy safeguards and supervision tools.

The energy transition process is very complex and it involves many actors, varying from country to country; therefore, there is no universal "most probable" or "most efficient" sequencing and timing.

As the energy transition process develops, many new doubts and problems will emerge, requiring new decisions to be taken. Given the large number of actors involved, the complexity of new, untested governance structures and the growing interaction among different regulatory authorities and jurisdictions, it is critical to ensure that new, specific decisions do not jeopardize consistency of the overall transition process. Therefore, it is very useful to set up a special Committee in charge of monitoring the evolution of energy systems (both local, national and EU), in order to ensure that existing investments, policies and operational developments are consistent and to propose legal or regulatory action whenever consistency is at risk, threatening consumer welfare or national climate change and energy targets.

In a multi-sector energy architecture, electricity flows in a local electricity network may be influenced by decisions in other sectors, such as (see Figure 2):

- waste management: waste may be converted directly into electricity or into gas that may be either injected into gas pipelines (not shown in the picture) or used to generate electricity;

- district heating and cooling: very often heating and cooling are associated with electricity generation in so-called combined heat and power plants;

- conventional electricity generation;

- demand participation: demand management has a direct impact upon global electricity demand and, therefore, upon electricity generation needs; increasingly, demand management is performed as part of a local distributed energy resources management process, taking into account local generation and storage facilities;

- electric vehicles (EV): the charging strategies of large-scale EV fleets can have a considerable impact upon electricity flows in the network, both as regards energy volumes and peak demand; moreover, EV batteries can be used as distributed storage resources and, under certain circumstances, may inject electricity into the grid.

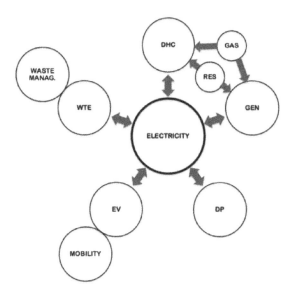

DHC	District Heating and Cooling	DP	Demand Participation
RES	Renewable Energy Sources	EV	Electric Vehicles
GEN	Electricity Generation	WTE	Waste-To-Energy

Fig. 2 Electricity as a service within a multi-sector architecture

7

According to the desired goal – e.g. minimize greenhouse gas emissions, minimize total primary energy consumption, minimize cost, etc. – different "dispatch strategies" should be followed to manage the available resources. In any case, all the above mentioned sectors are interlinked: decisions taken in one sector will affect all other sectors. In this new perspective, electricity should be seen as an "intermediate product" or a service, rather than as an "end product", like in the traditional perspective.

A market-based approach to the circular economy requires the existence of a level playing field where agents acting – sometimes simultaneously - in different sectors can compete and take decisions based on coherent and meaningful economic signals related to costs and prices. If the cost of externalities (e.g. greenhouse gas emissions) is not accurately and consistently integrated into prices in the different sectors, unfair distortions appear that will be responsible for economic inefficiencies. Subsidies are another factor that may lead to market distortions and undesired outcomes. Under these conditions, cross-sector transactions will inevitably be distorted and may lead not only to economic inefficiency, but also to unintended perverse environmental results. Creating a market design apt to support a "circular electricity" model is indeed a big challenge.

Defining the appropriate regulatory framework(s) is an equally demanding task. The "energy transition" is not about making the existing infrastructure just more efficient – it is about actively promoting the development of new resources and new business models. This implies moving away from "steady-state regulation" towards "transient regulation": a new kind of regulation that, by definition, aims at driving energy systems towards a new "steady-state". Regulation for liberalisation was concerned with incremental capacity additions. Regulation for the energy transition shall be more concerned with disruptive innovation and infrastructure transformation than with the efficient use of the existing infrastructure.

Regulation must provide the right incentives, not only for efficient short-term commercial and technical operation of the different sectors involved in the "circular electricity" compact, but also for long-term investments. Appropriate investments in the different infrastructures are crucial to ensure reliability, quality of service, technical and economic efficiency. Some infrastructures may compete against each other for customer preference and market share while other infrastructures may be inclined to cooperate and share resources. The regulatory framework may be carved from a single block but, most probably, it will result from the assembly of several regulatory bodies, reflecting different regulatory cultures and approaches.

For the circular economy to function properly, several sector policies must be aligned, providing a sufficient degree of consistency across the "encircled" economic sectors. As rightly pointed out by the OECD: *"For the most part, it is the sum of signals coming from misaligned policies which risks hindering the low-carbon transition"* [1].

3. THE CHALLENGES OF CHANGE

Meeting in 1992, shortly after the end of the Soviet Union, the Conference for Security and Co-operation in Europe (CSCE) assessed the big political transition of the late 20th century in a document entitled "The challenges of change" [2], in the following terms:

> "The transition to and development of democracy and market economy by the new democracies is being carried forward with determination amidst difficulties and varying conditions. We offer our support and solidarity to participating States undergoing transformation to democracy and market economy. We welcome their efforts to become fully integrated into the wider community of States. Making this transition irreversible will ensure the security and prosperity of us all. (…)
>
> The CSCE has been instrumental in promoting changes; now it must adapt to the task of managing them."

Managing change is indeed as challenging as promoting change. After two decades of energy market liberalisation and after the Paris Agreement entry into force, managing the energy transition in order *"to ensure the security and prosperity of us all"* is of paramount importance.

3.1 Changes impacting the electricity industry

Policy, technology and market forces, as well as human psychology, are among the sources of structural change in regulated industries.

The Paris Agreement, which entered into force on November 4, 2016, is a good recent example of policy-driven change. Its objective is to strengthen *"the global response to the threat of climate change, in the context of sustainable development and efforts to eradicate poverty"*. We have come a long way from the 1997 Kyoto Protocol, which the USA never ratified and binds just 37 industrialised nations to emissions targets. Now, action is real and the electricity industry is one of the major targets of the new

---

[1] http://www.oecd.org/env/Aligning-policies-for-the-transition-to-a-low-carbon-economy-CMIN2015-11.pdf
[2] http://www.osce.org/mc/39530?download=true

policy: on the one hand, through decarbonisation (which means closing fossil fuel power plants and building renewable energy plants), it becomes increasingly "green"; on the other hand, "green" electricity increasingly substitutes fossil fuels in sectors such as transport and heating. The Paris Agreement is both a threat (namely to old fossil fuel power plants and to their primary energy suppliers) and an opportunity (e.g. for those who invest on renewable energy and on new businesses like electro mobility, demand management, efficient buildings construction and management). Implementing the Paris Agreement is already changing the electricity industry worldwide, including the EU, the frontrunner of climate policy for decades.

Another example of policy-driven change is the introduction of competition in hitherto monopolistic industries. In the late 1980s/ early 1990s, many States decided to liberalize network industries, including the electricity sector. This political decision required deep changes regarding the way industry is organized and regulated; in some cases, it also affected ownership of former public utilities. Moving away from monopoly to a (fully or partially) liberalized electricity market had a tremendous disruptive impact in many countries throughout the world and market restructuring processes are still going on in many places, both at wholesale and at retail level. The EU implemented the most ambitious and comprehensive liberalisation programme worldwide, simultaneously introducing full liberalization at national level and at cross-border level, thus creating the largest integrated liberalized electricity market in the world.

Whenever a substantial change occurs in the relevant public policy framework or in the basic technical or economic conditions of a given network industry, the respective network infrastructure becomes, to some extent, inadequate to the new reality. Inadequacy may relate to any network property, namely: topology, capacity (insufficient capacity leads to congestion, latency or similar phenomena, while overcapacity means idle assets) and regulation (i.e., the technical and commercial rules governing infrastructure access and use).

Infrastructure inadequacy creates difficulties to the development of the emerging reality and it prevents some transactions from materializing; therefore, it is responsible for costs that would not exist if the infrastructure was perfectly adapted to the new policy requirements or technical/ economic conditions.

On the other hand, changing the infrastructure and the way it is used usually requires new investments that will increase the costs supported by network users. Moreover, some past investments may become useless under the new conditions ("stranded costs").

3.2 Reacting to change

Following the introduction of substantial changes in the policy framework or in basic network industry economics, network owners and operators, on the one hand, and regulators, on the other hand, must decide if, when and how to adapt the existing infrastructure. These decisions – even the decision not to act - will always have unequal impacts on network users (present and future) and therefore they should be explicitly described and justified.

When regulators justify these decisions - or when someone else assesses their regulatory decisions - the following aspects should be taken into account: compliance (enabling the achievement of the desired outcomes implied in the new policy framework), fairness and efficiency (providing the "right" incentives and signals, as well as promoting the "right" cost allocation, both during the transitional phase and in the new state).

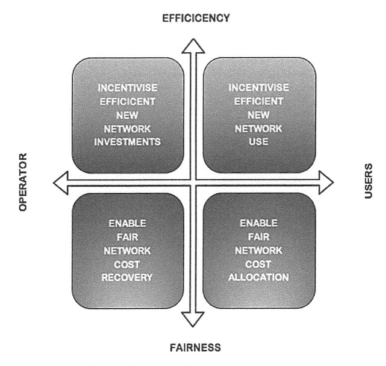

Fig. 3 Re-regulation main areas of concern

11

Regulation must promote the necessary infrastructure adaptation, providing appropriate signals both to infrastructure owners/operators and to infrastructure users. Change requires properly designed and implemented "re-regulation".

Re-regulation must address four symmetric issues, as described in Fig. 3: on the one hand, incentivize new investments and enable fair past cost recovery for network operators; on the other hand, promote efficient use of the available infrastructure and provide continuous fair allocation of costs among consumers (network users).

3.3 Information and control

After a long period of "information deficit", it seems that the energy industry is now entering a period of "information surplus" and concerns about "big data" management have surfaced in many countries, as well as concerns about data privacy and cyber security. However, the main challenge is not how to handle large amounts of data but how to guarantee that energy systems will be "under control" - i.e., how to ensure system integrity and reliability while allowing market participants as much freedom as possible; in other words, how to avoid that multiple, parallel uses of a large amount of data exposes the system to hazardous conflict or latency situations.

Modern ICT enable full monitoring and full control of energy systems in a cost effective way. Therefore, old hierarchical, centralized control systems based on many "educated guesses" may be easily replaced by decentralized, cooperative control systems based on real-time information. Nowadays, individual appliances may be remotely controlled, not only in factories, but also in households, offices and all kinds of consumption centers. Moreover, in terms of information and control flows, appliances may be effortlessly aggregated according to ownership, type, geographical location or any other criterion, thus enabling the introduction of innovative business models and more sophisticated optimization algorithms.

Control and communication devices are the same all over the world, but the way they are applied to energy systems (i.e., how they are interconnected and how information and control flows are organized) may differ, thus enabling implementation of different market structures, contractual arrangements and control strategies. "Control of energy systems" does not consist of just one function – it includes a large array of functions and variables associated with different physical resources. In the past, provision of the necessary "system services" was limited to a relatively small number of resources, mainly concentrated at the higher levels. New technologies, both internal to energy systems (e.g. storage, fuel cells, wind and photovoltaic electricity generation) and external (namely information and communication technologies), enable the provision of system services by lower levels, thus expanding the control space. If not properly managed, the multiplication and superposition of control loops may create stability and security problems. Therefore, decision-making and coordination roles must be (re)assigned in order to ensure that the whole system remains stable in spite of the multiplication of new types of transactions related both to the supply of "energy" (commodity and service) to end-users and to the supply of "system services".

Control complexity, more and above market complexity, is the major problem in the near future (cf. Fig. 4). Market redesign cannot be performed independently of system control redesign and this task, in turn, requires a full revaluation of the functioning of each layer of the whole energy value chain.

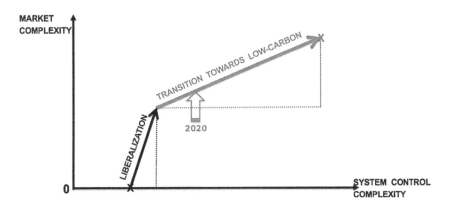

Fig. 4 Liberalisation and decarbonisation: impacts upon market and system complexity

In particular, the following three questions, composing the "control flow problem" inevitably arise:

1) How to ensure control at each level?

Within each layer, different control policies can be implemented, from a highly centralized approach, more or less replicating at each level the current national hierarchical structure, down to a fully decentralized structure.

2) How to define the functional interfaces between layers?

13

In order to ensure effective coordination of the whole system it is necessary to exchange information between layers and to establish clear communication and control procedures. Protocols must be implemented both for normal and for abnormal operational conditions.

3) Who is the "controller of the controllers" and "controller of last resort"?

4. RENEWABLES: BETWEEN CLEAN TECH AND NOT SO CLEAR POLICIES

Clean technologies are available in multiple fields – and many if not most of them were first developed and deployed in the EU. However, the widespread use of clean technologies requires appropriate policies and regulatory frameworks.

The EU was pioneer and world leader in renewable energy but has recently lost this position, as can be seen in the following table, comparing investments in Europe and China:

$ bn	Europe (decreasing since 2010)	China (continuously growing since 2004)
2004	25	3
2010	113	40
2015	49	103

Source: http://fs-unep-centre.org/sites/default/files/publications/globaltrends inrenewableenergyinvestment2016lowres_0.pdf

Since 2010, investment in renewable energy in Europe decreased 60%. This was mainly due to the policies adopted in several EU Member States aimed at limiting retail electricity price increases. Because subsidies paid to electricity producers are supported by electricity consumers, the more subsidized electricity is produced, the more prices increase. Instead of shifting the burden to other energy consumers (namely those using fossil fuels) or to tax payers (since decarbonisation is a policy goal of general interest), governments decided to stop subsidizing new generation capacity and, in a few cases, they even requested producers to pay back subsidies received in the past. This triggered a wave of litigation and created a climate of investment uncertainty in the EU.

At EU level, guidelines were issued that require subsidies to be awarded only through competitive tenders and "market premium" mechanisms.

Besides "competition for the market", several stakeholders also require renewables to be subject to "competition in the market", thus complying with technical and market rules designed for a completely different generation mix, under different assumptions.

Electricity markets in the EU were initially designed under the assumption of supply-side competition among thermal generators; renewable generation was either residual or, in the case of hydropower plants, largely amortized. It is illogical to expect that design to be fit under a completely different set of assumptions, namely competition including both supply-side and demand-side (comprising new types of demand such as electric vehicles and prosumers) and substantial amounts of generation based on renewable sources.

As I expressed in another paper[3],

"Talking about "the" electricity market is a conceptual mistake and a dangerous approach to market redesign because there is no such thing. Electricity markets are a very recent social construction, they exhibit very different features in different countries and, within any given country, they have changed substantially over the past two decades. To pretend that the electricity market today in any given country – conceived either as an imperfect, tangible reality or as an ideal, only partially fulfilled blueprint – is the only set of rules acceptable and accepted as axiomatic and universally binding, is a mistake. In energy markets, there is no such thing as a "canon".

When (re)thinking about energy markets it is not enough to look for ideas that are merely wrong; we need to look for troubled ideas that block progress by inspiring devotion out of proportion to their historical achievements."

When the EU liberalised energy markets, back in the 1990s, it did not provide a blueprint, a "market design" that Member States would be obliged to implement. There was no market design at all - neither for wholesale nor for retail markets; neither for electricity nor for natural gas; neither for national markets nor for the "single market". What followed was a process of trial-and-error, experimentation, both in the markets and in the institutional framework.

Some problems and barriers were overcome through innovative, cooperative processes under the Commission's leadership. Only seven

---

[3] https://d2umxnkyjne36n.cloudfront.net/documents/2016-03-16-JV-final-paper.pdf?mtime=20161004120859

years after the first liberalisation directive some substantial, concrete rules (and a corresponding Regulation) were approved.

What EU liberalisation legislation did initially was just to remove all legal barriers that had protected monopolies for decades, explicitly introducing new rights for consumers and producers, thus enabling the development of new business models and the emergence of new players (suppliers, traders, brokers, market operators, energy clearing houses, etc.)[4].

What is needed now is a similar approach: releasing the new, innovative market forces willing and able to challenge the status quo and to provide real benefits for consumers. To lead the changing process, to push digitisation. This may happen and will happen in many, different directions, with big successes and, most probably, some big failures too - as it has happened in the telecom industry and in all industries going through digitisation.

The new digital world is too dynamic and too complex for the European Commission or anyone to try to "tame" or even to frame this evolution through ambitious "market designs".

This is the moment for experimentation, as it happened 20 years ago with liberalisation; this is not the moment to try to "fix" all bugs of liberalised markets - as if digitisation was not already happening and challenging the main assumptions of the old market targets and designs: namely, the (now) ridiculous assumption that demand in inelastic.

In 2016, any "market design" initiative should be very modest, limited to a couple of critical points. Aiming at "keeping the lights on" while the new markets and business models take off, not aiming at accomplishing the perfectly integrated, well-functioning, efficient internal energy market. It shall not be about the target but exclusively about the transition. It shall enable the quick, safe and efficient "deconstruction" of the previous model, not the extension of its artificial life.

Empowering energy consumers is much more than just creating the conditions for them to benefit from the application of modern ICT to

---

[4] In 1991, the European Commission planned to issue a Commission Directive (based on article 90.3) to liberalise the energy industry. The reaction from the Member States and from the European Parliament (about to get codecision rights, also on energy matters, thanks to the Treaty of Maastricht) was so strong that the Commission felt obliged to change the legal base and to submit a proposal to the Council and Parliament. The primacy of legislation over competition law when (re)shaping the energy industry was clearly established in that moment...

energy. It means, also, to allow them to actively participate in the transition towards a low-carbon economy:

- Increasing their role in energy efficiency, namely at home and in transport (housing and energy account for about one third of average EU household expenditure), through new possibilities of demand management and financial incentives (e.g. for building renovation).

- Promoting their role as (thermal and electric) energy producers, both individually and collectively.

- Changing the current system that imposes upon electricity consumers the costs of decarbonising electricity (which becomes increasingly green) while fossil fuels are only slightly affected by ETS carbon prices.

5. FINAL REMARKS

At times society faces tough long-term challenges. At times society faces hard short-term challenges. Today, our society faces, at the same time, critical long and short-term challenges. We must meet both, engineering solutions that bring relief to our short-term social and economic problems and ensure the long-term sustainability of the planet.

In order to avoid the appalling consequences of climate change, we must act in a responsible way - preserving the planet for future generations and creating jobs now. The EU has the intellectual and financial resources to do this, turning climate change into an opportunity. But it is necessary to accelerate and to better coordinate the transition towards a low-carbon economy.

This transition requires a shift from fossil fuels to carbon free energy vectors; in other words, it triggers a deep transformation of our energy systems. However, the transition to a low-carbon economy is much more than mere fuel substitution: it implies, *inter alia*, structural changes in buildings, a new urban metabolism, different modes of mobility and redesigned, consumer-oriented, energy markets.

This vision lies at the origin of the Energy Union framework strategy and has been stepwise developed over recent months. The European Commission has already presented proposals related to ETS reform (2015), heating and cooling (February 2016) and low-emission mobility (July 2016), while other proposals are still under preparation, namely as regards energy efficiency and renewable energy.

Buildings and mobility deserve priority attention, not only because of their negative environmental impact and major contribution to greenhouse gas emissions, but also because of their economic and social relevance:

- The building industry represents 9% of EU GDP and employs circa 11 million people[5]. Housing and energy represents 24% of total average EU household expenditure. Following the financial and economic crisis, the building sector has successfully managed a transition to more renovation of existing buildings; renovation represents now almost 60% of the total building industry turnover.

- The transport sector (including equipment manufacturing) represents 6.3% of GDP and 6% of employment in the EU[6]. Transport represents 13% of total average EU household expenditure.

Moving to low-carbon buildings and mobility creates new jobs and increases households' disposable income. Trends in these sectors are already noticeable and must be accelerated and complemented by similar actions in other areas.

Implementing a coherent framework where policy guidelines, financial incentives, market signals and taxation are aligned across sectors and across countries favours the development of new services and new products that enable the virtuous transition to a low-carbon economy. A transition that creates new jobs, contributes to growth and improves the quality of life.

Under the umbrella of the Energy Union, measures that increase the required coherence and interaction among all relevant energy-related public policies and industrial sectors can be designed; moreover, it is necessary to systematically analyse and, whenever appropriate, remove, EU and national distortions and obstacles to the desired consistency of the transition to a low-carbon economy.

Improving the consistency and predictability of the path towards a low-carbon economy brings more investment, more quickly, creating more jobs now and ensuring the competitive advantage of European undertakings in one of the fastest growing world markets.

Very often, the new green services and products are based on digital technologies, exploring hardware and software developed by EU undertakings and research centres. The potential for mutual reinforcement of industrial skills and business volumes is sizeable and can be enhanced

---

[5] http://openexp.eu/sites/default/files/publication/files/Reports/energy_transition_of_the_eu_building_stock_full_report.pdf

[6] http://ec.europa.eu/transport/strategies/facts-and-figures/transport-matters/index_en.htm

through close coordination between the Energy Union and the Digital Single Market. projects.

Green services and products already represent 8% of total EU exports and their share keeps growing. EU trade policy actively supports initiatives and international agreements aimed at facilitating world trade of green goods and services. On the other hand, EU development and cooperation policy actively promotes diffusion of green services and technologies within the framework of bilateral and multilateral agreements, thus enhancing EU climate diplomacy.

A substantial part of the energy transition is already happening at local level, involving the active participation of citizens and consumers, urban planning authorities, municipalities, service providers and other stakeholders. These decentralized initiatives represent a powerful driving force and they enable implementation of the most suitable solutions according to geography, climate and culture. However, they do not preclude initiatives at EU level – for instance, improved standardisation and harmonisation of rules, as well as a suitable Energy Union governance architecture, are indeed very useful tools to increase economies of scale and to facilitate the diffusion of green products and services within the EU, stimulating innovation and enhancing overall competitiveness of the European industry.

Clean Energy and decarbonization objectives in the EU: impact on European energy model and implications for power markets

ALBERTO AMORES

Partner
Monitor Deloitte, Spain

1. EMISSION REDUCTION IS A GLOBAL CHALLENGE

GHG emissions such as carbon dioxide (CO_2), methane (CH_4) and nitrogen oxides (NO_x) have accompanied technological and economic development; nevertheless, until recent decades, their negative potential impact on our environment had not received sufficient attention. Between 1995 and 2013 GHG emissions increased by more than 25%[1] and, according to current thinking in the scientific community, in the absence of comprehensive and urgent action, climate change will have severe and irreversible impacts globally.

One of the great challenges facing our society in addressing climate change will be to decouple GHG emissions from economic growth (see Figure 1).

One of the most important factors for this correlation is the use of fossil fuels (mainly coal, oil and natural gas) for energy production, as a pillar of modern economic development until the end of the twentieth century. This was mainly due to:

- Their high calorific value compared with the replaced fuel, which was primarily wood and biomass.

---

[1] Source IEA: Energy and Climate Change.

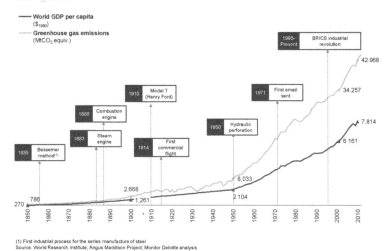

Historical evolution of global greenhouse gas emissions and their relationship with GDP growth

(1) First industrial process for the series manufacture of steel
Source: World Research Institute; Angus Maddison Project; Monitor Deloitte analysis

Figure 1

- Their availability in most Western countries or the accessibility from them, as well as the relative ease of extraction, which led to a low cost to consumers.

- The fact that they could be transported in large quantities at low cost and without significant energy losses.

- Ease of storage, thereby making it possible to ensure the supply of energy.

To a greater or lesser extent, these fuels are present in virtually all economic sectors, which indicates that a change in energy production and consumption patterns across all economic sectors will be necessary in order to achieve carbon neutrality. In this context, by 2013 the world was consuming annually a total of 9,120 Mtoe of final energy and emitting around 33,000 $MtCO_2$ (see **Figure 2**); coal, oil products and natural gas were the main causes of these emissions.

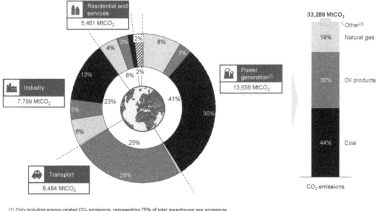

Global energy-related CO_2 emissions[1] in 2013 broken down by type of fuel and consumption segment

(1) Only including energy-related CO_2 emissions, representing 75% of total greenhouse gas emissions
(2) Including CO_2 emissions from heat generation
(3) including CO_2 emissions from industrial waste and non-renewable municipal waste
Source: World Energy Outlook 2015; Monitor Deloitte analysis

Figure 2

According to the most widespread opinion in the scientific community, our environment is already experiencing the effects of GHG emissions. In addition, scientist have developed further quantitative analysis: it is estimated[2] that the limit of cumulative emissions in the atmosphere to prevent global warming to 2°C above pre-industrial levels -a level above which there is a high risk of irreversible climate change- is 1 trillion tons of carbon. The most optimistic estimates indicate that the world has emitted about half of this limit (by 2011 0.52 trillion tons of carbon had already been emitted) and that this limit will be exceeded by 2040 if the world continues emitting at current rates (see Figure 3).

---

[2] An estimate made by the Intergovernmental Panel on Climate Change (IPCC), a scientific body established in 1988 under the auspices of the United Nations, whose main objective is to examine and evaluate all the literature on climate change and provide information about its causes, potential impacts and response strategies

Relationship between cumulative carbon emissions in the atmosphere and global warming

Cumulative carbon emissions in the atmosphere
(trillions t of carbon)

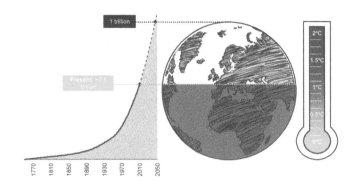

Source: Trillionthonne; UNFCCC; Monitor Deloitte analysis

Figure 3

In this context, as evidence of the international concern and mobilization, the international community has acquired the commitment to achieve carbon neutrality by 2050-2100. The Paris Agreement was a turning point for action to limit climate change below dangerous levels, stablishing an enduring, binding and transparent legal regime where all countries make commitments to reduce greenhouse gas emissions and manage the impacts of climate change.

In addition, the Paris Agreement, reached at the XXI United Nations Climate Change Conference (COP21) of the United Nations Framework Convention on Climate Change included the signing parties' commitment to limiting global warming to "well below 2°C" with respect to pre-industrial levels, to drive efforts to limit it to 1.5°C and to achieve carbon neutrality between 2050 and 2100. The "ambition mechanism" in the Paris Agreement means that countries will need to review and increase their emission reduction commitments every 5 years in order to meet the long term goal of greenhouse gas neutrality by the second half of century.

Although the agreement is not legally binding, the signing parties reached an agreement to organise, communicate and maintain national contributions in the future, implementing measures to achieve the overall objective set.

2. THE EU IS AT THE FOREFRONT OF DECARBONISATION EFFORTS

2.1 EU emissions and decarbonisation policies

The EU emitted 4,477 MtCO2 (see Figure 4) in 2013. Among the countries with the highest GDP in Europe, Germany is the country with the biggest amount of emissions in absolute terms and Poland is the country with the highest emissions rate relative to its energy consumption or GDP. For example, Spain lies somewhere in the middle (emissions per final energy consumption and emissions per unit of GDP) or below the European average (emissions per capita).

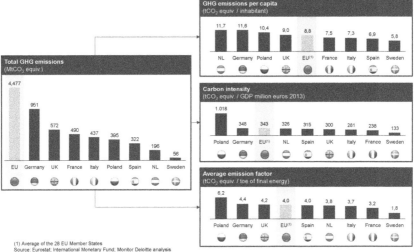

Figure 4

As far as the electricity generation mix is concerned, EU State members' energy policies in recent years have led to significant differences within the European Union (see Figure 5). Electricity generation is one of the most GHG emitting activity sectors on almost every EU country, with counted exceptions as in the case of Sweden or France. Thus, it is an activity sector that has an important necessity of being transformed by renewable energies penetration mostly.

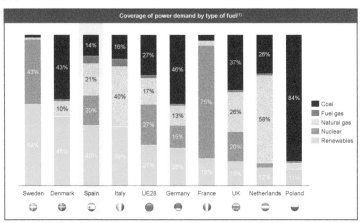

Comparison of renewable energy penetration level among the main EU countries in 2013

(1) Gross power generation
Source: European Commission

Figure 5

In the area of climate action, the EU is also committed to taking action to limit global warming. Europe is in the midst of a debate about medium and long-term climate and energy policies that would promote cost-efficient decarbonisation, and provide certainty for investments in long-lived energy infrastructure. To achieve decarbonisation, the EU has developed a set of benchmark policies and intermediate milestones for decarbonisation (see Figure 6), in particular:

The 2013-2020 Energy and Climate Change Package, adopted in 2007 by the European Council, laid the foundations for fulfilling the commitments on climate change and energy and included 2020 targets: reduce GHG emissions by at least 20% from 1990 levels, cover 20% of final energy consumption with renewable energy and reduce the consumption of primary energy by 20%.

The 2030 Framework, adopted in 2014 as a continuation of the previous Energy and Climate Change Package, included a binding target of reducing GHG emissions by 40% compared to 1990 levels. In addition, the Framework proposed another binding target of increasing renewable energy "by at least 27%", although this objective will not be translated into legally binding targets for EU Member States. An energy efficiency target of 27% was also set.

The Roadmap 2050, presented in 2011, states that by 2050 the EU must reduce its emissions to between 80% and 95% below 1990 levels, through domestic reductions.

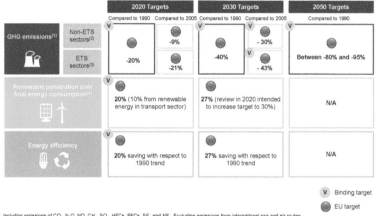

Analysis of EU environmental targets: 2020, 2030 and 2050

(1) Including emissions of CO_2, N_2O, NO_x, CH_4, SO_2, HFCs, PFCs, SF_6 and NF_3. Excluding emissions from international sea and air routes
(2) Sectors not covered by the Emission Trading System (ETS): transport except aviation, building construction, waste and agriculture
(3) Sectors covered by the ETS: industrial consumption, power generation and air transport
(4) Percentage of renewable energy consumption over total final energy consumption
Source: European Commission; Monitor Deloitte analysis

Figure 6

EU Member States are contributing to the achievement of the European objectives in accordance with the transpositions of these objectives to each of country.

2.1.1 EU progress towards climate and energy targets

The 2015 edition of the annual European Environment Agency (EEA) 'Trends and projections' report confirmed that the EU is well on track to meet its climate and energy targets set for 2020 (see Figure 7).

In addition, the report highlighted the positive impact of key 'drivers', in particular the steady roll-out of renewable energy and the decrease in the energy consumption in most EU Member States over the last decade.

Regarding the 2030 climate and energy policy framework agreed by the EU in 2014, the report showed that while projections show further decreases in EU GHG emissions beyond 2020, Member States project that the pace of these reductions will slow down. Planned reductions will only bring EU emissions between 27% and 30% below 1990 levels by 2030, which falls short of the 40% reduction target for 2030. Sustaining the current pace of growth in renewable energy sources could enable the EU

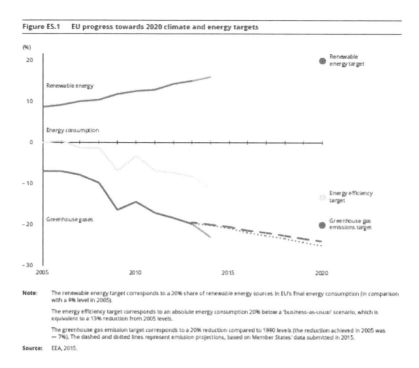

Figure ES.1   EU progress towards 2020 climate and energy targets

Note: The renewable energy target corresponds to a 20% share of renewable energy sources in EU's final energy consumption (in comparison with a 9% level in 2005).

The energy efficiency target corresponds to an absolute energy consumption 20% below a 'business-as-usual' scenario, which is equivalent to a 13% reduction from 2005 levels.

The greenhouse gas emission target corresponds to a 20% reduction compared to 1990 levels (the reduction achieved in 2005 was − 7%). The dashed and dotted lines represent emission projections, based on Member States' data submitted in 2015.

Source: EEA, 2015.

Figure 7

to achieve its target of a minimum 27% share by 2030. However, this will be challenging because market barriers persist, while support measures for renewable energy have been scaled back in various countries. Furthermore, as economies pick up across Europe, further efforts will be necessary to ensure that energy consumption continues to decrease in order to reach the objective of reducing Europe's energy use by at least 27% by 2030 compared to a baseline scenario.

Regarding EU objectives to 2050, although the EU and its Member States are making good progress towards their short-term goals on climate and energy, they will have to increase considerably their efforts to meet longer-term energy and decarbonisation objectives for 2050. For example, the reduction in GHG emissions needed between the 2030 target level (− 40% below 1990) and the 2050 EU objective (at least 80% below 1990) will have to be two to three times steeper than the necessary reduction between current levels and the 2030 target, which is itself steeper than the reductions achieved so far since 1990 (see Figure 8).

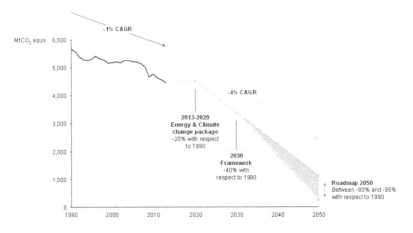

Source: UNFCCC; Monitor Deloitte analysis

Figure 8

In order to reduce GHG emissions is imperative a structural change on the ways energy is both produced and consumed from today until 2050. Coal, oil refined products and natural gas are the major causers of these emissions, both on a global and on an EU level. These fuels are consumed almost by all economic sectors to some extent, which will require a major shift on energy production and consumption patterns over all European economic sectors in order to reach emissions neutrality.

Against recent expectations, the energy model transformation along this century is not going to be motivated by the fossil fuels depletion but by the growth of two fundamental vectors: technological development and the aforementioned climate change fight.

2.2 Energy model implications for EU Member States: the Spanish case

2.2.1 The starting point of the Spanish energy model

Let's take the case of a specific country, Spain, which has a greater renewable penetration than the average of the EU, in order to analyze the transformation requirements yet pending for decarbonizing its economy and identifying priorities. Spanish GHG emissions amounted to 322 equivalent $MtCO_2$, of which 240 million stem from energy uses, whereas the remaining 82 million correspond to other non-energy uses (agriculture, livestock, land uses, etc.). Focusing on those emissions derived from energy uses, it can be observed (see Figure 9) a significant weight of transport and power generation.

Energy-related GHG emissions distribution by energy sectors and by primary energy

Distribution of energy-related GHG emissions by type of primary energy fuel and sector in 2013 in Spain
(%, MtCO$_2$ equiv.)

	Power generation	Oil refining	Road transport	Other transports[1]	Residential	Services	Industrial	Other[2]	
Coal	16%	0%	0%	0%	0%	0%	2%	1%	19% / 46
Oil products	3%	5%	31%	2%	4%	2%	3%	5%	55% / 132
Natural gas	5%	0%	0%	0%	3%	3%	13%	2%	26% / 61
	24% / 58	5% / 12	31% / 75	2% / 5	7% / 17	5% / 12	18% / 42	8% / 19	100 % / 240 MtCO$_2$

(1) Including railway, air and sea transport
(2) Including fugitive emissions, emissions from energy consumption in fishing, agriculture, solid fuel transformation and others
Note: the emissions from CHP/cogeneration are split between services, industry and oil refining. The emissions from international sea and air routes are excluded
Source: UNFCCC; MAGRAMA; IDAE; Monitor Deloitte

Figure 9

The transposition of the 2020 targets to Spain resulted in a goal of increasing GHG emissions by no more than 30%, taking 1990 as a reference. As for other EU Member States, Spain is on track to meet 2020 targets, whereas the target related to renewable energy penetration out of final energy final energy consumption will require an extra effort to ensure its compliance (see Figure 10).Furthermore, the progress made in achieving the objectives has basically been due to the development of renewable power generation and the economic crisis that has led to a reduction in energy consumption, but not to a structural change in final energy consumption.

Analysis of the achievement of environmental targets set for Spain within the framework of the European Union for 2020

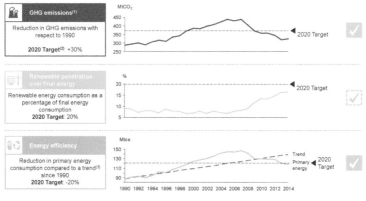

(1) Excluding emissions from international sea and air routes
(2) Different objective to that of the EU. The countries that were more industrialised in 1990 must make a greater effort (for example Germany -20%).
(3) Spain must make a 25.2 Mtoe reduction in the consumption of primary energy compared to the 2020 trend, which must represent 20% of its consumption. Straight-line growth with respect to 1990 has been assumed
Source: European Commission; Monitor Deloitte analysis

Figure 10

2.2.2 The Spanish energy model of the future

The European commitment of reducing GHG emissions between 80% and 95% in 2050 will imply for Spain, depending on the year of reference, that emissions will be limited to a very low level between 14 and 88 $MtCO_2$. Energy uses will concentrate a very significant part, if not all, of the emissions reduction effort, due to the greater complexity on reducing emissions for non-energy uses, an aspect that could be extrapolated to most member countries.

In order to achieve those objectives, it is clear that structural changes in the energy model will be necessary by the joint application of three decarbonization levers: shift to lower emitting energy carriers, emissions – free electricity generation and energy efficiency and conservation. In general, to illustrate, between 90% and 100% of electricity generation in 2050 will need to come from renewable sources, maintaining the required back-up capacity, either in the form of conventional generation technologies or in the form of new power storage technologies. One of the greater challenges for the stakeholders of the Spanish (and European) energy market will be renewable technologies' integration on the power market, with the efficiency, economic sustainability and security of supply requirements.

To the same extent, energy carriers will need to be shifted by others with lower emissions, mainly deriving on a massive electrification of the energy demand fed with renewable energies and almost displacing petroleum or coal from the primary energy mix, or using lower emitting fuels, for example, by using natural gas instead of oil derived products where electrification is not technologically feasible. This would imply, for example, that electric vehicle's share has to be increased to cover almost all the automotive industry in 2050, that a modal shift to between 40% and 60% of the heavy duty transport to railways has to be conducted, considering that today is mainly transported by road, and that the energy carrier shift to lower emitting fuels on residential, commercial and industrial sectors has to be intensified. Thus, electricity consumption should increase from 26% of final energy consumption to 64 – 70% in 2050 (see Figure 11).

Evolution of final energy consumption by energy carrier in Spain

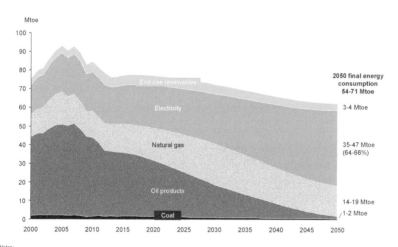

Notes:
Without considering heat generated by cogeneration units
Excluding consumption of international sea and air transport
Average values are shown
Source: IDAE; Monitor Deloitte analysis

Figure 11

In addition, ambitious energy efficiency measures will be needed in order to reduce final energy intensity between 1.6 and 2.2% annually through performances in new construction, renovation of existing buildings and new industrial processes.

In this way, in Spain (and on the majority of countries of the EU) electricity generation will precisely need to be based almost solely on renewable energies because the future power generation mix should reach a renewable energies share of 90-100% in 2050. In the case of Spain, as orders of magnitude, reaching this share of renewable energies will mean installing between 145 and 201 GW of renewable electricity generation capacity to satisfy an electricity demand that should increase to 410 – 570 TWh from an actual level of 220 TWh. Furthermore, due to the intermittency of these energies, sufficient back-up capacity will need to be installed to ensure that adequate levels of security of supply are guaranteed.

These relevant structural changes will demand a considerable investment effort that European economy will have to accomplish between 2016 and 2050. Continuing with the case of Spain, as an illustrative example, and with the current new technologies' cost evolution expectations, those investments will amount to €330.000-385.000 million depending on the considered scenarios.

However, all this effort will bring several positive externalities as a lower dependance on oil imports, a higher energy efficiency because usually electricity constitutes a lower energy consumption in comparison with other energy carriers, and possibly a lower electricity price, due to the high investment needs which will need to be recovered; the costs of these already mature technologies will be diluted along the higher demand derived from the electrification of the economy.

2.3 Policy issues and recommendations for the EU energy transition

There are high uncertainties on the transition to a decarbonized energy model, so solid and flexible energy policies are needed during this transition. The high investment needs, the long periods of recovering investments and the uncertainty of when certain technologies will reach maturity (on costs and performance) to be fully deployed require an intelligent transition. This transition must guarantee the efficient accomplishment of long term objectives and the resilience of the evolution of technology and costs. It must be a solid and flexible transition, composed by policies and measures of which we are not going to regret, not requiring investments possibly getting outdated or unnecessary due to technological development.

This situation will require relying on every available technology on the transition period. An early forego of several technologies or fuels (for example, nuclear, coal or natural gas) from today until 2030 will mean setting at risk economic efficiency or security of supply.

In order to achieve the maximum decarbonization potential, the previously described demand electrification must be accompanied by the development of free emitting electricity generation. The high necessity of new renewable power requires, likewise, a relevant back-up capacity during the transition to 2030, that must be provided by fossil fuel plants, hydro pump storage facilities, international interconnections, demand response mechanisms and by new storage technologies (that ensure not emitting as being charged with surplus generation of renewables).

It is complicated to estimate when new energy storage technologies will be available in terms of volume and at a competitive cost as to provide the required level of back-up during times of peak-load. By all means, it seems improbable that before 2030 these technologies could provide back-up during several hours. To the same extent, it could be argued that there are reasonable doubts about the short-term availability from international interconnections or from new demand response mechanisms. For these reasons, all available technologies are needed during the transition.

Hence, the early phase out of conventional generation plants, while storage technologies have not been sufficiently developed, will require new natural gas fired or even coal fired plants, which are highly emitting. This is the case which is being observed, for example, in Germany, with the nuclear phasing out decision for security risks reasons: nuclear plants contribute to climate change mitigation due to their lack of GHG emissions, but its early phase out has implied the construction of 7 GW of new lignite coal plants, one of the most pollutant and GHG emitting fuels.

With an appropriate management of the currently available generation fleet, the immense majority of the new generation capacity built in Europe from now should be renewable, except with high load growths, or when it has not been possible to develop other alternatives on time (for example, interconnections or pumping storage plants).

The effort to be done in terms of renewable energy penetration is massive, and is reasonable that it is shared by multiple stakeholders, fostering competition. The technological disruption that solar and battery storage technologies will imply, together with the energy self-sufficiency desire of consumers, will allow consumers to contribute to that investment effort.

In terms of energy efficiency, it will be required a continued annual reduction of energy intensity between 1.4% and 2% until 2030, with a similar continued path up to 2050. The initiatives to be implemented are numerous, highly different in nature and encompassing almost every activity sector. For example, edification sector and building rehabilitation, both residential and commercial, is one of the pending tasks of energy efficiency, which has to be purposefully addressed.

In addition, industrial sectors are highly sensible to price and economic return signals, so the efforts must focus on eliminating the price signal distortion and, given the case, on the inclusion of economic incentives or financing mechanisms that support the carrier shift (to electricity or gas) and the inclusion of greater efficiencies.

Government bodies and the European private sector need to undertake decided actions to lead the change of energy model. The fight against climate change requires consumption patterns changes, massively using renewable energies and performing enormous efforts on energy efficiency. All of which requires raising huge investments for power generation, infrastructure, R&D, new ways of construction, etc. This turnaround will require the combined commitment and awareness of Government and Regulatory bodies, companies and the whole citizenship.

Incentivizing policies of these structural changes and new legal and regulatory frameworks. An intense planning and execution coordination amongst different public institutions will be essential for the rational and efficient decision making from companies and consumers. In order to completing a gradual and competitive transition, but which has to be firm and with a commitment of changing the structures of our energy model, is necessary to determine a group of policy recommendations that sets the appropriate importance to security and energy model competitiveness. The group of Energy Policy actions that foster energy model evolution to decarbonization can be structured on four axis of recommendations (see Figure 12):

- Recommendations on the definition of targets and fiscal policy

- Recommendations on the transport sectors

- Recommendations on the residential, services and industrial sectors

- Recommendations on the electricity industry

Energy policy recommendations aimed at leading our energy model towards
decarbonisation

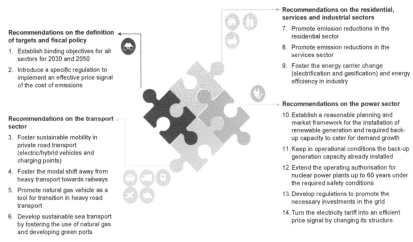

**Recommendations on the definition
of targets and fiscal policy**

1. Establish binding objectives for all
   sectors for 2030 and 2050

2. Introduce a specific regulation to
   implement an effective price signal
   of the cost of emissions

**Recommendations on the transport
sector**

3. Foster sustainable mobility in
   private road transport
   (electric/hybrid vehicles and
   charging points)

4. Foster the modal shift away from
   heavy transport towards railways

5. Promote natural gas vehicle as a
   tool for transition in heavy road
   transport

6. Develop sustainable sea transport
   by fostering the use of natural gas
   and developing green ports

**Recommendations on the residential,
services and industrial sectors**

7. Promote emission reductions in the
   residential sector

8. Promote emission reductions in the
   services sector

9. Foster the energy carrier change
   (electrification and gasification) and energy
   efficiency in industry

Recommendations on the power sector

10. Establish a reasonable planning and
    market framework for the installation of
    renewable generation and required back-
    up capacity to cater for demand growth

11. Keep in operational conditions the back-up
    generation capacity already installed

12. Extend the operating authorisation for
    nuclear power plants up to 60 years under
    the required safety conditions

13. Develop regulations to promote the
    necessary investments in the grid

14. Turn the electricity tariff into an efficient
    price signal by changing its structure

Figure 12

3. OTHER KEY IMPLICATIONS: THE IMPACT ON EU
INTERNAL ELECTRICITY MARKET

Cooperation on energy has been at the heart of European integration from the beginning, with the creation of the European Coal and Steel Community in 1952 and the European Atomic Energy Community (Euratom) in 1957. In this context, an internal market for electricity and gas in the European Union was established through three market liberalisation packages (adopted in 1990, 2003 and 2009), which provide for the 'unbundling' of energy production and supply from energy-transmission networks, as well as third-party access to gas storage facilities, reinforced consumer protection, and strengthened regulatory surveillance.

In this context, Electricity generation is a liberalized business in Europe, one in which the prices are set by market rules. The European Union Commission will have to integrate the derived requirements from the accomplishment of the environmental objectives with those of the development of the single European power market. In this way, the initial goals of the single market add up to those of the decarbonization; the Commission will need to analyze the compatibility of the measures to be developed and, in light of possible distortions, must facilitate new instruments for its joint attainment.

The shift of energy matrix will not be exempt of difficulties and considerations due to the difference in nature of the energy sources that will conform the power generation mix, both because of the intermittency of renewable energies and because of the different cost functions that present these new technologies with respect to conventional energy sources. In such a way, the European power market design must allow stakeholders decision making for recovering all the costs and obtaining a return on investment through their bids in the market.

Renewable energies, even though have high generation costs, their variable costs are low, since the primary resource they use (the sun or the wind) can be renewed by the very nature. Thus, they will only be able to run in moments when the primary resource is available, which is the reason for requiring back-up capacity to function when that primary resource is not available. If renewable energies, with a variable cost close to zero, are able to bid on wholesale power markets, thus competing with conventional technologies, wholesale electricity prices will be increasingly depressed (in cases when the displaced energy comes from conventional power plants with higher variable costs) as the share of these technologies is increases.

In addition, the high requirements of new renewable capacity requires, in turn, a relevant flexible back-up capacity that, initially will be provided by the actual nuclear, thermal and hydro generation fleet. In such a way, for example, back-up power plants with high variable costs will be condemned to operate a reduced number of hours, challenging the complete recovery of their costs.

Thus, it is crucial to adapt wholesale markets design, in order to correctly assess firmness, which does not occur in existing only-energy markets. In addition, it is noteworthy that the actual price signal does not incentivize the investment in new generation, neither conventional nor renewable (without incentives), which might put at risk security of supply.

To the foregoing, it adds the main problem of electricity markets, which even relying exclusively on conventional technologies, sufficient revenues to recover investments are not obtained, specifically because of "system reliability". This is known as "missing money": the average revenues obtained by generation is lower to the average cost of a new generation entrant, which discourages investments on new generation capacity. On several markets, this problem has been addressed with complementary regulatory payments, capacity payments, for guaranteeing cost recovery.

This gap will need to be filled up with mechanisms that remunerates capacity and "remuneration complements" to renewable energies. These additional regulatory payments are implemented for ensuring full recovery of investments not jeopardizing security of supply by a lack of generation investments. This situation could be reverted on the medium term if the advances on the decarbonized technologies' learning curves advances (nuclear and renewable) are sufficiently intense.

In that way, the market will shift to a scheme which, even though wholesale market revenues and ancillary services' revenues may be reduced, capacity remuneration mechanisms are defined and, where appropriate, incentives for renewable energies.

In terms of renewable energies integration on the electricity system, it has to be accomplished without affecting system security and under the principle of optimizing its integration for minimizing energy spills. To this extent, System Operators (OS) must be granted with the required tools, as for example, a greater minimum load for combined cycle units, when technically feasible, for ensuring the operation with the minimum spill levels or the management of high response generation that ensures load recovery in spite of the lack of renewable energies due to the lack of primary resources. Moreover, a fundamental coordination between the neighbors OS for them to use the excess of renewable energy on their ancillary services.

Based on the above mentioned, policies dedicated to power market during the energy transition will be crucial. In this way, in order to ensure efficiency and security of supply, it will be critical to stablish a reasonable planning and market framework for installing the required renewable and back-up generation capacity for meeting load increases. This framework will be the foundation for developing and continuously updating a medium to long term (5 – 10 years) capacity planning; and for developing an electricity market reform for triggering a long term economic signal, efficient for investments, that ensures stability and which fosters the installation of more mature technologies with lower costs.

According to the generation capacity under operation, it will be necessary to efficiently take advantage its operating life for minimizing investments and unnecessary costs on the transition period, as explained above. In order to achieve it, it will be necessary to maintain back-up capacity under operation while a technically an economically viable storage technology is developed; as well as to convey an electricity market reform for stablish the appropriate price signal for remunerating firm capacity. In such a way, mechanisms should not incentivize investments on capacity which in the future could be underused (thermal generation) or early investments on not yet mature technologies (storage).

In summary, in order to make possible a generation mix based almost exclusively on renewable energies, actions leading to that mix will need to be put in place and granting it with a regulatory framework which generates the appropriate economic signals for investments to be accomplished; the investors must have an adequate visibility of cost recovery.

Finally, and to existing interrelations, accompanying the transition with the development of the interior European power market will be other of the main challenges of the European Union policy. Regulation of the power market initiatives, such as interconnection impulse, national policies coordination, promotion of forward markets in order to foster investment, or market support systems will be aspects whose development will be critical in the decarbonization process of the European Union.

The Energy Union – catalyser or roadblock for Europe's energy transition?

CHRISTOPHE SCHRAMM

Former adviser to the French energy minister

«L'Europe se fera dans les crises.» (Jean Monnet)

The following text builds on a paper jointly published in November 2015 by the French think tank Terra Nova, the German Friedrich Ebert Foundation and the Polish Institute of Public Affairs: http://tnova.fr/system/contents/files/000/001/108/ original/231115_-_The_ Energy_Union_at_a_crossroads.pdf?1448635463

1. THE RECENT CHALLENGES IN EUROPE'S ENERGY POLICY

Since the establishment of the European Coal and Steel Community in 1951, energy has been one of the backbones of the European project. The physics of existing electricity systems – i.e. that supply and demand have to be balanced at all times – make the Europe-wide connection and integration of energy systems across the continent a foremost necessity.

The geopolitical nature of energy also makes a coordination of national energy policies a must if Europe wants to be heard on the international scene. The EU, with its scarce and declining primary resources, needs to be able to speak with one voice to our external suppliers and to rely on solidarity mechanisms in case of supply disruptions.

More importantly, energy policy has had from its beginning a strong social and industrial component. Most of us have a house to heat, a car to fuel, a mobile phone to charge or various household devices to power with electricity. And energy industries have been important players of Member States' economies, be it as providers of a basic good for all other industries, as employers or as "industrial champions". So European energy policy debates have always been about more than just energy, they have been the expression of the Member States' conceptions about economic and industrial policy, social justice and their own sovereignty.

It is this founding European project that has been going through a crisis in recent years.

Though Europe's energy policy has been based from the outset on a triptych of objectives – competitive access, sustainability, and security of supplies – it is the first objective that has dominated the Commission's thinking on energy policy until recently, as embodied by the efforts to create an internal energy market.

Launched about 30 years ago with the idea that liberalisation and free markets would increase competitiveness and reduce energy prices, the internal market agenda has suffered from national opposition tactics and has proven unsuitable to tackle the other objectives of energy policy.

Tensions and conflicts close to Europe's borders (Eastern Ukraine, Syria, Iraq, Libya, Algeria etc.) and the recent decline in oil prices have revealed the insufficiencies of Europe's foreign energy policy and its dependency from external fossil fuel suppliers for decades to come.

More recently, the European Union has been criticized for the impact its policies have on energy poverty, even if the responsibility for identifying vulnerable energy consumers and putting measures in place to protect them lies with Member States. Indeed, around 54 million people in Europe (11% of the population) suffer from rising energy prices, low income and poorly energy efficient homes, in particular in Central Eastern and Southern Europe[1].

This has led to increasing doubt about the capacity of the European Union to design, let alone implement a coherent energy policy to deliver on its three objectives of security, competitiveness, and sustainability of energy supplies.

2. A POLICY CAUGHT UP BETWEEN THE ENERGY TRANSITION AND TECHNOLOGICAL DISRUPTION

Among the many possible causes for this state of affairs, two stand out.

Looking backward, the main cause is internal to Europe's policy making and is the shift towards more climate-focused energy transition policies over the past 20 years. In line with the Kyoto protocol, European energy policy makers have since the years 2000 progressively focused their attention on reducing the environmental impact and in particular the carbon intensity of the energy systems.

---

[1] Source : https://ec.europa.eu/energy/en/news/energy-poverty-may-affect-nearly-11-eu-population

Germany launched its *Energiewende* in 2000 when the Social Democratic / Green coalition government announced the exit from nuclear energy and the shift towards renewable energies. In 2011, this decision was confirmed by the then conservative government, with an objective of 80-95% economy-wide emission reductions by 2050.

In 2009, the European energy and climate package set out ambitious targets for the reduction of carbon dioxide emissions (-20% compared to 1990), the development of renewable energies (20% of final energy consumption) and the increase in energy efficiency (+20% compared to 1990) by 2020 ("20-20-20").

In 2012, France launched its own energy transition, with similar emission reduction objectives as Germany and the plan to reduce the share of nuclear energy in the electricity mix from about 75% to 50% by 2025.

The climate priority in Europe's energy policy has been further strengthened with the adoption of a global climate agreement in Paris in November 2015 that aims at limiting the increase in temperatures at the globe's surface to a maximum of 2°C above pre-industrial levels and that enshrines the objective of global carbon neutrality before 2100.

While the 2008 package has allowed the European Union to establish itself as a role model for global climate action, it contained two fundamental flaws. First, the Commission did not make a clear choice in terms of policy instruments to achieve its objectives. A strict emissions target complemented by an emissions trading scheme could have been sufficient to drive emissions down in the sectors covered, notably electricity. Instead, the Commission proposed additional renewable energy and energy efficiency targets and European rules on how to achieve them. This created interferences between the three policies that have overall been detrimental to the functioning of the European emissions trading scheme.

Second, decision makers and market players alike underestimated the tensions that would arise in the internal market from the European renewable energy policy. The fundamental challenge derives from the replacement of formerly centralised systems of energy production and distribution by increasing shares of decentralised renewable energy systems. Over the past years, decreasing demand in the context of the economic crisis, prices favouring the use of coal over gas power plants and the increase of renewable capacities have all led to overcapacities in conventional base load power generation. At the same time, more flexible solutions (storage, demand-side response, investments in grid and back-up capacities to cover demand peaks) are needed to tackle the higher volatility of power production. Europe is moving away from fossil fuel based systems whose costs are mainly operating costs, towards systems based on more volatile renewable capacities, whose costs are mainly capital costs.

While the European internal market legislation has provided for short-term market signals for operational decisions, it has not integrated the need for additional price signals for adequate long-term investments in such a new system ("missing money problem"). The long term signal for developing renewable energies has been developed outside of the market through national support schemes, thereby increasing volatility in the market and creating other unwanted effects. The existing "energy only" electricity market has become more and more unsustainable.

Policy makers at national and European level were taken by surprise by the combined effects of their own policies for more market and competition on the one hand and more renewables on the other hand. Struggling with the task of making their national energy transition a success, each Member State chose unilateral action to address the problems. 28 different types of mechanisms were created in the United Kingdom, France, Germany, Italy, Poland, Spain and 6 other Member States, to ensure that sufficient production capacity is available when the sun does not shine and the wind does not blow despite high electricity demand. Environmental NGOs have accused these mechanisms to favour fossil fuel based technologies, while others see the perspective of a single energy market with the same rules for all moving further away.

Afraid of the possible state-aid nature of certain renewables support schemes, the European Commission also tried to harmonise the aid that can be given to renewable energy projects, using its powers in the field of competition policy to favour market premia and competitive bidding processes over feed-in systems.

In addition, the trans-European energy infrastructure package of 2013 came too late and was not powerful enough to appropriately address national and cross-border network development needs arising from the rapid development of new renewable power capacities. As a consequence of insufficient grid infrastructure, operators today have to use more and more often "re-dispatch" measures that ensure a balance between supply and demand (i.e. order conventional power stations to reduce generation, in order to "make space" in the grid for the high influx of wind power; temporarily shut down wind turbines; order conventional power stations to produce more electricity to meet demand from consumers who cannot be served with wind power because of insufficient grid capacity). This is particularly true in Germany, where installed wind capacity now exceeds 30 Gigawatts in the North of the country, while consumption still mainly takes place in the more industrial South. The cost of these re-dispatch measures amounted to 400 million euros in 2015 and could reach 1 billion euros by 2020[2]. Building and refurbishing the necessary infrastructure could even cost around 55 billion euros by 2025[3]. But the consequences also cross borders: On certain windy days, the massive amounts of electricity produced on the German coast were pushed through the Polish electricity network to reach customers in Austria (so called "loop flows"), forcing Poland to install additional infrastructure allowing it to control energy flows on its network. Facing the fact that the almost 3,000 km of additional high voltage transmission lines cannot be built fast enough through Germany – notably due to low public acceptance –, Germany is now considering the split of the power market it has been sharing with Austria since 2002.

The second cause came like an external shock to European policy making and is technological disruption. One disruption has come from the massive cost reduction for renewable energies. Since 1980 photovoltaic modules have decreased in cost at an average rate of about 10% per year[4]. Costs for wind power have decreased more slowly, but nevertheless significantly. This has accelerated the roll-out of solar and wind installations in the European Union and across the globe, thereby further accelerating technological progress and cost reduction. Traditional energy giants such as E.On, RWE and Engie (ex *GDF Suez*) were unprepared for the speed, with which wind and solar power have crowded out their coal and gas fired power plants. Billions of assets had to be written off in the last few years, leading to the isolation of fossil fuel based assets in "bad bank" like entities.

Looking forward, the bigger disruption for traditional energy players however probably comes from the rise of digital technologies and the new services they allow to offer in a world with more decentralized renewables where up to half of all EU citizens could produce their own energy by 2050[5]. The key here is access to data: Traditionally, consumer data was in the hands of distribution system operators who operate the lines running to individual (household, commercial or industrial) consumers. Things are changing rapidly, as more and more individual households start to store and sell to the grid the electricity or heat they produce. With the rise of cheap

---

[2] Source: https://www.cleanenergywire.org/factsheets/re-dispatch-costs-german-power-grid / https://www.cleanenergywire.org/news/loops-and-cracks-excess-german-power-strains-europes-grids-0.

[3] Source: http://www.insm.de/insm/Presse/Pressemeldungen/Pressemeldung-Studie-EEG.html

[4] Source : http://www.sciencedirect.com/science/article/pii/S0048733315001699

[5] Source : http://www.rescoopv.be/sites/default/files/Prosumer%20Potential.pdf

sensor, data transmission and data analytics technologies, competition has emerged from new companies offering smart metering, self-consumption and other energy-related services. It is still unclear who, between energy utilities, equipment providers or digital giants such Google or Apple, will be most successful in extracting value from the data generated. But digital disruption is already creating huge uncertainty among all players in the energy field, making the definition of a common European energy approach and the implementation of effective energy policies even more challenging.

So while Europe's transition towards a cleaner customer-centric energy system should be a formidable, unifying political project for 500 million citizens and a unique catalyser for investment, jobs and growth, it appears that the choices made in the various Member States have so far created more of a disunion.

3. THE ENERGY UNION: (SLOWLY) ACCELERATING EUROPE'S ENERGY TRANSITION

The Energy Union should help in solving some of the challenges described above.

The idea of some new European energy initiative has been maturing in Brussels' policy circles for several years. In 2010, Jacques Delors and Jerzy Buzek threw their political weight behind the concept of a "European Energy Community", which however remained only an issue for Brussels' think tanks and other Europhile circles. Things changed when the now president of the European Council, Donald Tusk, in the wake of Russia's annexation of Crimea, called for an "energy union" to break Russia's energy "stranglehold" on Europe in April 2014.

Though initially focussed on security of supply, the idea of a much broader union finally reached the highest political level. The newly elected Jean-Claude Juncker adopted the initiative, identifying five dimensions – energy security, solidarity and trust; full integration of the European energy market; energy efficiency as a means to moderate demand; decarbonisation of the economy; research, innovation, and competitiveness – which would take into account the concerns of all Member States. These were developed into 15 action points[6] in a Framework Strategy published on 25 February 2015.

---

[6] Implementing existing energy legislation, in particular the third internal energy market package; diversifying EU gas supplies, improving resilience in case of supply disruptions; making intergovernmental agreements more transparent; promoting trans-European energy infrastructure; rethinking the EU's electricity market design; strengthening the role

The document lacked hierarchisation and a real diagnosis on the most pressing issues such as making the EU's existing market rules compatible with its climate and renewables ambition. This "business as usual" approach made it impossible to honestly take stock of where European energy policy has really succeeded or failed so far, and – rather than muddling through as before – what areas Europe should focus its attention on in the coming years to really achieve progress, such as the energy transition.

The Commission's "Clean Energy for All Europeans" proposals published on 30 November 2016 are – partly – responding to this challenge.

The EU agreed in October 2014 on a new set of objectives for 2030 in the run-up to the Paris climate summit, including a 40% cut in greenhouse gas emissions compared to 1990 levels, at least a 27% share of renewable energy consumption, and at least 27% energy savings compared with the business-as-usual scenario. The European Commission had proposed a more ambitious 30% for the share of renewables and energy savings, but carbon-intensive energy producers such as Poland traded a lower number in exchange for accepting the 40% emissions reductions.

The 30 November package contains a whole array of measures in the fields of energy efficiency (including eco-design and the renovation of buildings), renewable energy, and electricity market design.

The revised energy efficiency directive stands out as the Commission is coming back to its initial 30% energy efficiency target for 2030.

By contrast, the renewable energy directive keeps the 27% target and does not – as done in 2009 – fix any national objectives that would add up to the 27% European objective. This weakness in ambition is compounded by the fact that the directive in itself only proposes marginal improvements to the existing framework for renewables development in view of reaching the 27% objective: the one-stop-shop and time limit for renewable energy permit granting procedures is a welcome novelty; the attempt to open national support schemes to installations from other Member States seems unlikely to be more successful than the 2008 provisions on joint projects. The proposal also contains an attempt by the Commission's Energy directorate to take back control from the Competition directorate regarding renewable support schemes, through an article that describes – in much more general

of European regulators and network operators as well as regional cooperation initiatives; increasing transparency on energy prices; advancing towards more energy efficiency, notably in buildings; speeding up decarbonisation in transports; achieving the EU's GHG emission reduction and renewable energy objectives for 2030; developing a stronger European research and innovation agenda for energy and transport; speaking with one voice to the outside world on energy and climate issues terms than the 2014 state aid guidelines – how support schemes should be designed to avoid market distorsions. Finally, as explained in the proposal's impact assessment, the EU's emissions trading scheme alone would allow achieving 24.3% of renewables by 2030, so the additional effect of the renewables directive itself is a meagre 2.7 percentage points (assuming the 10-year forecast is precise). One can wonder in the light of the Commission's drive for simplification to what extent such a text is indispensable.

The Commission's package also contains a revision of the regulation and directive on the internal energy market that tries to address market design problems. The text is a clear step towards establishing rules regarding the operation of electricity markets, including day-ahead, intra-day, balancing and forward markets. The Commission also tries to harmonise Member State approaches to capacity mechanisms, although only after the approval of several capacity mechanisms, notably in the UK and France, by DG Competition. The proposal aims at the transparency and non-discriminatory nature of these new schemes, while making only the most CO_2-efficient gas and coal power plants eligible to these mechanisms. The regulation also puts an end to the priority access for renewable electricity to the grid as established by the 2008 renewables directive (with exceptions for small installations). Internal market supporters explain these measures are necessary to ensure that renewables and conventional power sources play well together, while energy transition activists interpret them as clear signs of Europe's lack of clear vision on where it wants to go on renewables. The text clearly is a compromise proposal that tries to reconcile the contradicting views between Member States with different energy mixes and hence different views on their energy future.

Interestingly, the Commission also proposes to set up an EU-level body to coordinate the operation of distribution system operators, based on the existing and well-functioning model of transmission system operators. This entity will have a role in better integrating renewables, developing demand-response and accelerating the roll-out of smart grids.

In any case, given the massive development of renewables capacities in China, the United States and India, it remains to be seen whether this legislative package will be enough for the European Union to become (again) "the world number one in renewable energies" as promised by Commission President Juncker.

4. WHAT MORE CAN THE ENERGY UNION DO TO FURTHER EUROPE'S ENERGY TRANSITION?

The key question today is whether Member States can agree on fully coordinating the development of their power plant parks and the corresponding grid and storage infrastructure, i.e. the evolution of their respective energy mixes. To this end, they need to agree at the highest political level on the priority objectives they want to reach with the Energy Union: Is the Energy Union only the new name for Europe's existing and partially contradictory energy policies? Or can it be a catalyser for Europe's transition towards a low carbon energy future, on which everyone agrees in principle?

We believe the Energy Union has the potential to be the second.

For that, it needs first to be based on a strong and transparent governance structure.

The 30 November package has made interesting proposals in this regard. Its governance regulation obliges Member States to produce a national integrated energy and climate plan for the period 2021 to 2030 and foresees a consultation process that will allow both the Commission and other Member States to comment on each plan. This measure will help in aligning national energy and climate policies and facilitating a more European approach to energy transition policies across Europe.

However, one can doubt whether this measure will be sufficient to close the gap between European and national policy debates and politics and to ensure national political orientations are as coordinated as possible and together shape a coherent European energy system.

National lawmakers have their say on key aspects of energy policy such as the energy mix or renewable energy support schemes, and they make the link with citizens in each Member State. A renewed and strengthened governance framework should thus make sure members of national Parliaments are on board when European energy policy decisions are taken.

This could be achieved by creating a "European Parliamentary Platform on Energy", which would bring together representatives from the committees in charge of energy in each of the 28 national Parliaments and the European Parliament, to discuss the future of energy policy in Europe. Such a platform could enable the involved groups to engage in a dialogue with civil society actors and thereby to progressively harmonise their views on the further development of the Energy Union. This body could also create spaces for enhanced cooperation to discuss regional policy issues affecting only a subgroup of Member States.

Secondly, an energy system reform is necessary to achieve the Union's long-term energy policy goals.

Pivotal to the transformation of energy production and consumption is joint planning, a market design reform, a stable framework for investment and network development as well as clear priorities for research, development and innovation policies.

Member States will not adopt the same strategies concerning the energy mix, but all share the same long-term goal of a more sustainable energy system. To get there, joint planning will be necessary. Member States should plan their respective investments in the energy system in a much more coordinated way, if they want to build an integrated European energy system that leaves space for the specific choices of each country. Current reporting obligations of Member States regarding energy policy need to be both streamlined and strengthened, to become proper impact assessments: they should be sufficiently detailed to get a common understanding of the potential impacts of national energy policies on neighbouring countries, highlighting expected costs and benefits at both national and European levels. The proposed regulation foresees that the national integrated energy and climate plans will be the result of regional collaboration between all concerned Member States and will contain an impact assessment. These measures go definitely in the right direction and need to be effectively implemented.

The design of electricity markets will also have to change, both to allow further integration of short-term markets and to give the right long-term signals for new capacities Member States want to develop in renewables, storage and back-up facilities, while accelerating the phase-out of inefficient, carbon intensive base load overcapacities. National capacity mechanisms and strategic reserves alone will not get us there. Rather, their existence reflects the flaws of the current market design. One solution to be explored is the creation of regulated or publicly controlled entities at regional level, which would allow investments following European interests in renewables, storage and back-up facilities to happen by entering into long-term contracts with generators, while ensuring competition between them. This in fact already applies today, albeit in an uncoordinated and thus costly way, through national renewable support schemes and capacity reserve mechanisms, which in many cases boil down to long-term contracts with regulated Transmission or Distribution System Operators or publicly controlled entities. This new scheme would not replace short-term markets, which could still provide the appropriate incentives for operational decisions and dispatch. It would require an in-depth coordination at regional level to define the objectives of the regulated or publicly controlled buyers when it comes to entering into long-term contracts with investors in renewable, storage or back-up capacities, while being flexible enough to accommodate different national energy policy choices. While the recent proposals do not contain such a measure, it is interesting to note that the Commission is considering additional action, should national efforts be insufficient to meet the objectives of the Energy Union: Indeed, in the technical memo accompanying the governance regulation, the Commission mentions the possibility to set up a "financial instrument managed by the Commission, which would be used to support cost effective renewable energy projects across the Union"[7].

Whatever the strategies of each Member State are, grids will play an ever-increasing role in accommodating the evolving energy mix. Regional integration of network operators – through smart grids, joint control centres and integration into regional operators – is necessary to speed up the integration of national markets. This is fully in line with the regional operational centres that the Commission proposes to create as part of the 30 November package. Having 4 or 5 fully integrated regional network operators in the EU should be the mid-term objective.

In order to meet our goals for 2050 one has to be aware that neither a linear extrapolation of the past is possible, nor can a step-by-step policy account for the need to completely change our mode of energy generation and consumption. We have to innovate: most of the technologies that will dominate the energy world of the 2050's have still to be invented or developed. This is why the Energy Union should step up Europe's efforts in developing strategic energy and climate technologies with a focus on a few key topics and sufficient funding. Energy efficiency, energy storage, smart grids and clean mobility are the areas in which a massive push on R&D would be a no regret move. Furthermore, we have to think all sectors, namely electricity, heat and transport together and connect them in a smart way, taking advantage of the possibilities of digitalisation. To increase the impact of support, national research and innovation agencies should jointly elaborate their funding programmes, merge available funds at European level, thereby spreading best practices in terms of innovative financing, and develop early on common technical standards to allow for the emergence of strong European industrial players for the energy transition. Unfortunately, the Commission's 30 November communication

[7] Source: https://ec.europa.eu/energy/sites/ener/files/documents/technical_memo_energy uniongov.pdf

on "Accelerating Clean Energy Innovation" does not propose any joint funding measures.

Thirdly, the robustness of Europe's energy policy in the longer term depends on its integration with Europe's broader policy goals. In this area, the recent proposals tabled by the European Commission remain too general and incomplete.

If energy policy has been a controversial issue for such a long time, this is also due to it being linked to and entangled with so many other policy fields, from transport policy to fiscal, social, trade, economic or foreign policy. The Energy Union will only succeed if it manages to take a holistic approach and reconcile the various policy objectives.

To increase energy security, no Member State should be left entirely dependent on one single supplier. The necessary infrastructure should be implemented to make sure all Member States can diversify their supply portfolio and to prevent abuses from dominant suppliers. European funds available for energy networks should be clearly prioritised towards such projects.

Integration is also needed with Europe's climate policy instruments. While the European emissions trading scheme (EU ETS) needs to be strengthened and extended, the sectors not subject to EU ETS (e.g. buildings, agriculture, transport) should receive a price signal through a European-wide carbon tax that would prevent the current market distortions created by the existence of different national taxation schemes.

Clean mobility is a central piece of the energy system we are aiming for. This is why the Energy Union should dedicate significant means to this objective, beyond research & development. The EU should develop a network of European transnational green mobility corridors and support their equipment with charging stations for electric and hydrogen vehicles.

Europe should finally integrate its energy policy objectives with economic competitiveness, industrial and social policy objectives, making sure that the energy transition leads neither to burdening the competitiveness of energy-intensive industries that operate in global markets, nor to social costs that are such that large parts of the population will oppose it. A more comprehensive and concrete approach is needed: rather than focusing exclusively on harmonised wholesale market prices, a truly European energy policy should strive to harmonise the overall cost of energy, notably for energy-intensive consumers across the Union, by considering wholesale prices, but also network costs and taxes, while also establishing protection measures for vulnerable consumers. This should start with renewed efforts to harmonize energy-related taxes, tax exemptions and state aid.

5. CONCLUSION

The positive dynamic created by the Paris climate agreement should help the European Union to really decide in the ongoing negotiations on the "Clean energy for all" package where it wants to go with its Energy Union project. It is time for Europe to merge conflicting interests in order to achieve its energy, and beyond that its ecological transition, in the spirit of Robert Schuman's declaration on 9th May 1950: « Ainsi sera réalisée simplement et rapidement la fusion d'intérêts indispensable à l'établissement d'une communauté économique qui introduit le ferment d'une communauté plus large et plus profonde entre des pays longtemps opposés par des divisions sanglantes. »

Environment & Motorsport. A Race To Sustainability

ENRIQUE BUENAVENTURA

General Counsel, Formula E Operations Ltd, United Kingdom

1. INTRODUCTION BY ALEJANDRO AGAG[1]

Five years ago, Mr. Jean Todt, president of the Fédération Internationale de l'Automobile ("**FIA**"), expressed his interest in an electric "Formula 1" racing series in response to the European Commission's desire to entice the car industry to adopt more sustainable forms of energy.

A year later, the FIA granted my company, Formula E Holdings Limited, a licence to promote a new championship for 100% electric formula cars. Thus the Formula E project was born. Our dream to drive the future was about to begin.

At that time, we needed much more than a new racing series concept to convince teams, cities, sponsors, investors and employees to embrace the project. The widespread belief that Formula E could support behavioural changes for transport users, plus the idea to develop and promote innovative solutions to ensure that transportation remains environmentally friendly, were key factors to obtaining immediate interest from different stakeholders around the world.

But Formula E is not just a R&D platform to develop electric cars. We also want to show to young generations that electric cars can also be fast and cool. These children and teenagers will be the potential buyers of future cars, and we want these cars to be electric. A change in the perception of electric cars could definitely improve its development and directly affect the environment in city centres.

I am now writing these lines after the end of our second season. Now, leading car manufactures have joined us and are competing around the most iconic cities of the world to become Formula E champions. We, as the promoters of the championship, together with the teams, cities, investors,

---

[1] Alejandro Agag is the CEO of Formula E Holdings Limited the company holding the FIA licence to promote the FIA Formula E Championship

sponsors, partners and suppliers, are all racing towards a better and more sustainable future. The race for sustainability has begun.

2. MOTORSPORT, SUSTAINABILITY AND LAW

One of the key principles in Environmental Law is "Sustainable Development", defined by the World Commission on Environment and Development[2] as *"the development that meets the needs of the present without compromising the ability of future generations to meet their own needs"*. With this principle in mind and understanding the background of the recently created Formula E Championship, I would like to show how racing can be linked to the concept of sustainability.

To achieve this, I want you as reader to understand a bit more about motorsport history, the role of the FIA and how this organisation reaches and influences the perceptions of so many people. I would then like to go on to the recently created "Formula E Championship" and look at how it has united many different stakeholders around the creation of a new global racing series with a sustainable DNA. It is an event that aims to increase electric car usage, impact the air quality in our cities and thus improve our quality of life. Therefore, it is directly linked to one of the key principles of Environmental Law.

3. FIA [3]

In the race to sustainability, the FIA has a fundamental role. To the general public the FIA is seen solely as the governing body for motorsport events like Formula 1 or the World Rally Championship. But there is a long history behind this non-profit association that aims to safeguard the rights and promote the interests of motorists and motorsport across the world.

In the early 20th century, when city-to-city racing was becoming popular, there were no rules governing safety or fair competition. The Automobile Club de France allied itself with 12 clubs from around the world to form, in 1904, the Association Internationale des Automobile Clubs Reconnus, the direct predecessor of the FIA. The initial goal of this association was to bring coherent governance and safety to motorsport. The FIA's evolution into a global motorsport organisation started in 1950, when the federation inaugurated the Formula 1 World Championship.

---

[2]   The World Commission on Environment and Development released a report called "Our Common Future" also known as the "Brundtland Report" in 1987. Such report defined the meaning of "Sustainable Development"
[3]   Information available at www.fia.com

Since then, the FIA has been regulating and adjudicating at hundreds of events in a huge variety of series each year. The Formula 1 World Championship, the World Rally Championship, the World Endurance Championship and the Formula E Championship are just some of the competitions under the FIA's umbrella.

The FIA discusses issues on an international level defining global public policy positions. As a direct result of this work, the FIA is officially recognised by the United Nations, where it has special consultative status and sits as on several of its transport-related working parties.

4. CO2 EMISSIONS - POLICY RECOMMENDATIONS FOR DECISION MAKERS

As an example of the FIA's consultative role and with the goal of contributing to the global CO2 emissions reduction debate, the FIA issued in December 2015, in light of COP21[4], a policy paper entitled *"Global Reduction in CO2 emissions from cars: a consumer's perspective"*. In this document, the FIA and its global network of automobile clubs presented a number of key recommendations in relation to the reduction of CO2 emissions.

It is very interesting in this paper, the FIA's position in relation to the fuel tax and fiscal policies.

Fiscal incentives are a useful instrument to reduce CO2 emissions and fuel consumption, especially when paired with national CO2 regulation.

The FIA belives that goverments should ensure that broder taxation on motoring is consistent with climate change objectives: petrol, diesel or other fuels or propulsion systems should be taxed according to their enviroemental performance and revenues should be reinvested. Under this idea, the FIA highlights a new set of fiscal policies that have been used by governments kwown as feebate programms. A feebate programme is a "transfer", not a "tax". Those who choose to buy higher CO2 emitting vehicles pay fees which are used to give rebates to those who buy lower CO2 emitting vehicles.

The FIA considers that, if properly designed, a feebate programme can create a continuous incentive for vehicle manufacturers to improve the environmental performance of their vehicles, including the most efficient ones. For that reason, it should provide financial incentives to consumers

[4] COP21: Was the 2015 United Nations Climate Change Conference, held in Paris, France, from 30 November to 12 December 2015. It was the 21st yearly session of the Conference of the Parties (COP) to the 1992 United Nations Framework Convention on Climate Change (UNFCCC) and the 11th session of the Meeting of the Parties to the 1997 Kyoto Protocol

and manufacturers without collecting additional revenue: any fees collected should be balanced out by the rebates awarded, without imposing any net tax.

But FIA's most notorious step towards sustainability, especially from its motorsport angle, is the creation of a new 100% electric racing cars championship. This opens a new door to innovation and development of transportation towards sustainability.

5. FORMULA E - A BABY BORN TO CHANGE THE PERCEPTION OF ELECTRIC VEHICLES

The Formula E Championship was born out of a desire to develop and foster electric transportation. Its ultimate goal was to serve as an R&D framework for electric vehicles, whilst also increasing the general interest in electric cars and promoting sustainability. But Formula E is becoming much more than just a racing series, it is turning into a wider global movement.

The announcement made on August 27, 2012 about the understanding reached between FIA and Formula E Holdings Limited[5] ("**FEH**") to launch a worldwide racing series with electric formula cars was met with much scepticism from the world's motorsport media. Comments such as, *"that will never happen"*, and, *"we'll believe it when we see it"*, rang out across the news pages.

Yet little by little the foundations of this incredibly ambitious project began to be laid in a very short period of time.

In January 2013, in Kidlington, Oxfordshire, the series turned a corner as the first ever team was unveiled giving much needed credibility to the project. Drayson Racing would be led by Lord Paul Drayson, a former UK Minister for Science who shared the same passion as the new environmentally friendly championship. *"The most exciting aspect of Formula E is the opportunity to make motorsport much more relevant to the challenges of the car industry,"* said Lord Drayson at the time. *"Motorsport needs to be the leader in this and to help shape perceptions of what is cool and exciting,"* he added.

As the year, and the hype surrounding Formula E progressed, so did its ability to attract sponsors. Michelin, TAG Heuer and Renault, all leaders in their respective fields, committed at a very early stage and became key partners in the Formula E movement.

---

[5] Formula E Holdings Limited (FEH) is the holding company owner of the FIA licence to promote the FIA Formula E Championship.

As other teams and important partners like Qualcomm or DHL joined the project, September 2013 would also prove to be a game-changing month for Formula E which at that stage still only consisted of around 10 full-time staff. Despite its embryonic stage, it was that month when the FIA's president unveiled to the world the new Formula E car at the Frankfurt Motor Show.

In November 2013, and just over a year since FEH had been named as the promoter of the new FIA electric series, comments from journalists were shifting from *"that will never happen,"* to, *"this could be happening"*.

In June 2014, and now with all the 10 teams on board, Formula E rose to one of its biggest tests to date. Behind closed doors, the teams' first ever shakedown of their cars took place at Donington Park. The reliability and smooth running of these first ever electric racing cars was celebrated with great joy by all involved.

Then in September 2014, the 10 teams together with their 40 cars, equipment and drivers made the short journey from Donington Park to East Midlands airport to leave for China for the first ever Formula E Championship Electric Prix.

The eyes of the world fell on a 3.44km stretch of asphalt in Beijing as these noiseless electric cars were about to race for the first time. A project started by a few optimistic dreamers was about to become a reality and signal the start of the future of motorsport and the car industry. In the media centre, journalists waiting for the five start lights to go out had one common headline in their minds: *"well, it's happened then"*.

6. A ROOM FULL OF CONTRACTS

Behind the scenes, there have been many legal challenges to build the whole series. When the CEO, Alejandro Agag, was trying to convince me to join the project four years ago, he described Formula E not as a racing series full of cars, but as a "future room full of contracts".

He was right. The mountain of contracts drafted and negotiated during the early years of the project included agreements with teams, cities, promoters, suppliers, investors, partners, and broadcasters, and each required the complex legal advice that a start-up needs (things cannot stop from happening) together with the assurance that all the risks associated to long term commitments (with powerful and experienced partners) were stablished to form the pillars and precedents of this new international event.

Applying the learnings from experience with other similar series (both the mistakes and the wise decisions), and managing to have a well-balanced structure from the outset (i.e. internal lawyers understanding all the commercial details of the project and commercial people respecting all the legal work required for each matter), the Formula E project has managed to create a safe and robust legal structure to face the challenges and difficulties of a pioneering worldwide event.

But this legal structure is only one part of the well-organised ecosystem that surrounds the Formula E project. And this happens when different parties join forces to identify common goals. There has been a common denominator among our partners since the early negotiations. Aside from teams wanting to win each of the races, all the stakeholders joining the project have prioritised, above their own individual interest, the challenge of making Formula E a reality and helping to create a better and more sustainable world.

7. THE STORY: UNDERTAKING THE MOBILITY CHALLENGE - SUSTAINABLE DEVELOPMENT FUELLED BY INNOVATION

This combination of the common efforts and goals shown by all Formula E partners is perfectly captured at the end of the first season in a white paper put together by Formula E and its partners under the guidance of its Official Logistics Partner DHL. The eStory: Undertaking the Mobility Challenge, is a document where readers can find examples of innovations developed at Formula E during its first season and it shows how motorsport, through the FIA Formula E Championship, is managing to directly participate in a Sustainable Development around electric mobility. FEH has defined rules that guide innovation, but the individual partners are fully responsible for contributing necessary resources and finding the right balance between different needs of their core business. Formula E's objective, together with its partners, is to minimize the footprints at each of the racing events, not only in terms of carbon but also considering ecosystems quality, natural resources and human health across all of Formula E's activities.

Through its partners, Formula E has created collaborative platforms capable for game changing developments which have the potential to grow on a greater scale. I will reproduce below some examples and relevant data captured in this white paper, associeted to the work and solutions provided by the different partners involved in the Formula E Championship:

Aquafuel and the power of glycerin: one of the main objections from the anti-electric car lobby is that the pollution caused by the production of the electricity in the first place negates their environmental credentials.

This argument carries some weight in countries where the main supply to the national grid comes from coal-fired power stations (although it still overlooks the fact that the amount of carbon produced in the process of creating and distributing petrol or diesel is greater still). Nevertheless, if electric cars are to make a significant difference to the quality of air we breathe, charging them with electricity produced by low-emission sources is crucial.

As Formula E wants to play a key role in advancing the technology surrounding electric car ownership not just the cars themselves, the bold decision was taken that the charging of the racing cars had to come from a sustainable source.

The British company Aquafuel Research Ltd was commissioned to build clean mobile generators which can be packed inside a shipping container and sent as freight to each race. Aquafuel patented its own renewable energy generators which run on glycerin. This fuel is clean in terms of emmissions as it has no carbon and low particulate and nitrous oxide emmisions. The fuel has a positive effect on the injection system parts and the exhaust of the cars. It is expected that in the next 3-5 years the production of glycerin from salt water algae will be commercially demostrated, thus creating a fully sustainable production process. The Aquafuel generators used by Formula E provide 42kW of electricity per car. This means that if all 20 cars are plugged in at once, the power generated is equivalent to the amount of electricity 2000 UK homes would consume. In addition, the pollution reduction in comparison to a standard production diesel engine is impressive. In just one hour, nearly half a kilogramme of poisonous nitrous oxide emissions is avoided.

Logistics and offsetting the impact on climate change: DHL has also successfully risen to the chalenge of handling the logistics of the Championship in a fast, efficient and environmentally caring manner in order to minimise the carbon footprint of each event's logistics. DHL has been involved with Formula E since its early stages and contributed to the setup of the race calendar in a smart way by avoiding unnecessary transportation. A total of 41 batteries were transported directly inside the cars while complying with specific UN regulations. Aluminium battery cases were used to transport the additional ones. Formula E and its sustainable approach requires innovation on the logistics side too, so in that sense, Formula E is also a driving force for its logistic partners like DHL.

Wireless charging technology: Innovation around Formula E has no barriers. Imagine a race where the entire race track has dynamic pads under the surface wirelessly charging the batteries and allowing the electric cars to race for an infinite distance. This is the goal of Qualcomm and its Qualcomm Halo wireless electric vehicle charging technology (**"WEVC"**). The BMWi8 Safety Cars used in the Championship during the first two seasons have been using Qualcomm Halo WEVC. This technology goal could be transported to the city centres where electric cars could be charged at a parking space, whilst waiting in a traffic light or, why not in the future, as they move around the city using dynamic pads placed under the street surfaces.

Like the above examples, all Formula E partners have developed their own innovation strategies to be implemented and/or showcased around the Formula E events. Michelin and its tyre recycling program or BMW using energy from renewable sources in the production process of the Official Championhip Medical Car, the all-electric BMW i3, are other good examples.

Roborace and the future of vehicles: The entire Formula E ecosystem could be the perfect prototype for smart cities in terms of transportation.

In light of this idea, it is interesting to mention one of the latest partners to join the Formula E family: Roborace. This is a new racing event that will showcase electric driverless cars using artificial inteligence technology. Again, Formula E will be the platform for innovation and helping to develop what could be the future of transport. There are still many questions around this new support event, even from a regulatory point of view. Can autonomous cars be regulated by the FIA if the main definitions of vehicle or even the concept of sport require the participation of a human being? Would Roborace be just a showcase for driveless cars or could it become a new global series? What is true though, is that Roborace will help to develop one of the most challenging and promising technologies concerning mobility under extreme racing circumstances. Another testing ground for future smart cities.

5. CONCLUSION

I would like to come back to the Brundtland Report released by the World Commission on Environment and Development in 1987. In such report Brundtland explains how in the middle of the 20th century, we saw our planet from space for the first time in history. He believes how historians may eventually find that this vision could have a greater impact on thought than did the Copernican revolution of the 16th century, which upset humans' self -image by revealing that the Earth is not the centre of the Universe. "From space" - he describes – "we see a small and fragile ball dominated not by human activity and edifice but by a pattern of clouds, oceans, greenery and soils".

No matter how important we think our activities are, we need to take a step back from our human centric vision and try to fit, as much as possible, such activities into the Earth's patterns. From Formula E, we are trying to take this approach. We want people to enjoy motorsport but in a way that meets the environmental needs of the present, fostering the social awareness and infrastructure investment for sustainable mobility in the future. We have tough opponents, but we are all committed to win this race!

Clean Energy and environmental tax regime

MARTA VILLAR EZCURRA

CEU San Pablo University, Spain*

1. INTRODUCTION

Making ours the words of Ban Ki-moon "we have entered in a new era of clean energy growth that can fuel a future opportunity and greater prosperity for every person in the planet".[1] Promoting clean energy with environmental tax regimes means not only introducing new carbon taxes as part of the energy tax system, but reviewing in a broad manner, if necessary, the scope of the energy taxes to include polluter sectors, exclude non-polluters, and also, address tax reliefs in order to promote environmentally friendly targets (e.g. energy efficiency).

Nevertheless, energy taxes are often introduced with the main purpose of raising revenue rather than influencing energy consumption and provide for tax benefits to some sectors such as agriculture or energy-intensive users. Therefore, they should also be reviewed to check their coherence in terms of environmental protection objectives and to guarantee that they are well-co-ordinated with other economic and market instruments like emission trading systems, control on prices and environmental relief for tax purposes.

Sometimes the gap between theory and execution is significant from economic and political perspectives. This is particularly the case of clean energies and environmental concerns. So, as it has been suggested by Janet Milne there is also a need to explore the idea of expanding the use of environmental fees as a complement to environmental taxes in the environmental pricing toolbox.[2]

---

*   Professor of Tax Law, CEU San Pablo University, Madrid. Coordinator of the Jean Monnet Project ETSA-CE (Ref.: 553321-EPP-1-2014-1-ES-EPPJMO-PROJECT) and IP of the National Project (2004-58191-P), RID: 0-7484-2015.

[1]   See Global Trends in renewable energy investments 2016, Frankfurt School FS-UNEP Collaborating Centre for Climate & Sustainable Energy Finance (2016), 5.
[2]   See J Milne, Environmental taxes and fees: wresting with theory, in L Kreiser *et al* (ed) Environmental Taxation and Green Fiscal Reform. Theory and Impact, Critical Issues in Environmental Taxation Vol XIV (2014), 5-22.

The limits on States' power to use tax incentives to achieve clean energy goals, in Europe or elsewhere are particularly important in an era when countries are confronting the challenges of climate change. As States designing policy instruments to reduce greenhouse gas emissions, they must grapple with the question of how to achieve their environmental goals without violating legal rules, and among others, the ones designed to protect internal markets.

Environmental and energy issues intersect in a particularly strong and significant way in the arena of fight against climate change given the need to reduce emissions from fossil fuels and shift to clean energy practices. Yet trade and clean energy objectives can conflict. Sometimes governmental policy instruments that promote clean practices can skew market competition at the international, national or sub-national level. For example, they may intervene in the market by providing subsidies o tax benefits to encourage renewable energy and energy conservation or protect industries at risk during the transition to a greener economy.

This Chapter deals with one specific subject of tax law – environmental taxation dimension – connected with rules on competition and market regulation within the legal frame of the European Union law. Though interesting, the economic dimension will be let aside.[3] The ultimate objective is to analyse the most legal relevant factors and constraints that could explain the role of taxation related to clean energy resources in the European Union region. Four main sections will structure this analysis. Section 2 will discuss the need to coordinate tax measures with other instruments, policies and actions and will address the issue of the distribution of powers between the European Union and the Member States. Section 3 will examine the Energy Taxation Directive pointing out the lack of a truly environmental component in its current version. Section 4 will explain the reason of the relevance of the State aids rules in the energy taxation regimes. Section 5 will analyse some leading European Court of Justice (ECJ) cases and finally, Section 6 concludes.

---

[3] Energy taxes often provide exemptions for energy-intensive industries, with the effect of reducing the macroeconomic costs in exchange for increased emissions because the disburden companies that otherwise would have been heavily affected. For further economic analysis on the topic see, among others, A Dannenberg *et al*, What does Europe pay for clean energy? – Review of macroeconomic simulation studies, Energy Policy 36 (2008) 1318-1230, at 1327.

2. THE NEED TO COORDINATE TAX POLICY WITH OTHER POLICIES AND ACTIONS

Although significant progress is being made in completing the internal energy market according to the European Commission's Internal Energy Market progress report adopted on 13 October 2014, before the internal energy market can be completed further integration of energy markets will be necessary for meeting the medium to long-term objectives.[4] In this context, the European Commission called in 2012 for a more co-ordinated European approach and for an increased use of renewable energy trading among Member States.[5]

Since the very early approach of European Union law to renewable energies, Member States were permitted to support renewable energies, as an exemption to a free market. Currently, the 2009 Directive[6] allows Member States to employ tendering schemes for new capacity, which may take into account the interests of environmental protection and the promotion of emerging technologies. The EU target of achieving a share of renewables in gross final energy consumption of 20 per cent by 2020 is distributed among Member states. The national targets range from 10 per cent for Malta to 49 per cent for Sweden.[7]

The issue of harmonization in the European region is ever more important, to avoid market distortion by means of bad financial support schemes and energy and CO_2 taxes. However, tax harmonization cannot successfully tackle all the distortions and should be co-ordinated with other legal measures such as the approximation of legislation on prices, environment, energy efficiency and security of supply.

Taxation is typically an area in which the European Union has few exclusive powers, mainly expressed in the Union Treaties in order to harmonize tax regulations, although many powers of taxation straddle the areas of shared competences between the European Union and the Member States. Thus, the European Union does not tax, spend, implement or coerce, and, in many areas it does not hold a legal monopoly of public authority. On the contrary, in the European Union, Member States keep

---

[4] See Communication from the Commission to the European Parliament, the Council, the European Economic and Social Committee and the Committee of the Regions, Progress towards completing the Internal Energy Market (COM (2014) 634 final).
[5] COM (2012) 271 "Renewable Energy: a major player in the European energy market".
[6] Directive 2009/28/EC of the European Parliament and of the Council of 23 April 2009 on the promotion of the use of energy from renewable sources and amending and subsequently repealing Directives 2001/77/EC and 2003/30/EC, OJ (2009) L 140/16.
[7] For the analyses of the tax legal evolution of the renewables in the European Union see D Pérez-Bustamante, La fiscalidad de las energías renovables en la Unión Europea in M Lucas Durán (dir) Fiscalidad y energías renovables, Thomson-Reuters Aranzadi (2013), 741-775.

their tax powers and even in areas of the European Union's greatest fiscal activity (the common agricultural policy, structural funding and development aid), most public findings remain national.[8] However, some multilateral agreements cover trade and investment[9] in particular sectors and impose obligations concerning taxation in the sectors covered. In contrast, Article 4 of the Treaty on European Union (TEU) enumerates the shared competences between the European Union and the Member States, several of which are also relevant to the major objectives of the Union: internal market, economic, social and territorial cohesion, environment, transport, trans-European networks and energy.

The internal market has long been the exclusive objective and the rationale of the European Union in shaping its tax policy. However, the attribution to the European Union of other competences must be considered in all subareas of European tax law. The competition rules which are, of course, the core of this internal market, are the exclusive domain of the Union. In addition, the Union already has extensive legislation in place with respect to the internal market. Therefore, there is no doubt that the centre of gravity of the legislative power with respect to the internal market lies with the Union but tax power's allocation lies with the States.

From these considerations, in the absence of Europea Union standards (e.g. through harmonized environmental taxes), it is clear that European Union Member States may use tax incentives to promote clean energy and specifically to: (i) achieve higher levels of environmental protection; (ii) reduce pollution and other negative impacts on the environment; and (iii) introduce national environmental regulation, going beyond European Union standards.

Nevertheless, these tax benefits have to be checked directly against article 107(1) of the Treaty of Functioning of the European Union (TFEU) through the 2014 Guidelines on State aids regarding environmental protection and energy 2014-2020 (EEAG)[10]. Besides, they could conflict with the fundamental freedoms[11] and with specific limits imposed on the

---

[8]   A Moravcsik, Reassessing legitimacy in the European Union, JCMS, Journal of common market studies, vol. 40, no 4, (2002), 603-624.
[9]   In relation to trade and WTO legal restraints, see H J Ault and J Sasseville, Taxation and Non-Discrimination: A reconsideration, World Trade Journal 22, (2010) 120. See also R H. Weber, Renewable energy: subsidies and taxes as competition distortion, in L Kreiser *et al* (ed), Environmental Pricing. Studies in Policy Choices and Interaction, Critical Issues in Environmental Taxation Vol XVI (2015), 161-176.
[10]   Communication from the Commission, Guidelines on State aid for environmental protection and energy 2014-2020, OJ 2014/C 200/01. This statement is made by the Court on *Republic of Austria v. European Commission* case (see T-251/11, EU:T:2014:1060).
[11]   On this question see E Traversa and S Wolff, Energy Tax Policy in an EU Context: Non-Discrimination Free Movement and Tax Harmonization, in P Pistone and M Villar Ezcurra

European Union Member States' tax powers because of the need to fulfil the requirements of the Directive 2003/96/EC of 27 October 2003 restructuring the Community framework for the taxation of energy products and electricity (ETD).[12]

3. THE ENERGY TAXATION DIRECTIVE FRAMEWORK

The Energy tax policy in European countries shaped significantly by the Energy Taxation Directive (ETD)[13], which sets minimum tax rates for a variety of energy commodities. The main goal of the ETD is to ensure the proper functioning of the internal market as regards the taxation of energy products and electricity. According to the preamble to this Directive, this goal requires minimum levels of taxation to be laid down for most energy products. Being the "right" level of taxation a question of debate there is not a precise theoretical basis[14]. For the purpose of the ETD the level of taxation means *"the total charge levied in respect of all indirect taxes (except VAT) calculated directly or indirectly on the quantity of energy products and electricity at the time of release for consumption".*[15]

This structure makes the ETD potentially suitable instrument for these products to reflect in their prices the cost to the society of the CO2 emissions resulting from their use. In particular, the taxation of energy products allows the European Union to combine the incentive role of taxes in favour of an energy efficient and environmentally friendly role with the ability also to generate revenues. However, the ETD sacrificed its environmental pretension in exchange for a greater role in European Union´s energy taxation harmonization. Essentially, the current minimum rates based on the volume of energy products consumed do not reflect the energy content or the CO2 emissions of each energy product, leading to a contradiction with the energy and climate change European objectives, since, for instance, it promotes the use of cola as heating fuel.

One key aspect of the discussions of the ETD in the Council focused on the connections between tax reductions and/or exemptions and EU State aid rules and that, compulsory or facultative nature of certain tax

---

(eds), Energy Taxation, Environmental Protection and State Aids, Tracing the Path from divergence to convergence, 2016, IBFD, 397-411.

[12] The Council Directive 2003/96/EC of 27 October 2003, restructuring the Community framework for the taxation of energy products and electricity (OJ L 283, 31.10.2003). The Proposal for a Council Directive amending Directive 2003/96/EC (COM (2011) 169/3) was given up. The Commission decided on the withdrawal of 73 pending legislative proposals and the list has been published in the Official Journal of the EU (OJ C 80/17, 7.3.2015).

[13] See supra note 12.

[14] See J Milne (2014), supra note 2.

[15] Art. 4(2) of the ETD.

reductions and/or exemptions must be considered. Member States and the industry needed certainty that the reductions and exemptions they were negotiating would not be prohibited by the Commission under State aid rules when transposed in national legislation.[16] Thus, the ETD is closely related to the State aids regime, since it includes exemptions and authorises Member States to grant tax incentives.[17] If the tax exemption derives from a Community measure such a Directive, without leaving any scope for discretionary application at national level, the measure is not "imputable" to the State and cannot therefore be considered to be a State aid. The first condition that the aid must be imputable to the State, different from the need to be granted through State resources is hence not met.

Also, in the interests of protecting the environment, the ETD authorizes European Union countries to grant tax advantages to businesses that take specific measures to reduce their emissions. Although Member States may apply tax exemptions – including the implementation of a level of taxation down to zero – and reductions under articles 15-17 of the current ETD, these measures have to be notified following article 26 of the ETD and may be checked by the Commission under State aid rules. Nevertheless, since it is difficult to subsidize all the environmentally beneficial alternatives to a harmful activity, tax expenditures inevitably involve "picking winners" which may put other good alternatives at a disadvantage.

Moreover, ongoing economic uncertainties and changing government policies have led to a reduction in incentives for clean energy in many countries, especially in the European Union. However, under article 14(1) (a) of the ETD, Member States shall exempt from taxation energy products and electricity used to produce electricity and electricity used to maintain the ability to produce electricity.

However, they may, *"for reasons of environmental policy"*, subject these products to taxation without having to respect the minimum levels of taxation laid down in this Directive. In that case, the taxation of these products shall not be taken into account for the purpose of satisfying the minimum level of taxation on electricity laid down in article 10. In the *Kernkraftwerk Lippe-Ems* case, regarding the German nuclear fuel tax,[18] the ECJ clarified that article 14(1)(a) of the ETD is to be interpreted *"as not*

---

[16] See D Boesherz, Community State aid policy and energy taxation, EC Tax Review 4 (2003), 214-219.
[17] For further information about this topic see M Villar Ezcurra EU State Aid and Energy Policies as an Instrument of Environmental Protection: Current Stage and New Trends. European State Aid Law Quarterly (4), 611-620 (2014) and M Villar Ezcurra State Aids and Energy Taxes: Towards a Coherent Reference Framework. Intertax 41 (6-7), 340-350 (2013).
[18] See DE: ECJ, 4 June 2015, Case C-5-14, *Kernkraftwerke Lippe-Ems GmbH v. Hauptzollamt Osnabrück.*

precluding national legislation which levies a duty on the use of nuclear fuel for the commercial production of electricity", firstly because the nuclear fuel that is the subject of the German law (KernbrStG) does not constitute an energy product for the purposes of the ETD and it is not, therefore, covered by the exemption laid down in this article of that Directive, and secondly, because it cannot be applied by analogy to the nuclear fuel that is the subject of KernbrStG.[19]

Furthermore, the current European Union energy taxation framework needs to be changed to improve the functioning of the internal market and use energy taxation more effectively for environmental purposes. One important step had been attempted to reach environmental targets. On 13 April 2011, the European Commission presented its proposal for amending the ETD,[20] considering a series of demanding, legally binding climate and energy targets. In this proposal, the European Commission remarked that one of the problems of the current ETD is that Member States can compensate differences in production costs by applying favourable tax treatment according to article 16 of the ETD.

The main objective of the revision of the ETD was to bring it more closely in line with the European Union's energy and climate change objectives, in particular to address CO_2 emissions in the non-ETS sector, avoid negative interference with the EU ETS, facilitate energy saving and the deployment of renewables, and allow revenue generation in a non-distortive way.

The new proposed rules aimed to restructure the way in which energy products are taxed, in order to remove current imbalances and take into account their CO_2 emissions and energy content as well. Existing energy taxes based on the volume of energy products consumed would be split into two components that, taken together, would determine the overall rate at which a product is taxed: one part would be based on CO_2 emissions of the energy product and would be fixed at EUR 20 per ton of CO_2; the other would be based on energy content, i.e. on the actual energy that product generates measured in gigajoules (GJ).

This approach is clearly in accordance with the aim of promoting a higher level of environmental protection. A more efficient tax structure on energy products and electricity in itself would provide better and more consistent price signals and would ensure more effective use of energy taxation both for environmental and fiscal purposes. Unfortunately, the proposal for amending the ETD has been abandoned[21] and the current tax regime remains inappropriate in terms of environmental protection and the

---

[19] See *Kernkraftwerke Lippe-Ems GmbH* (Case C-5-14), paras. 47-48 and 53.
[20] COM (2011) 169, see SEC (2011) 409 and 410.
[21] See OJ C80/17, 7.3.2015.

need to co-ordinate taxes with other economic or market instruments. As we have already mentioned, the existing ETD does not provide incentives or even price signals to encourage alternative energy.

4. THE RELEVANCE OF THE STATE AIDS RULES IN THE ENERGY TAXATION CONTEXT

It is clear that any kind of tax measure which certain undertakings may enjoy, including in the context of the energy taxation and clean energies, should be checked - as any "aid"- objectively, against the notion of article 107 (1) TFEU[22] under their well-known four circumstances: The measure has to be granted by the State or through State resources; it has to favour an undertaking or the production of certain goods; it has to be selective; and it has to affect trade between Member States in such way that it leads to a distortion of competition.

Basically, the structure of State aid law consists of two main levels. At the first level, the general prohibition of State aid can be found in Article 107(1) TFEU and it is developed in the definition of State aid. Article 107(1) states as follows:

"Save as otherwise provided in the Treaties, any aid granted by a Member State or through State resources in any form whatsoever which distorts or threatens to distort competition by favouring certain undertakings or the production of certain goods shall, in so far as it affects trade between Member States, be incompatible with the internal market".

The second level is based on Article 107(2) and (3) TFEU. These two provisions provide for exemptions to the general prohibition on the granting State aids. Automatic justifications mentioned in paragraph 2 are declared to be compatible with the internal market and no discretion is possible.[23] Conversely, regarding the list included in paragraph 3 concerning the discretionary justifications[24], as is settled law, the Commission *"enjoys a*

---

[22] See Communication from the Commission, Commission Notice on the notion of State aid as refer to in Article 107 (1) TFEU, Brussels 2016, available at http://ec.europa.eu/competition/state_aid/modernisation/notice_of_aid_en.pdf.

[23] Moreover, the exhaustive list regarding, in summary, "social aids", "disaster aids" and "German aids" *"must be construed narrowly"*. See Case C-156/98, *Germany v. Commission*, Judgment of 19 September 2000 (EC:C:2000:467), para. 49.

[24] The most important categories of exemptions are enumerated in paragraph 3 (a), (b), and (c) as follows: *"(a) aid to promote the economic development of areas where the standard of living is abnormally low or where there is serious underemployment, and of the regions referred to in Article 349, in view of their structural, economic and social situation; (b) aid to promote the execution of an important project of common European interest or to remedy a serious disturbance in the economy of a Member State; (c) aid to facilitate the development of certain economic activities or of certain economic areas, where such aid does not adversely affect trading conditions to an extent contrary to*

wide discretion, the exercise of which involves assessments of an economic and social nature which must be made within a Community -Union- context". The Court would here *"restrict itself to determining whether the Commission has exceeded the scope of its discretion by a distortion or manifest error of assessment of the facts or by misuse of powers or abuse of process"*.[25] Among the activities referred to in paragraph 3, c, the Commission has included aids related to environmental protection and energy. The Commission may, of course, decide to structure its discretion through the adoption of formal or informal regulatory acts.

Acting on the basis of Article 109 TFUE, the Council has granted the Commission the power to adopt block exemptions in a number of areas[26] and the Commission has used this power to adopt the General Block Exemption Regulation (GBER).[27] The current GBER and particularly its article 44 are greatly relevant for several energy taxes and environmental tax reliefs and a distinction has to be made between tax reliefs covered by the GBER and those that have to be individually examined. As in addition to formal secondary law, the Commission has also introduced a range of soft law measures, which are generally labelled as "guidelines" or "communications" and these "guidelines" and "communications" informally structure the Commission's discretion, the Guidelines on State aids regarding environmental protection and energy 2014-2020 (EEAG) and in particular the more specific criteria to assess the necessity and proportionality in the case of tax reductions or exceptions of harmonized and non-harmonized environmental taxes, has to be taken into account.[28]

What constitutes an "aid" in with respect to tax in the energy sector depends on the ECJ interpretation based on a case-by-case approach. Such clarification is particularly important in view of the procedural requirements that stem from designation as aid and of the consequences where Member States fail to comply with such requirements.

The wording of Article 107 *"granted by a Member State or through State resources"* suggests that the prohibition outlaws two forms of State interference. In a number of cases, the ECJ has come to clarify that the two

---

the common interest".
[25] Case C-225/91, *Matra SA v. Commission,* Jugement of 15 June 1993 (EU:CE1993:239), paras. 24 and 25.
[26] One of these areas is "environmental protection". See Council of the European Union (2015), Article 1 (1)(a)(iii).
[27] European Commission (2014) Commission Regulation (EU) No 651/2014 of 17 June 2014, declaring certain categories of aid compatible with the internal market in application of articles 107 and 108 of the Treaty (OJ L 187, 26.6.2014).
[28] See supra note 10.

conditions are cumulative[29], among others, in *PreussenElektra* under the following terms: *"The distinction made in that provision between aid granted by a Member State and aid granted through State resources does not signify that all advantages granted by a State, whether financed through State resources or not, constitute aid but is intended merely to bring within that definition both advantages which are granted directly by the State and those granted by a public or private body designated or established by the State"*.[30] Concerning the State imputability of the aid, the measure is regarded as not being imputable to the State to the extent that the implementation of the text was in compliance with a legal measure adopted at EU level with a clear and precise content.

In relation to the criterion of "advantage", it covers a very large range of situations (the advantage can be temporary, either direct or indirect -*"in any form whatsoever"*-). Therefore, the fact that an advantage is labelled as a tax, a parafiscal levy, a charge or a duty, does not prevent the Commission (nor at times the ECJ) from carrying out a deep research into the economic consequences of a specific government regulation in order to establish whether certain elements of the regulation constitute unlawful State aid or not.

Despite the difficulties in identifying the tax advantage the Commission distinguished, in its 1998 Notice, three main categories of tax advantages that may be provided through a reduction in the firm's tax burden: a reduction in the tax base (such as special deductions, special or accelerated depreciation arrangements or the entering of reserves on the balance sheet); a total or partial reduction in the amount of tax (such as exemption or a tax credit); and the deferment, cancellation or even special rescheduling of tax debt. Moreover, the Commission defined the advantage by reference to a measure, which confers *"on recipients an advantage which relieves them of charges that are normally borne from their budget"*.[31]

Only the measures granting an advantage in a selective way to certain undertakings or categories of undertakings or to certain economic sectors fall under the notion of aid. Thus, general measures, which are effectively open to all undertakings operating within a Member State on an equal basis, are not selective.

---

[29] Then, the term "or" should be interpreted as "and". For a clear example, see Case C-189/91, *Petra Kirsammer-Hack v. Nurhan Sidal*, Judgment of 30 November 1993 (EU:C:1993:907), paras. 16-19.
[30] Case C-379/98, *PreussenElektra v. Schleswag*, Judgment of 13 March 2001 (EU:C:2001:160), para. 58.
[31] European Commission (1998), Notice on the application of the State aid rules to measures relating to direct business taxation (OJ C, 384, 10.12.1998), at para, 9.

Finally, in relation to the criteria of "affectation of trade, distortion of competition and adverse effects", the ECJ case-law has developed an extensive interpretation of the conditions of affectation of trade and competition and they are assumed as soon as the State grants a financial advantage to an undertaking in a liberalised sector where there is, or could be, competition.[32]

5. LANDMARK ECJ CASES

It is remarkable that several landmark cases in the area of taxation, parafiscal charges and minimum price systems like *PreussenElektra*[33], *Adria Wien-Pipeline*[34], *British Aggregates*[35], *Transportes Jordi Besora*[36], *Kernkraftwerke Lippe-Ems GmbH*[37], and *Republic of Austria v. European Commission*[38], dealt with energy taxes or levies. These cases represent a significant step towards the clarification of the notion of State aid and the compatibility of tax benefits for clean energies with the internal market. However, since a few years ago, new trends may increase the problems due to the effects-based approach, according to which only the effect of the measure on the undertaking is relevant, and not the cause or the objective of the State intervention.[39]

According to settle case-law, in the absence of harmonization of particular tax provisions, Member States are not prohibited from granting tax advantages in the form of exemptions or reduced rates, applicable to certain products or undertakings. Indeed, tax advantages of this kind may serve legitimate economic, environmental and social purposes[40] and

---

[32] European Commission (2016), at para. 187, supra note 22.

[33] Case C-379/98, *PreussenElektra v. Schleswag*, Judgment of 13 March 2001 (EU:C:2001:160), see para. 58.

[34] Case C-143/99, *Adria-Wien Pipeline GmbH and Wietersdorfer & Peggauer Zementwerke GmbH v Finanzlandesdirection für* Kärnten, Judgment of 8 November 2001 (EU:C:2001:598), see paras. 52-55.

[35] Case C-487/06 P, *British Aggregates Association v Commission of The European Communities and United Kingdom* (supra note 75), see paras. 85 and 89.

[36] Case C-82/12, *Transportes Jordi Besora SL v Generalitat de Catalunya*, Judgment of 27 February 2014 (EU:C:2014:108), see paras. 32-36.

[37] Case C-5/14, *Kernkraftwerke Lippe-Ems GmbH v. Hauptzollamt Osnabrück*, Judgment of 4 June 2015 (EU:C:2015:354), see paras. 48-54 and 79.

[38] Case T-251/11, *Republic of Austria v. European Commisssion* (EU:T:2014:1060), see paras. 160-171.

[39] See case C-173/73, *Italy v Commission*, para. 13, ECLI:EU:C:1974:71, and C-487/06 P, *British Aggregates v Commission* (supra note 75), paras. 85 and 89, ECLI:EU:C:2008:419. The effects-based approach contribute towards the policy goal of "less and better targeted aid" and is helpful in terms of increasing the effectiveness and predictability of state aid control. See H W Fiederiszick *et al* European State Aid Control: economic framework, MIT Press, 2006, 2, 54.

[40] Case C-148/77, *Hansen jun. & O.C. Balle GmbH & Co. v Hauptzollamt Flensburg*, Judgment of 10 October 1978 (EU:C:1978:173), para. 16.

differential treatment of economic activities may be always justified by reference to their respective statutory and regulatory conditions.[41]

Nevertheless, under State aid law, the objectives of the measure are not taken into account and it is common ground that the tax measure is examined only in the light of its effects which prevail over its objectives. The ECJ has constantly maintained that article 107 (1) TFEU defined aids in relation to their effects and neither economic, nor fiscal nor environmental objectives can be taking into account for the appraisal of State aid. If there is one question that could be raised is that to whether the objective pursued by the tax measure could be taken into account. In that regard, it should be note that the commonly known as the `three-step analysis'[42] cannot be applied in certain cases to analyse material selectivity, taking into account only the practical effects of the measures concerned.

This means that in some exceptional circumstances, to apply State aids rules, it is also necessary to evaluate whether the boundaries of the system of reference have been designed in a consistent manner (is the levy itself the right reference system as it was stated in *Adria-Wien Pipeline?*[43]) or, on the contrary, in a clearly arbitrary or biased way, so as to favour certain undertakings which are in a comparable situation with regard to the underlying logic of the system in question.[44]

Although acceding to the ECJ case-law only the effect of the measure on the undertaking is relevant and not the cause or the objective of the State intervention,[45] in *Adria-Wien Pipeline*, the ecological considerations

---

[41] Case C-353/95P, *Tiercé Ladbroke SA v Commission,* Judgment of 9 December 1997 (EU:C:1997:596), para. 35.

[42] First, the system of reference must be identified. Second, it should be determined whether a given measures constitutes a derogation from that system insofar as it differentiates between economic operators in light of the objectives intrinsic to the system, are in a comparable factual and legal situation. Assessing whether derogation exists is the key element of this part of the test and allows a conclusion to be drawn as to whether the measure is *prima facie* selective. If the measure in question does not constitute derogation from the reference system, it is not selective. However, if it does, it needs to be established, in the third step of the test, whether the derogation is justified by the nature of the general scheme of the reference system. If a prima facie selective measure is justified by the nature or the general scheme of the system, it will not be considered selective and will thus fall outside the scope of Article 107(1) of the Treaty. See Commission Notice (para. 18), supra note 22.

[43] The advantageous terms granted in this case to undertakings manufacturing goods were intended to preserve the competitiveness of the manufacturing sector within the EU. Then, providing an energy taxes rebate for an entire sector of the economy, such as the manufacturing sector, would be regarded as entailing a State aid. See Case *Adria-Wien Pipeline GmbH* (supra note 34), paras. 52-55.

[44] See on that regard, the 2016 Commisssion Notice (para.129) and case-law references, supra note 22.

[45] See case C-173/73, *Italian Republic v Commission of the European Communities,* Judgment of 2 July 1974, (EU:C:1974:71) para. 13, and C-487/06 P, *British Aggregates Association v Commission*

underlying the national legislations at issue were relevant and "*do not justify treating the consumption of natural gas or electricity by undertakings supplying services differently than the consumption of such energy by undertakings manufacturing goods*" because "*energy consumption by each of those sectors would be equally damaging to the environment*".[46]

Similarly, in the *British Aggregates* case, the Court rules that "*it is appropriate to examine whether within the context of a particular legal system that measure constitutes an advantage for certain undertakings in comparison with others which are in a comparable legal and factual situation*".[47] In some cases the Court refers to the objectives pursued by the "system" in question while in other cases it mention the objectives pursued by the "measure" in question. As has been observed, this can bring about different outcomes.[48]

Regarding the features to an "energy tax" (although based on the harmonizing Directive of hydrocarbon taxes), the ECJ held that the concept must be related to its legal setup for its admission as "environmental tax", especially in the case *Transportes Jordi Besora*. Since every tax necessarily pursues a budgetary purpose, the mere fact that a tax is intended to achieve a budgetary objective cannot, in itself, suffice to preclude that tax from being regarded as having, in addition, a `specific purpose' within the meaning of article 3(2) of Directive 92/12. According to the ECJ "*a tax such as the IVMDH could be regarded as being itself directed at protecting the environment (...) only if it were designed, so far as concerns its structure, and particularly the taxable item or the rate of tax, in such a way as to dissuade taxpayers from using mineral oils or to encourage the use of other products that are less harmful to the environment*".[49]

On *Kernkraftwerk Lippe-Ems* case, regarding the German nuclear fuel tax[50], the ECJ clarified that article 14(1)(a) ETD is to be interpreted "*as not precluding national legislation which levies a duty on the use of nuclear fuel for the commercial production of electricity*", first because the nuclear fuel that is

---

of the European Communities, paras. 85 and 89.

[46] See para. 52. The advantageous terms granted in this case to undertakings manufacturing goods were intended to preserve the competitiveness of the manufacturing sector within the EU. Conversely, in *Stadtwerke Schwäbisch Hall GmbH v Commission*, the CJEU held that the treatment of tax reserves for the decommissioning of nuclear power stations and the safe disposal of nuclear waste in Germany did not constitute State aid since it was based on generally applicable provisions allowing for the creation of reserves by all undertakings satisfying the relevant criteria (see Case T-92/02, Judgment of 26 January 2006 (EU:T:2006:26) para.93.

[47] See supra note 35, para. 82.

[48] See C Micheau, State Aid, Subsidy and Tax Incentives under EU and WTO Law, Wolters Kluwer (2014), 287.

[49] See para. 32.

[50] See case C-5/12 (EU:C:2015:354).

the subject of the German Law (*KernbrStG*) does not constitute an energy product' for the purposes of the ETD and it is not, therefore, covered by the exemption laid down in this article of that Directive, and secondly, because it cannot be applied by analogy to the nuclear fuel that is the subject of *KernbrStG*.[51]

Besides, this case is also interesting because of the selectivity criteria analysis held by the Court which may be seen in this statement: "*methods of producing electricity, other than based on nuclear fuel, are not affected by the rules introduced by KernbrStG and that in any event, they are not, in the light of the objective pursued by those rules, in a factual and legal situation that is comparable to that of the production method based in nuclear fuel, as only that method generates radioactive waste arising from the use of such fuel*".[52]

Finally, most of interesting issues on State aids and energy taxation are extensively considered in the case T-251/11, concerning parafiscal levies in the Austrian Green Electricity Act. The ECJ held that while extra cost or additional cost are comparable to a special tax levied on electricity, the rules governing reductions of energy taxes under the law of the Union cannot be applied to para-fiscal charges by analogy.[53] It is important to highlight that the Court stated, in this case, that the whole Austrian scheme is a State aid incompatible with the internal market, against the Community guidelines on State aid for environmental protection. The Court stresses that the exemption does not reflect harmonisation at EU level regarding taxation in the area of renewable energy.

6. CONCLUSION

Concern for environment is fairly new in public policies. Even though the transition to a carbon free society may not go as far as many in Paris COP21 thought possible, environmental issues require a global approach as to the desired objectives, the desired strategies to achieve them and the instruments to implement the strategy. The European Union climate change and energy policies trust on renewable energies as the significant future sources. The need to diversify European Union energy sources lead to renewable energies.

It is clear that reinforce the share of renewable energies in the European Union is very much dependent on taxes. However, taxes need to be wisely

---

[51] See paras. 47-48 and 53 of the referred Judgment.
[52] See para. 79 of the referred Judgment.
[53] See para. 68 and 169 of the referred Judgment (supra note 38) and case-law cited on these paragraphs. See M Villar Ezcurra, Avances en la relación de tributos ambientales y ayudas de Estado al hilo de la sentencia del Tribunal General de la Unión Europea, de 11 de diciembre de 2014, Quincena Fiscal 14 (2015), 151-181.

combined and complemented with other economic and market instruments to guaranty that all the steps are done on the right direction. We need to move forward in the way to establish the basis for a tax system consistent with national and European environmental and energy policies. The law should provide solutions tailored to the needs of promoting the objectives set at the European and international level with the correct use of economic instruments and legal concepts.

For these reasons, to our mind in the European Union area, the legal and tax framework should evolve adapting the ETD and State aid rules in order to really play a significant role for environmental purposes.

II

CLEAN ENERGY
REGULATION AND
TECHNOLOGICAL CHANGE

Clean energies in México after and before the last energy reform

FRANCISCO X. SALAZAR DIEZ DE SOLLANO

Non-resident fellow, Institute of the Americas
Executive Fellow, School of Public Policy, University of Calgary
Chair, Mexico's World Energy Council Committe
Coordinator, International Confederation of Energy Regulators (ICER)
Enix, Founding Partner

1. ABSTRACT

In less than a decade, Mexico has been successfully designing energy policy and regulation in order to promote the penetration of clean energies as part of the generation bundle. Before the very broad energy reform that took place in late 2013, when private participation was limited to generation for self-supply purposes to sell capacity and energy to CFE, the Energy Regulatory Commission (CRE) found ways to incentivize private generation with intermittent sources while the Ministry (SENER) designed a policy to complement private investment resulting from these incentives through the state owned utility (CFE). Since the reform, policy and regulation now rely heavily on a market for Clean Energy Certificates (CECs) where auctions to meet the requirements of the regulated load serving entity (or Basic Services Supplier as it is named in legislation) play a very important role in the development of a long term market that is complemented with the spot market. What is interesting is that in both schemes, before and after the reform, Mexico has been able to find ways to promote in an efficient and effective way the use of clean energies in the electricity sector.

2. EVOLUTION OF ENERGY POLICY

Energy policy to promote clean energies in Mexico has been based on 4 legal instruments. The first one was the so called Renewables Act, issued in 2008. Four years later came the Climate Change Act. Then, as result of the 2013 energy reform, came the Electricity Act in 2014 and finally the

Energy Transition Act in late 2015. All of these gave place to the policy and regulations to be described in this chapter.

The Renewables Act, the Climate Change Act and the Energy Transition Act all set penetration goals. In the case of the first Act, the transitional 2nd article specified the following:

> In accordance with Art. 11th, section III, the Secretary of Energy will establish a goal of maximum 65 percent fossil fuels based generation for 2024, 60 percent for 2035 and 50 percent for 2050 (Ammendment published on the Official Gazette the 1st of June, 2011).

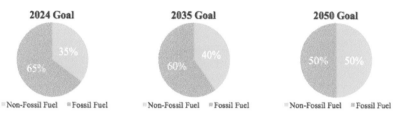

Figure 1: Non-fossil fuels goals set in the Renewables Act

The first of these goals was reinforced by the Climate Change Act in its 3rd transitional article:

> a)   ...

> e)   In coordination with the Electricity Federal Commission (CFE) and the Energy Regulatory Commission (CRE), the Secretary of Energy will promote a goal of at least 65 percent of clean energies in electric generation by 2024.

The only difference was the rephrasing of the goal: instead of citing non-fossil fuels, it made reference to clean energies, setting the stage for a definition that would include non-fossil energy with clean energy, as it is done now in both the Electricity Act and the Energy Transition Act.

The Energy Transition Act confirmed the target for 2024 but, different from what was stated in the previous legislation, instead of detailing goals beyond 2024, the Act sets goals for previous years, setting a short term path, as detailed in its 3rd transitional article:

> The Secretary of Energy will set a clean energies penetration goal in electric generation of minimum 25 percent by 2018, 30 percent by 2021 and 35 percent by 2024.

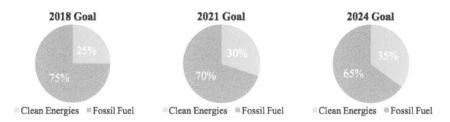

2018 Goal **2021 Goal** **2024 Goal**

Clean Energies   Fossil Fuel   Clean Energies   Fossil Fuel   Clean Energies   Fossil Fuel

Figure 2: Clean energies penetration path in the Energy Transition Act

It is interesting to note though that since the Energy Transition Act abrogated the Renewables Act, strictly speaking from a legal point of view, from 2024 onwards there are no binding goals now. On the other hand, on the 29th of June of this year, President Barak Obama, Prime Minister Justin Trudeau and President Enrique Peña Nieto announced "a historic goal for North America to strive to achieve 50 percent clean power generation by 2025". While this announcement puts a lot of political pressure, it may be difficult to achieve because is much stricter than the previous goals and it is not binding unless passed by Congress, at least in the case of Mexico.

3. REGULATION PREVIOUS TO THE REFORM

Interestingly, the building blocks found in the old regulation that made possible most of the investments in renewable energy were designed before the issuance of the Renewables Act. Nevertheless, it was thanks to this law that the regulation became rooted and supported by policy. Among the resulting regulatory instruments, four are noteworthy. One was meant for small scale, distributed generation type developments, while the other three were designed for large projects.

The first one was a 1:1 net metering scheme for consumers at the generation point. It considered two cases: small and medium scale. Small scale meant being interconnected at low tension, i.e. below 1 kV, and allowed for two options: residential users up to 10 kW, and commercial users up to 30 kW. Medium scale implied an interconnection at medium tension, i.e. below 69 kV, and was open to a wide range of users up to 500 kW in capacity. The scheme allowed for a roll-over or virtual accumulation of energy that could be used within a period of up to 12 months. It was very attractive for relative large residential and commercial consumers that were previously paying rates that were high above costs (supposedly cross-subsidizing poor consumers) and that saw their invoices dramatically reduced and a short payback of the investment.

In regards to the large scale regulatory instruments, the first one was the interconnection contract for renewable and efficient cogeneration plants. This contract had a feature popularly known as the "energy bank". This worked as a massive scale net metering mechanism where an accounting balance was made between the value of the energy calculated with the corresponding hourly rates at the generation point and the consumption nodes. A 12 months roll-over accumulation of the value of energy at the generation point was allowed, and any excess energy not accounted to the load (if any) could be sold to CFE at the end of this period at 15% discount of the marginal cost in the interconnection node.

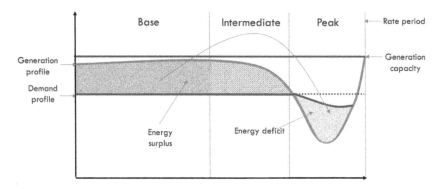

Figure 3: Energy Bank mechanism

The second instrument was the transmission agreement again for renewable and efficient cogeneration plants. This agreement included particular wheeling rates different to the conventional rates that were calculated based on energy flows and location of both generation and loads so charges were higher when electricity went with the flow and lower in the opposite case. Even if sensible, the old conventional rate methodology did not consider that clean energy projects are not located at will but at places where the resource is available. Because of this, CRE issued a postage stamp type rate for them to pay according to the tension levels used to supply the loads. The initial rates were calculated based on long run marginal costs and considering the benefits of substituting expensive fuel oil marginal generation in the short run. Since then, they have been adjusted on a monthly basis by inflation. Values for October 2016 are:

Tension level	Rate (MXN/kWh)	Rate (USȼ/kWh)[*]
High tension	0.04065	0.214
Medium tension	0.04065	0.214
Low tension	0.08130	0.428

Table 1: Special rates for renewables and efficient cogeneration

The final instrument is related to the two previous ones since it defines what is considered an efficient cogeneration. This was a result of the Renewables Act that specified that cogeneration with efficiencies higher than the minimum standard set by CRE were subject to the benefits applicable to renewable energy. Based on this consideration, CRE issued the efficiency minimum standards (η_{min}) described in table 2, using the following formulae to calculate efficiency (η):

$$\eta = Elc/Econv = AEP/Fe \qquad (1)$$

$$AEP = EP - F \qquad (2)$$

$$EP = E/RefE' + H/RefH \qquad (3)$$

$$Fe = F - Fh \qquad (4)$$

Where:

Elc   Electric energy free of fossil fuel

Econv   Electric energy produced by a conventional efficient plant

AEP   Primary energy savings

Fe   Fossil fuel used for electric generation

EP   Primary energy

E   Net electricity generated

RefE'   Reference performance for electric generation taking into account T&D losses

H   Net thermal energy

RefH   Reference performance for heat generation

[*] Exchange rate considered: 19.0046 MXN/USD as published by the Central Bank for 10/14/2016

Plant size (MW)	η min (%)
Name plate < 0.5	5
0.5 ≤ Name plate < 30	10
30 ≤ Name plate < 100	15
Name plate ≥100	20

Table 2: Minimum efficiency standards

Considering the end of 2015 as a date to make an assessment of the results, the following graph and table show that the regulation was effective in attracting investments in the sector. Because of that success and as a signal of certainty to investors, during the debate of the energy reform it was decided that the projects developed under this regulation would be grandfathered. Furthermore, in the case of efficient cogeneration, the minimum standards set by CRE will continue to be used under the new regime as the criteria to grant CECs to this kind of projects, while the net metering scheme continues in place and will be the backbone of the new regulation for distributed generation.

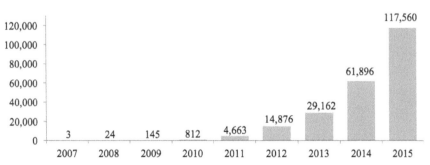

Chart 1: Evolution of installed capacity under the net metering scheme

Technology	Permits	Operating MW	Developing MW	Inactive MW	Total MW	Percentage as a whole	Percentage operating
Wind	103	1,882.10	6,594.10	-	8,476.20	44.32%	64.35%
Mini-hydro	102	409.04	684.50	20	1,113.90	5.82%	14.00%
Solar PV	290	49.70	7,684.90	-	7,734.60	40.44%	1.70%
Biomass	58	520.40	371.40	8	899.80	4.70%	17.79%
Biogas	38	63.30	180.50	-	243.80	1.27%	2.16%
Geothermal	2	0.00	65.00	-	65.00	0.34%	0.00%
Total (12/2015)	593	2,924.90	15,580.40	28.0	19,126.30	100.00%	100.00%

Table 3: Projects developed by the private sector under the grandfathered regulation

Before moving to explain the new regulation, this last table helps to explain the implicit logic of policy to meet the goals set by the Renewables Act. In effect, the government projected the amount of clean energies produced by CFE and the private sector. As the following figure 4 describes, the gap was supposed to be filled by CFE, who would be instructed by SENER to develop the projects by itself (essentially large hydro, nuclear or geothermal) or through IPP tenders (mostly for wind).

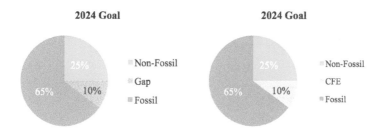

Figure 4: Policy mechanism to meet clean energy target in the previous regime

4. NEW REGULATION

Since the constitutional reform on energy passed by the Mexican Congress in December 2013, the industrial organization of the electricity sector has changed deeply. CFE was both vertically and horizontally separated and the market was opened to full competition and private participation in generation, supply and ancillary services as shown in figure 5. CENACE was established as the Independent System Operator. Transmission and distribution remained controlled by the State but open to participation of the private sector through public bids organized by SENER. And the reform did not stay there: it aimed to guarantee the transit from a high-carbon to a low-carbon generation bundle by introducing clean energy obligations to the demand side of the market. These obligations will need to be met through CECs that will be acquired in the market.

In a certain sense the new policy mechanism to meet the target resembles the previous one in that its logic is to fill the gap between the clean energy generated by existing facilities plus those in the pipeline and the one that is needed to comply with the goal established in the law; that is, the clean energy obligations imposed on the demand side represent the forecasted gap in three years. Indeed, starting in 2015, every year (t) SENER will make a forecast of the energy demand (TWh) in three years time ($t + 3$) and the amount of demand that will be supplied with clean energies from existing facilities and projects in the pipeline. The difference with the goal for the $(t + 3)$ year is translated into a percentage of consumption for that year and will become the clean energy requirements (see figure 6). Since requirements will be met by CECs, this mechanism creates a demand for them within this period of time[1].

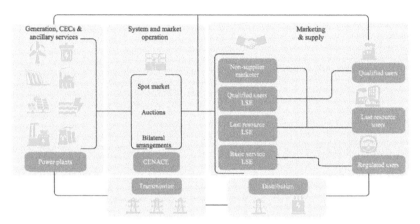

Figure 5: New industrial organization in the electric sector

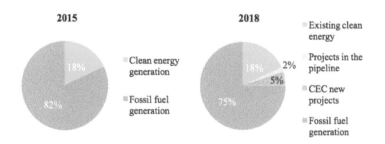

2015

2018

- Existing clean energy
- Projects in the pipeline
- CEC new projects
- Fossil fuel generation

- Clean energy generation
- Fossil fuel generation

Figure 6: Policy mechanism to meet clean energy target after the 2013 energy reform

That demand will be satisfied either by existing facilities that migrate to the new regime[2] or by projects that will be ready in a 3 year time span. Suppliers will offer CECs to the agents with clean energy obligations:

---

[1] 3 years is considered to be a reasonable time to construct new clean energy facilities

[2] CECs will not be granted to existing facilities that choose to remain under the grandfathered regulation. Those that wish to exit the old regime will be eligible to obtain CECs for the time corresponding to the remainder of the legacy interconnection contract when they migrate. The idea is that no facility should be benefited simultaneously by regulatory incentives from both regimes.

"Qualified Users[3]" participating directly in the market in the spot market; Load Serving Entities (LSE[4]); final users under off-grid supply (isolated supply), and loads under legacy interconnection contracts supplied by fossil fuel based generation. CECs will be sold under private bilateral contracts, as the result of auctions or in an organized market for unbalances. Essentially, an entitled clean energy facility will receive one CEC for every MWh that it generates.

Figures 7 and 8 describe in more detail the process of compliance with obligations and the cycle of CECs.

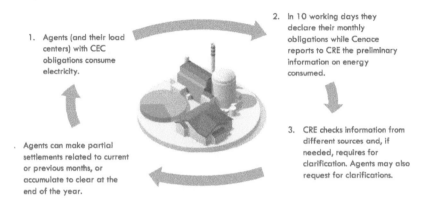

1. Agents (and their load centers) with CEC obligations consume electricity.

2. In 10 working days they declare their monthly obligations while Cenace reports to CRE the preliminary information on energy consumed.

3. CRE checks information from different sources and, if needed, requires for clarification. Agents may also request for clarifications.

. Agents can make partial settlements related to current or previous months, or accumulate to clear at the end of the year.

Figure 7: Compliance of obligations mechanism

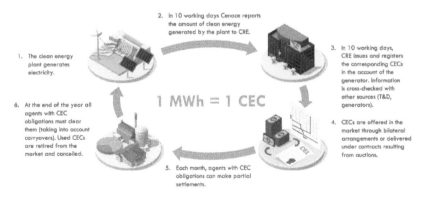

1. The clean energy plant generates electricity.

2. In 10 working days Cenace reports the amount of clean energy generated by the plant to CRE.

3. In 10 working days, CRE issues and registers the corresponding CECs in the account of the generator. Information is cross-checked with other sources (T&D, generators).

4. CECs are offered in the market through bilateral arrangements or delivered under contracts resulting from auctions.

5. Each month, agents with CEC obligations can make partial settlements.

6. At the end of the year all agents with CEC obligations must clear them (taking into account carryovers). Used CECs are retired from the market and cancelled.

1 MWh = 1 CEC

Figure 8: CEC's cycle

---

3 Shown in Figure 5, a Qualified User is a load over certain consumption or demand defined by SENER that allows him to participate directly in the market or through a lightly-regulated LSE called a "Qualified Supplier".

4 See figure 5: "Qualified Supplier", "Last Resource Supplier" and "Basic Supplier".

As mentioned before there is a market for imbalances and long term markets related to auctions and long term bilateral contracts. In regards to the market for imbalances, the left graph in figure 9 describes two features that would allow flexibility: CEC's obligation carryover and accumulation. The graph on the right describes a market where such features do not exist and market does not clear (as has happened in several regions).

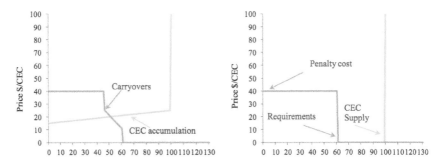

Figure 9: CEC's market with and without flexibility

A critical element for the well-functioning of the CEC's market is an adequate level of non-compliance penalties. In the case of Mexico, the penalty applies per MWh of non-compliance and is calculated as a multiple of daily minimum wages[5]. Table 4 shows the applicable penalties, which vary in accordance with whether a carryover was asked or not, and depending on the number of times that non-compliance has occurred[6].

Non-compliance range (%)	Without carryover				With carryover			
	$0 \leq 25$	$25 \leq 50$	$50 \leq 75$	$75 \leq 100$	$0 \leq 25$	$25 \leq 50$	$50 \leq 75$	$75 \leq 100$
1st time	6	8	10	12	8	10	12	14
2nd time	12	16	20	24	16	20	24	28
3rd time /contempt	18	24	30	36	24	30	36	42

Table 4: Non-compliance penalties

[5]   As of 2016, the daily minimum wage is MXN 73.04, equivalent to 3.84 USD at an exchange rate of 19.0046 MXN/USD.

[6]   It is worth mentioning that, in the end, payment of penalty does not release the obligation to acquire the CEC.

Although necessary, the market for imbalances will not be as important as the resulting from long term auctions. This is not only because at least in the beginning most of the demand for CECs will come from the regulated LSE, the "Basic Supplier" – who is required by law to buy energy, capacity and CECs through competitive processes such as auctions – but also because once a clearing house is ready, other LSE and qualified users that can participate directly in the market will be able to join these auctions.

The four objectives of the auctions as designed for the electricity market in Mexico are: (i) to have a level playing field for competition between different technologies; (ii) to pay according to the value of the power plant to the system; (iii) to allow projects to be bankable, and (iv) to minimize costs to the LSE. As mentioned before, the products to buy in the auctions are CECs, associated energy and capacity. Winners sign 20 year contracts for CECs and 15 years for energy and capacity.

The auction is run as an optimization process for a package of CECs, energy and capacity where the objective is to maximize the consumer surplus. It is interesting to note that location receives a value used to compare offers on a level-playing field. That is, for the optimization process, the package offer is adjusted by a positive or negative x amount of pesos (a delta) per MWh depending on the location of the offer. That delta reflects the difference in nodal marginal prices. It is important to stress that although the optimization process is run taking into consideration differences in location, winning bids will be paid the full amount submitted for the auction.

So far, two auctions have taken place. In the first one, the volumes solicited by CFE (as the Basic Supplier LSE) were 6.3 million CECs, 6.3 million MWh of associated energy and 500 MW of capacity. It received 227 offers from 69 prequalified bidders, resulting in 18 offers granted to 11 companies. The auction assigned 5.4 MWh of energy (85.7%), and 5.38 CECs (85.4%). Although there were no allocations for the 500 MW of capacity requested, this was included in the second auction. The total value of the contracts was 4,456,817,815 MXN or around 234 million USD[7]. The lowest bid implied a price of 614.14 MXN/(MWh + CEC) or 32.32 USD/(MWh + CEC)[8] for the package of CECs and energy; the highest bid allocated was 1,169.78 MXN/(MWh + CEC) or 61.55 USD/(MWh + CEC)[9]. The projects represent 2,191 MW of Solar PV and 562 MW of wind.

---

[7]   Same as in previous sections, an exchange rate of 19.0046 MXN/USD is used.
[8]   A 330 MW Solar PV Project offering 269,155 MWh and 263,815 CECs. It meant a record low price at that time.
[9]   A 30 MW Solar PV Project offering 54,974.5 MWh and 53,477 CECs. This project was located in Yucatan, the zone with the highest location delta per MWh.

For the second auction, the volumes solicited were 10.6 million CECs, 10.6 million MWh of associated energy and 1,483 MW of capacity (including the 500 MW unallocated in the first auction). 28 offers were allocated to 17 companies. The auction assigned 8.91 MWh of energy (84%), 9.28 CECs (87.5%) and 1,187 MW of capacity (80%). For this auction, according to the latest information by SENER and aggregating the offers by technology, the resulting prices were as follows: 31.9 USD/(MW + CEC) for solar; 35.8 USD/(MW + CEC) for wind; 37.3 USD/(MW + CEC) for geothermal and 7.3 USD/CEC for hydro (no energy was offered). In terms of capacity, again by technology, prices were as follows: 21,044 USD/MW-yr for solar; 19,220 USD/MW-yr for wind, 43,534 USD/MW-yr for geothermal and 36,360 USD/MW-yr for natural gas combined cycle (the only product it can offer). The projects imply 1,854 MW of Solar PV plants (out of which 184 MW offered as capacity); 1,129 MW of wind plants (out of which 128 MW as capacity); 25 MW of geothermal plants (including the 25 MW as firm capacity), 68 MW of hydro plants (offering only CECs) and 899 MW of natural gas combined cycle plants that offered 850 MW as firm capacity (the only product that can be bid by this technology – can't offer clean energy or CECs).

A key element that is important to notice from this "3 products package" auction introduced in Mexico is that, thanks to this feature, technologies like geothermal can be competitive and can result in winners based on its packaged price. Clearly, geothermal technology would not be competitive in pure clean energy auctions or capacity auctions; it is only as a package that they can compete.

5. FINAL REMARKS

Even if previous regulation was effective in attracting investments in clean energy generation, there was a problem with the competitiveness of the whole sector. The lack of full competition in the market and the restrictions to private investments required a profound reform. However, introducing full competition and changing the regulation accordingly was perceived by some actors as a risk to the growth of clean energies. As reality has been demonstrating, that risk did not materialize and the new regulation is proving to be attractive and efficient to the benefit of the whole new electric market in Mexico.

Renewable Energies in Peru

ALFREDO DAMMERT L.

Director of Masters Program on Regulation of Public Services
Director of Masters Program on Mining Regulation, Management and
Economy, Pontifical Catholic University of Peru

1. GENERAL REGULATORY FRAMEWORK IN PERU AND THE INCLUSION OF RENEWABLE ENERGIES

The regulatory framework in Peru differentiates between sectoral policy (related to license awarding), legislation, and planning, in charge of the Ministry of Energy and Mines (MINEM, Ministerio de Energía y Minas), and the regulation and supervision in charge of the Supervising Body of Energy and Mining (OSINERGMIN, Organismo Supervisor de la Energía y la Minería), whereas the National Institute of Competition and Protection of Copyright (INDECOPI, Instituto Nacional de la Competencia y de la Protección de la Propiedad Intelectual) is responsible for ensuring free competition in the sector. On the other hand, the Operation of the Electrical System and the Operation of the Electrical Market are in charge of the Committee for the Economical Operation of the System (COES, Comité de Operación Económica del Sistema), with electricity companies as its members. Finally, when the MINEM deems it appropriate, it commissions PROINVERSION, the state investment promotion agency, to create the request for bids of investment in the electricity sector.

The Peruvian corporate structure of Generation, Transmission and Distribution is shown in Chart 1.

	Generation		Transmission		Distribution
	Capacity MW	Number of Companies	Extension Km.	Number of Companies	Number of Companies
Hydroelectric	2,961	16			
Thermal	5,458				
Non-Conventional Renewable Energies	616	18			
Total	9,035	33	8,350 (Main Transmission)	11	11

Source: COES, Peru, 2015

Chart 1. Peru: Corporate Structure of Electricity Generation, Transmission and Distribution Companies

Generation

On the motion of the Executive Power, on July 2006 the Congress passed the Law to Secure the Efficient Development of Electrical Generation (Law 28832), including its amendments for the regulation of generation and transmission. A procedure for bidding of contracts between distributors and generators was established under that law. Its characteristics are as follows:

Regulated Market comprising the distributors and their clients of a capacity smaller than 2500 kW (consumers between 200 kW and 2500 kW can choose between being regulated or free customers):

1. The request for bids must be done by all distributors so as to cover 100% of their needs for the first year of contract, and it must be done three years in advance.

2. Other distributors or free consumers may join the bid of the distributor that initiated the bidding, and the quantities are assigned and prices obtained proportionally to the required capacities.

3. The price of electricity is obtained as a result of each bidding, and the bids of the generators are sorted from lower to higher price until the demand to be contracted by the distributor is covered.

4. Bids are subject to a maximum price, which is determined by the regulator and presented in closed envelope.

5. The duration of the contracts is 5-20 years.

6. The price of energy is determined annually by the regulator.

7. Subsequently, with the purpose of encouraging investment in hydroelectric projects, a 15% decrease in the bid price of hydroelectric plants was introduced, only for comparing bids.

8. Short term bids for up to 10% of the needs of each distributor may be defined by the regulator with the purpose of covering the missing offer.

Apart from the bids carried out under the Efficient Generation Act, in previous years, with the purpose of encouraging hydroelectric generation, the state has called for bids through PROINVERSION for the installation of hydroelectric plants for a capacity of approximately 1,000 MW, with the priority of supplying electricity to the network.

There is also a free market for consumers of more than 200 kW. Free clients may celebrate their contracts freely with electricity generators under contracts that have been determined by both parties under conditions that are the result of negotiations between the parties. As it has been indicated previously, companies with energy consumption between 200 and 2500 kW can choose either the regulated or the free market. It has also been established that free users can be incorporated to the bids of distributing companies.

In 2010, through Legislative Decree 1002, the Government approved the Promotion of Investment in Renewable (non-conventional) Energy Resources with the purpose of improving the quality of life of the population and of protecting the environment. The said decree offers the following incentives:

- Priority in dispatching the COES.

- Priority in access to transmission and distribution networks.

- Long-term stable tariffs, established through bids.

Transmission

Under the Efficient Generation Act, a new regulation was created for the transmission of electricity in Peru. It consists of:

1. Creating a unit in charge of planning the transmission based on the identification of future transmission needs, the analysis of alternative projects, and the determination of the beneficiaries. The entity assigned by the MINEM has been the COES, which presents the transmission plan to the MINEM for its approval, with the non-binding opinion of the OSINERGMIN.

2. The establishment of a Guaranteed Transmission System (SGT, Sistema Garantizado de Transmisión) constituted by those facilities included in the transmission plan. The lines of the SGT are built by licensed companies that have been awarded bids called by the MINEM and carried out by PROINVERSION. Each bid is awarded to the company that asks for the smaller annual remuneration. Contracts are of the BOOT type for a period of 30 years.

3. A Supplementary Transmission System (SCT, Sistema Complementario de Transmisión) which arises out of specific agreements between generators, distributors and large users according to their particular needs (for example: extending a transmission line from the main line to the facilities of a mining company).

4. The income of the SGT derives from the tariff income resulting from system losses, and the toll derived from payments of users

proportionally to their consumption ("postage stamp" rate), the latter being the largest.

The electrical distribution toll of the Guaranteed Transmission System is the only one which may be assigned to all users of the system, so the government adds to that value all the other charges it requires for its promotional schemes, including payments to renewable energies, subsidies to rural electrification, and subsidies to the natural gas transportation network, among others.

Distribution. Distribution fees in Peru are defined as a result of applying the model efficient enterprise approach together with the "yardstick competition" approach. The objective is to obtain distribution tariffs that yield appropriate profit to companies under efficient practices. To that end, each distributing company is divided into several typical sectors, defined by network density and consumption levels, among other factors. Then, studies about model efficient enterprises are carried out (adjusted by topology, equipment and costs) through a sample for each typical sector. After that, the efficient tariffs for each distributor are calculated through means that are obtained according to the share of each typical sector in its network. Finally, the "yardstick competition" model is used to make sure that the resulting tariffs yield a profit of 8-16% to each distributor.

Marketing

In the case of regulated users, the distributing companies are also marketers. In the case of free users, they can choose to purchase electricity from generators, distributors (when they are within the distribution network), or marketers.

2. PROMOTION OF RENEWABLE ENERGIES

The investment on renewable energies in Peru is the result of three regulatory policy measures:

I. One oriented towards investment in conventional hydroelectricity. The hydroelectric generation capacity in Peru is 2,961 MW, which represents 33% of the electrical generation capacity in the country. The promotion of conventional hydroelectricity is carried out through two mechanisms. The first one is based on the comparison of electricity tendering prices (see previous section), where electrical generation bids have a 15% discount. The second one are the previously mentioned PROINVERSIÓN tenders—until now for 1,000 MW in construction—in which the offered price is guaranteed to the winners for 20-year periods with priority in dispatching.

II. Tenders carried out under Legislative Decree 1002, which include solar, wind, urban- and agro industrial-waste biomass, and small hydroelectric (less than 20 MW) generators. The decree sets a goal to bid for non-conventional renewable energies for up to 5% of the national generation capacity, excluding small hydroelectric plants from that percentage. These bids are for each technology. The process is as follows:

a) MINEM defines the total of energy required.

b) Within this total, MINEM assigns an initial share to each technology, where it is possible to reassign the percentages in case the total for some of them is not reached.

c) OSINERGMIN defines a maximum price for each technology.

d) The envelopes with the bids are opened, and sorted by price from cheaper to more expensive, until the maximum capacity assigned by technology is reached, and those bids that exceed the maximum price are discarded.

e) In case the bids for one technology are not sufficient to cover the maximum assigned capacity, the capacity is reassigned to other technologies.

The settlement of revenues and assignments for the RER comes from two sources:

a) revenues from sale of energy at marginal cost; and

b) a charge for bonus or difference between the bid price and the marginal cost, which is assigned to all users through the transmission toll.

III. The investment contract for electricity supply with solar panels in areas which are disconnected from the network, celebrated in 2015 between MINEM and a private investor who won the tender under the said project. Even though this initiative is not strictly a part of the promotion of RERs, but destined to favor rural population that don't have access to electricity, it is oriented exclusively towards the installation of that type of energy. The aforementioned contract establishes as a goal the installation of 500,000 photovoltaic solar systems in rural locations that are not connected to the network, divided in the task to install at least 150,000 solar systems or panels, leaving the rest at the discretion of the investor. As per the contract, the investor shall be in charge of the design, construction-installation, operation, maintenance and replacement of the installations for 15 years, and shall receive a monthly remuneration. The remuneration shall come in part from the payment from users, and the rest from resources from funds for subsidizing low-income energy consumers; these funds are constituted with contributions from electrical users (through a charge on the transmission fee) and consumers of other types of energy (hydrocarbons). For commercial management, the investor can count on the participation of the electricity distribution companies of each area, or of the body of MINEM in charge of rural areas when these are not included in the licenses of distributors. The commercial start-up of the project was defined initially for August 2016, but as of now (November 2016), it has not yet started.

3. RESULTS OF THE TENDERS OF NON-CONVENTIONAL RENEWABLE ENERGIES

This section presents the results of tenders of non-conventional RER under legislative decree 1002. As of today, four tenders have been held in: 2009, 2011, 2013 and 2015. The awarded capacity for each technology is shown in Chart 2, and the prices of each tender are presented in Graph 1.

Technology	Capacity (MW)
Biomass	23
Bio gas	11
Wind	394
Solar	280
Small Hydro	566
Total	1,274

Source: Osinergmin

Chart 2: Awarded capacity in non-traditional RER tenders - Peru 2009-2015

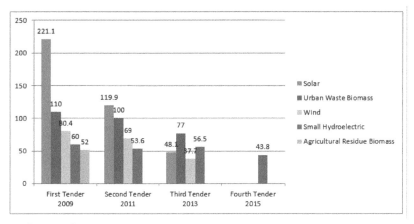

Source: Osinergmin

Graph 1: Result of tender prices for non-traditional RER - Peru 2009-2015

As it can be seen in the four tenders, noticeable results have been obtained in the capacity offer for small hydroelectric (566 MW), wind (394 MW) and photovoltaic solar (280 MW). The results assigned to energy derived from biomass are much smaller, due to the restrictions of raw materials and the supply logistics. The total of capacity assigned as of today is 1,274 MW (the small hydroelectric plants are not considered for the 5% established by the law). An important issue for the tenders is that the prices decreased considerably between tenders, moving from a photovoltaic solar energy price of USc22/kWh in the first tender to USc4.8/kWh in the third tender, and in wind energy from USc8/kWh in the first tender to USc3.8/kWh in the third tender. Therefore, the prices of the third tender have been competitive with traditional energies; although non-conventional RERs (wind and solar) still have the problem of intermittency, thus requiring backup technology.

4. IMPACT OF RENEWABLE ENERGIES IN THE MITIGATION OF CLIMATE CHANGE

According to OSINERGMIN[1], non-conventional RER generation in Peru between 2010 and 2016 has prevented the emission of 2.6 million tons of equivalent carbon dioxide, or expressed otherwise. Whereas at a global level, 42% of greenhouse gases belong to the electrical sector, this figure is of only 18% in the case of Peru. This positive impact (non-emission of

[1] Peru - Operation and Supervision of Energy Markets, 2016.

greenhouse gases) is due only to non-conventional energies, including small hydroelectric plants. If we consider that the conventional hydroelectric energy represents 4.8 times the capacity of RERs, the prevented carbon dioxide emissions are much larger.

Based on this, non-conventional RERs in Peru are an important contribution to a decrease in the greenhouse effect, but since Peru has significant hydroelectric resources (only 5% of the assessed hydroelectric resources are being exploited), the generation of electricity through large hydroelectric plants constitutes also a valuable potential to contribute to the mitigation of greenhouse gases at a global level.

5. CONCLUSIONS

Renewable energies, conventional and non-conventional, represent in Peru 40% of the electricity production capacity, which is higher than the global average of 20%. This is due both to the promotion policies by the Peruvian government and to the energy resources of the country, especially its hydroelectric and solar potential.

The government of Peru has a policy of promoting renewable energies, which considers two aspects:

A decrease in greenhouse effect gases, with a program focused on the generation of non-conventional RER energies; and

Promotion of investments with the purpose of supplying the demand of electricity in general (the case of large hydroelectric plants), and promotion of photovoltaic solar energy to supply rural areas without access to the national electrical network.

Even though these are two different objectives, they both contribute to the decrease of greenhouse effect gases.

BIBLIOGRAPHY

Batlle, C., L. Barroso, and C. Echevarría. Assessment of the Normative and Institutional Framework of Peru for the Promotion of Electrical Energy from Renewable Resources. Inter-American Development Bank, 2012, Lima-Peru.

COES. Diagnostic Report of the Operational Conditions of the SEIN 2017-2026, 2016, Lima-Peru

Dammert Alfredo, Raúl García and Fiorella Molinelli. Regulation and Supervision of the Electrical Sector, Fondo Editorial PUCP, 2008, Lima-Peru.

Dammert Alfredo, Fiorella Molinelli and Max Carbajal. Technical and Economical Foundations of the Peruvian Electrical Sector. OSINERGMIN, 2011, Lima-Peru.

MINEM. Plan for Universal Access to Energy 2013-2022, Ministry Resolution 203-2013- MEM/DM of 2013 and Supreme Decree 029-2013-EM of 2014. Lima-Peru.

MINEM. National Energy Plan 2014-2015, The Golden Book, COP20, 2014. Lima-Peru.

OSINERGMIN. Peru - Operation and Supervision of Energy Markets, 2016. Lima-Peru.

OSINERGMIN. Corporate Portal of the Supervision Body of Investment in Energy and Mining. Peru.

The Regulation of Renewable Energy in Latin America: The experiences of Brazil and Mexico

GABRIEL CAVAZOS VILLANUEVA

Dean for the Northern Region, School of Social Sciences and Government
Tecnológico de Monterrey, México

CAROLINA BARROS DE CASTRO E SOUZA·

Federal University of Alagoas, Brazil

The purpose of this chapter is to analyse the regulatory framework on renewable energy in the two most important Latin American markets: Brazil and Mexico. Both countries were among the top ten investors in 2015 in terms of total new renewable energy investment.[1] For both cases, this chapter will discuss the legal commitments Brazil and Mexico have made, at the international and domestic levels, to have an energy transition from fossil fuels to renewable resources such as the wind, solar, biofuels and others. Both countries have signed and ratified the Protocol to the United Nations Framework Convention on Climate Change, also known as the Kyoto Protocol. In this context, Brazil and Mexico have established in their internal regulations an objective to comply with standards established in this Protocol. This chapter begins discussing the Mexican regulatory framework on renewable energy followed by the Brazilian. In both analyses, the discussion is focused on the constitutional and legislative provisions at a federal level, other relevant regulations and the challenges and opportunities that both countries face for the adequate implementation of their regulations.

---

[1] *See* Frankfurt School – UNEP (United Nations Environment Programme) Collaborating Centre for Climate & Sustainable Energy Finance, *Global Trends in Renewable Energy Investment*, [2016]. Available at: http://fs-unep-centre.org/sites/default/files/publications/ globaltrendsinrenewableenergyinvestment2016lowres_0.pdf. Last visited on July 14, 2016. .

1. MEXICO

On December 20th, 2013, some important amendments to the Mexican Constitution were published, allowing the investment of private capital both in the hydrocarbons and the electricity sectors, for the first time in seventy five years.[2] This fundamental reform in Mexican modern history created two companies to substitute the former State –owned monopolies of oil and electricity: PEMEX (the Mexican oil company) and CFE (the Federal Commission of Electricity), became what the law calls "State productive companies," a concept of which there is not a clear definition but that situate the companies in a competitive market with the possibility of private investment.[3]

Although the most salient aspect of the Energy Reform is the possibility of private investment – both domestic and international – in the previously restricted sectors of hydrocarbons and electricity, it is important to highlight that the Constitutional amendments, and the relevant implementing statues, also considered the renewable energy sector as a very important part of the new energy policy in Mexico.

In fact, Article 25, paragraph 6 of the Mexican Constitution, establishes environmental protection as a relevant public policy: "Criteria of social equity, productivity and sustainability will support and encourage enterprises of the social and private sectors of the economy, subjecting them to the modalities dictated by the public interest and to the use, in the general benefit, of productive resources, taking care of their conservation and the protection of the environment." On the other hand, Interim Article Seventeen of the Decree that amends different Constitutional provisions in the matter of energy establishes that for the electricity sector, the relevant statute shall establish obligations of the electricity industry participants for the use of clean energy and for the reduction of pollutant emissions.

As a result of the energy reform, the Mexican Congress passed a new Law for the Energy Transition (LTE) on December 24th, 2015.[4] This legislation abrogates two previous federal statutes: The Law for the Use of Renewable Energy and the Financing of Energy Transition (LAERFTE) and

---

[2] *Decreto por el que se reforman y adicionan diversas disposiciones de la Constitución Política de los Estados Unidos Mexicanos, en materia energética.* Published in "Diario Oficial de la Federación", December 20th, 2013. Available at: http://dof.gob.mx/nota_detalle. php?codigo=5327463&fecha=20/12/2013 (Last visited: February 27, 2015).
[3] For a description of this concept *See* Article 4 Ley de Petróleos Mexicanos (Law of PEMEX), published at *Diario Oficial de la Federación* on August 11th, 2014. Available at: http://www.dof. gob.mx/nota_detalle.php?codigo=5355990&fecha=11/08/2014 (Last visited: July 15th, 2016).
[4] *Ley de Transición Energética* (hereinafter LTE). Published at the *Diario Oficial de la Federación* on December 24th, 2015. Available at: http://www.diputados.gob.mx/LeyesBiblio/pdf/LTE. pdf (Last visited: July 15th, 2016).

the Law for the Sustainable Use of Energy (LASE) of 2008.[5] It is important to mention that, since Mexico signed and ratified the Kyoto Protocol in 2005, there has been a consistent but somehow weak process to implement public policies for the mitigation of climate change. Another legislation which is still in force, is the General Law of Climate Change (LGCC) of 2012, which allocates powers in this matter among the Federal, State and Municipalities levels.[6]

The basis of the Energy Reform in the matter of renewable energy is the mitigation of climate change. Mexico has committed itself to a 30% reduction in emissions with respect to the projection of emissions for 2020 if Mexico continued with the same trend of emissions that it currently has.[7] These commitments are contained in the LGCC and in the Copenhagen Climate Change Conference of December 2009.

As part of these international commitments, Mexico has implemented a series of public policy instruments (some of them contained in the relevant legislation discussed below) such as the Special Program of Climate Change (PECC). This program is based on the provisions of the LGCC and establishes as one of its key objectives to diminish the emission of greenhouse effect gases. In this context, the use of clean energy is an essential element of Mexico's public policy in this matter. As it is discussed in the preamble of the LTE, Mexico is highly dependent of hydrocarbons for the generation of electric energy. 82 % of the energy in this sector is generated by hydrocarbons, while the world average is 68%. If the high scale hydroelectric generation is not considered in the analysis, Mexico only has an installed capacity of 3,5 GW of renewable energy, when the total capacity for electric energy amounts to 61GW. In this context, only 5% of this energy is renewable. In a per capita analysis, Mexico's indicator is very low: 0.09 TWh/person, while in Germany is 1.42 TWh/person.[8]

The previous legislations, LAERFTE and LASE, were implemented to face these poor indicators, but their effects were very deficient. The new LTE, in the context of the Energy Reform, focuses in the correction of some of the most salient shortcomings of the abrogated laws. It is

---

[5] *Ibid.* Interim Article Second.
[6] Ley General de Cambio Climático (Hereinafter LGCC). Published at the *Diario Oficil de la Federación* on June 6th, 2012. Available at: http://www.diputados.gob.mx/LeyesBiblio/ref/lgcc.htm (Last visited: July 15th, 2016).
[7] Preamble of the Bill to enact the LTE (Hereinafter Preamble). Available at: http://sil.gobernacion.gob.mx/Archivos/Documentos/2014/11/asun_3178017_20141125_1413904279.pdf (Last visited: July 15th, 2016)
[8] *Ibid.*

important to mention that both the LGCC in 2012[9] and the LTE[10] have been challenged by industrial organizations in Mexico. Entrepreneurs allege that many industries will be affected in their competitiveness because of the implementation of these regulations and the commitments in terms of reduction of emissions with which they have to comply.

Notwithstanding the above, the LTE came into force in 2015, establishing as an objective in its Article 1 the regulation of the sustainable use of energy, as well as the obligations with respect to clean energy and the reduction of pollutant emissions in the electric power industry, maintaining the competeveness of the productive sectors. It is clear that the last part of this general objective was included because of the allegation of loss of competitiveness by the industrial sector.

It is important to mention that the LTE in most of its provisions, refers to clean energy in general. Clean energy is defined by the Law of the Electric Power Industry (LIE) and it includes sources that are not necessarily considered "renewable." The concept of renewable energy for the purposes of the LTE includes the following sources: a) the wind; b) the solar radiation; c) the movement of water in natural waterways or in artificial ones, with generation systems with a capacity lower or equal to 30 MW; d) oceanic energy; e) geothermic energy; and f) the bioenergy. There is a special legislation to promote and develop bioenergy (LPDB) enacted on February 1, 2008. This law establishes incentives for the production and use of bioenergy sources such as biodiesel, biogas, and others.

Article 4 of the LTE provides that the Strategy of Transition to Promote the Use of Cleaner Technologies and Fuels (the Strategy) shall establish goals of clean energy and energy efficiency, to promote the generation of electric power from clean energy sources to the levels established by the LGCC. As has been stated, the general goal is a 30% reduction by 2020.[11]

The subjects obliged to comply with the goals established in the LTE and the LGCC are all the participants of the electric power industry in general.[12] In this context, Article 9 of the LTE establishes that the State will promote the legal, regulatory and tax conditions to facilitate the compliance of all participants of the electric power industry with the goals and objectives established by this law.

---

[9]   *See* the newspaper article at: http://expansion.mx/negocios/2012/03/01/canacintra-vs-ley-de-cambio-climatico. (Last visited: July 15th, 2016).
[10] *See* the newspaper article at: http://www.negociosreforma.com/aplicaciones/articulo/default.aspx?id=758229. (Last visited: July 15th, 2016).
[11] Interim Article Second of the LGCC.
[12] Article 6 of the LTE.

Because the LTE is a federal legislation, the authorities with jurisdiction conferred by the law are those in the Executive Branch: the Secretariat of Energy, the Secretariat of Environment and Natural Resources (SEMARNAT), the Energy Regulatory Commission (CRE), and the National Commission for the Efficient Use of Energy (CONUEE). The CONUEE is an agency created by this law, dependent of the Secretariat of Energy but with an operational and technical autonomy. In general terms, it is the agency in charge of the promotion of energy efficiency and it is the technical entity in the matter of sustainable use of energy.[13] Among its functions, the CONUEE elaborates and proposes to the Secretariat of Energy the above-mentioned Strategy and the National Program for the Sustainable Use of Energy (PRONASE).

In general, the three planning instruments established by the LTE are the Strategy, the Special Program of Energy Transition and the PRONASE. The Strategy is the leading instrument of the national public policy with respect to the mid and long-term obligations on clean energy. It establishes de goals and the "roadmap" for the implementation of such goals. The Strategy defines policies and actions to be executed by means of the Special Program of Energy Transition and the annual programs derived from the Special Program. The current Strategy was published on December 19th, 2014[14], before the entry into force of the current LTE. The Special Program is applied on a yearly basis and it establishes – *inter alia* - the goals of the Strategy for a determined period of time, as well as the different mechanisms and incentives to promote the use of clean energy.[15]

The PRONASE[16] is the instrument through which the Executive establishes actions, projects and activities derived from the Strategy. In contrast with the Special Program, it provides a mid-term implementation. The current one covers the period from 2014 to 2018 and it is aimed at the implementation of specific actions on energy efficiency with the participation of the different agencies of the Federal Government. It also identifies priority areas for scientific and technological research in the matter of sustainable use of energy.

---

[13]   Article 17 of the LTE.
[14]   Statregy published at the Diario Oficial de la Federación on   December 12th, 2014. Available at: http://dof.gob.mx/nota_detalle.php?codigo=5376676&fecha=19/12/2014. (Last visited: July 15th, 2016)
[15]   *See* the *Estrategia de Transición para promover el uso de tecnologías y combustibles más limpios.* Available at: http://www.conuee.gob.mx/wb/Conuee/estrategia_de_transicion_para_prom over_el_uso_de_t (Last visited: July 15th, 2016)
[16]   Available   at: http://www.conuee.gob.mx/work/sites/Conuee/resources/LocalContent/ 182/4/PRONASE20142018FINAL.pdf. (Last visited. July 15th, 2016).

Financing is an important element in the Mexican regulation of renewable energy. The LTE provides that the necessary resources for the Federal Government to comply with the its functions provided by the law, shall be established in the Appropriations for the corresponding fiscal year as approved by the Federal Congress. The LTE also provides for the possibility of private contributions.

As it was provided by the former LAERFTE, a Fund for the Energy Transition and the Sustainable Use of Energy was established by the Federal Government in the shape of a public trusteeship.[17] For the fiscal year of 2014, the Fund administered a budget of MX $1.030 million, for different projects of energy efficiency and implementation of renewable energy. It is important to mention that the LTE does not establish a compulsory minimum amount for this Fund or other funds implemented to finance renewable energy projects.

An important aspect of the LTE is that it provides for the use of Clean Energy Certificates, known in other countries as Renewable Energy Certificates or "Green Tags."[18] Again, it is noticeable that the LTE avoids the concept of renewable energy and uses a more general definition of clean energy. Although these certificates have been proved in other countries as a successful tool to facilitate the compliance with commitments for the reduction of pollutant emissions, in Mexico they have been one of the most controversial issues in the law and the source of legal challenges from industrial associations that consider them as obstacles for the competitiveness of the manufacturing sector.[19]

Another public agency created by the LTE is the National Institute of Electricity and Clean Energy.[20] The Institute – inter alia – coordinates studies and projects of scientific and technological research on electric energy, clean energy, renewable energy, energy efficiency, sustainability, etc. It also provides technical and scientific support to agencies and to the Productive State Companies (such as the CFE), and to the private sector.

The LTE also provides for the establishment of an Advisory Board for Energy Transition, which is a permanent consultative organism of citizen engagement, with the objective of rendering opinions and advise

---

[17] Abouy the Fund *See*: https://www.gob.mx/sener/articulos/el-fondo-para-la-transicion-energetica-y-el-aprovechamiento-sustentable-de-la-energia-es-un-instrumento-de-politica-publica-de-la-secretaria. (Last visited: July15th, 2016)

[18] Article 68 of the LTE.

[19] *See* newspaper article available at: http://www.milenio.com/negocios/Certificados_de_Energia_Limpia_de_Sener-acereros-Secretaria_de_Energia_0_715728506.html. (Last visited: July 15th, 2016)

[20] Article 78 of the LTE.

the Secretariat of Energy with respect to the necessary actions to comply with the objectives related to clean energy and energy efficiency, as well as with respect to the various planning instruments established by the LTE. The advisory Board is chaired by the Secretary of Energy, and includes the participation of representatives of the different relevant agencies involved in the implementation of the provisions of the LTE. Also, it includes the participation of representatives of the energy industry, of academic institutions, and non-governmental organizations.

The LTE provides for the establishment of an Information System on Energy Transition, which is responsible for the registry, organization and dissemination of relevant information. On the other hand, the CONUEE shall publish a catalogue of equipment and devices that should include information with respect to their energy consumption. This catalogue should include devices and equipment with a significant consumption of energy and an important number of units sold in the market.[21]

With respect to the powers of inspection and to impose sanctions for violations of the law, both the CRE and the Attorney General's Office for Environmental Protection can conduct actions of oversight and inspection of the participants of the electric power industry. The CONUEE can impose fees for those electricity consumers with a high pattern of energy consumption, that do not provide the necessary information in the terms of the LTE or provide false information.[22]

In general, the LTE is an important legal instrument that provides certainty in the promotion of the use of clean energy and renewable energy in Mexico. As has been stated before, it is not the only piece of legislation devoted to mitigate the effects of climate change: the LGCC establishes the general commitments that Mexico has expressed before the international community for the reduction of greenhouse effect emissions and also, there is a special legislation to promote and develop bioenergy (LPDB) such as biodiesel and biogas.

The regulations on clean energy and renewable energy have been legally challenged for different reasons: On one hand, the private sector has expressed its concerns with respect to the lack of competiveness that the goals and objectives emissions' reduction impose on the manufacturing industry. On the other hand, some very important projects of wind energy have been legally and materially blocked by indigenous communities that are opposed to the establishment of these facilities. In sum, it is probably too soon to conclude that the regulatory framework in Mexico is going to

---

[21] *See* Article 103 of the LTE.
[22] Article 120 of the LTE.

be successful in terms of compliance with the objectives of a true energy transition.

According to a Report published by the Secretariat of Energy, as of the first semester of 2015 the participation o renewable energy in the total capacity of the electric power sector, represented only 25.3%. In contrast, the participation of non-renewable energy sources represented 74.7%. [23]

2. BRAZIL

Increasing consumption and environmental impact caused by traditional energy resources forced Brazil to explore clean alternatives of energy production. Brazil is now between the top 10 investing countries in renewable energy,[24] after all, more than 90% of the Brazilian territory extension is in the tropical region, ensuring excellent solar resources, plenty biomass and good wind regimes, which places this country in a favourable position when it comes to renewable energy production.

In the decades of the 1950's to the 1970's of the last century, Brazil public policy in the energy sector was characterized by a strong and direct State participation, reflected in the creation of several State owned companies.[25] In turn, the 1980s (also known as "the lost decade") were marked out by a fiscal and economic crisis that affected Brazilian capacity of investing in the electric sector.[26]

Such conditions were responsible for the inception of a completely new program for the production of energy and its commercialization in Brazil. The strong need of a reform in the electric sector, alongside with a new environmental awareness strengthened by the Brazilian participation in

[23] See "Informe sobre la participación de energías no renovables en la generación de electricidad en México." Available at http://www.gob.mx/cms/uploads/attachment/file/44323/Informe__1sem_2015.pdf, at p. 10 (Last visited: July 15th, 2016)

[24] In 2015, Brazil invested $BN 7.1. Frankfurt School – UNEP (United Nations Environment Programme) Collaborating Centre for Climate & Sustainable Energy Finance, *Global Trends in Renewable Energy Investment*, [2016]. Available at: http://fs-unep-centre.org/sites/default/files/publications/globaltrendsinrenewableenergyinvestment2016lowres_0.pdf. Last visited on July 14, 2016.

[25] For instance, in this period Eletrobras, Eletronorte and others companies were incorporated. In 1964, a military dictatorship was established in Brazil, which explains the nationalization process that these companies had been through. – J. P. P. Gomes, M. M. F. Vieira, *O campo da energia elétrica no Brasil de 1880 a 2002*. Revista de Administração Pública – Fundação Getúlio Vargas. Rio de Janeiro, nº 43, vol. 2, Mar/Apr [2009], pp. 306-308.

[26] After the oil crisis, the government started to encourage industries to use energy produced by hydroelectric plants instead of fossil fuels. In order to increase energetic capacity, Brazil got into a huge international debt, which got worse due to the execution of monumental projects such as Itaipu Hydroelectric Plant. Alongside Brazilian government impossibility of investing in electric sector, levels of consume were increasing rapidly and there was the chance of Brazil to run out of hydroelectric resources.

Stockholm Conference of 1972,[27] impelled environmental legislation. Until then, Brazilian regulatory framework was mainly focused on protecting the economy, putting aside any environmental concern.[28]

The Federal Constitution of 1988 was the first one to regulate the environment. Previously, this matter was merely mentioned indirectly in hierarchically lower laws.[29] It established a duty to avoid environmental degradation, to make private property greener, to increase public participation in environmental issues and, most importantly, it established the fundamental right to live in a clean and ecologically balanced environment.

Moreover, the Constitution of 1988[30] provided that the State would only intervene in economic activities in special situations, enduring its regulatory function. In other words, the State adopted a normative role rather than being a direct participant in the sector. Its role was to regulate the sector and to provide a favourable environment for competition. In this context, it was the Brazilian Constitution the one that led to the beginning of the denationalization of the infrastructure sectors, including the energy sector,[31] at the same time that lifted environmental concern to another level.

Subsequently, the enactment of Law 8.031/1990, established the possibility of granting attempted concessions of electric energy production to private investors, removing the State direct participation in the sector. Later, Laws 8.987 and 9.074, both from 1995, established several criteria for the concession of public services, including that electricity had to be granted through a bidding process.

Therefore, in less than 10 years, the Brazilian legislation on the energy sector changed completely, moving from a period when there were no contracts with private investors in this matter to a compulsory procedure, including the mandatory assignment of a contract.[32]

---

[27] United Nations Conference on the Human Environment, 1972, Stockholm. The report of this Conference is available in http://www.un-documents.net/aconf48-14r1.pdf.
[28] The enactment of three laws marked a restructuring process in the environmental sector. Law 6.938/81 established the National Environmental Policy, Law 7.347/85 provides the civil action for liability for the damage caused to the environment and Law 9.605/98, which provides for criminal and administrative sanctions derived from harmful acts to the environment.
[29] J. A. Silva, *Direito ambiental constitucional*. 5. ed. São Paulo: Malheiros, 2004, p. 46.
[30] See articles 173, 174 and 175 of the Brazilian Federal Constitution of 1988 in http://www.planalto.gov.br/ccivil_03/constituicao/constituicaocompilado.htm.
[31] J. P. P. Gomes; M. M. F. Vieira, *O campo da energia elétrica no Brasil de 1880 a 2002*, [Mar;Apr/2009]. Revista de Administração Pública, 43 (2), pp. 295-321. Rio de Janeiro.
[32] S. M. G. R. David, Geração de energia elétrica no Brasil: uma visão legal-regulatória sobre riscos para o desenvolvimento da atividade e mecanismos de incentivo estabelecidos pelo poder público. São Paulo, [2013], p. 19.

Also, for the first time in Brazilian history, with the enactment of Law 8.631/1993 and Law 9.648/1998, not only one company would produce, transmit, distribute and commercialize energy: all these activities were isolated now, and they would be operated by different agents.[33]

However, in spite of these changes, Brazil was not capable of expanding energy supply sufficiently, which led the country to a great rationing in 2001, paralyzing the privatization process of the sector.[34]

By 2002, rationing was finally over, but the concern about Brazilian capacity of energy production remained as an issue.

As one of the rationing causes was the instability of hydroelectric power plants, which are very sensitive to hydrological factors, Brazilian government instituted the Programme of Incentive to Alternative Sources of Electric Energy (PROINFA), through the enactment of Law 10.438/2002, aiming to diversify resources of electricity production in order to guarantee electric supply and to reduce gas emissions. Its focus was to stimulate wind power, biomass and hydraulic sources.

Hence, a new chapter in the history of Brazilian electricity sector started. Still in 2002, Brazil ratified the Kyoto Protocol[35], and in 2005 it came into force through Decree 5.445.

Nonetheless, until the Copenhagen Conference of 2009, Brazil had not established strong and serious goals for reducing greenhouse emissions, especially given the fact that the Kyoto Protocol had not provided for any specific obligation and since developed countries, the biggest responsible for most of the concentration of gases in the atmosphere, did not ratify the Protocol or simply could not reduce their emissions as they have committed to.[36]

This excuse legitimated the execution of non-environmentally friendly projects, since they were considered as absolute necessary for the Brazilian

---

[33] M. P. Zimmermann, Aspectos técnicos e legais associados ao planejamento da expansão de energia elétrica no novo contexto regulatório brasileiro, [2007], pp. 15-17.

[34] C. A. J. Schmidt; M. A. M. Lima, *A demanda por energia elétrica no Brasil*. Revista Brasileira de Economia, vol. 58, nº 01, Rio de Janeiro, [Jan/Mar 2004].

[35] Although the Kyoto Protocol had not imposed any specific obligations to Brazil, it stablished the Clean Development Mechanism, which allowed developing countries to benefit from their low level of greenhouse gas emissions and their efficient reduction programmes of greenhouse gas emission, also including the possibility of selling Certified Emission Reductions. See the Brazilian report guidance about the subject: *O mecanismo de desenvolvimento limpo*, [2009]. Available in: http://www.bndes.gov.br/SiteBNDES/export/sites/default/bndes_pt/Galerias/Arquivos/conhecimento/livro_mdl/mdl.pdf. Last visited on: July 15, 2016.

[36] R. Abramovay, *Desenvolvimento sustentável: qual a estratégia para o Brasil?*, Revista Novos Estudos, nº 87, [Jul/2010], pp. 98-99.

economic and growth as a developing country, such as new hydroelectric power plants projects[37] and sources of emissions like the Amazon deforestation.[38]

Then, in 2010, Brazil informed the United Nations Framework Convention on Climate Change its volunteer commitment to reduce greenhouse gas emissions between 36.1% and 38.9 % of the emissions expected for 2020. Law 12.187 of 2009 had enacted such commitment through the establishment of the National Policy on Climate Change and had determined several plans for the adaptation to the climate change.[39]

The possibility of extending deadlines for generation concessions, electric transmission and power distribution were already set forth in Decree 9.074/1995, but because it did not establish the allowance of extending deadlines more than once, it was necessary to come up with a legal instrument that would permit further extension of long-term contracts of concessions for generation, transmission or distribution already extended, especially because in 2015 many important concessions were going to achieve their deadlines.

Thus, Interim Measure 579 of September 2012, subsequently converted into Law 12.783/2013, provided that generators and transmitters could renew their concession contracts, but their prices would now be regulated by the National Agency of Electric Energy - ANEEL (Agência Nacional de Energia Elétrica). Therefore, the idea was that companies could renew their concessions, but with a new contract, with lower prices, so the consumers could enjoy lower energy costs.

Mainly due to this price regulation, there was a significant change in the institutional context of the electricity sector: generating companies that once operated in a competitive environment now had regulated prices, like as distributors and broadcasters, which were considered natural monopolies.

Currently, Brazilian energy sector is extremely regulated. A strict system of contract auctions,[40] "in which total long-term demand from the various distribution companies is matched, in a bidding process, to

---

[37] For example, Jirau, Tapajós and Santo Antônio projects.

[38] R. Abramovay, *Desenvolvimento sustentável: qual a estratégia para o Brasil?*, Revista Novos Estudos, n⁰ 87, [Jul/2010], pp. 98-99.

[39] According to the Brazilian government. Available in: http://www.brasil.gov.br/meio-ambiente/2014/05/entenda-como-funciona-o-mecanismo-de-desenvolvimento-limpo-mdl. Last visited on July 15, 2016.

[40] These contracts of concessions of public service are especially disciplined by the National Agency of Electric Energy, which is also competent to discipline federal politics on utilization and exploration of electric potential in Brazil.

different combinations of potential supply, with the most competitive bids then receiving long-term power supply contracts,"[41] provides the Brazilian Government an efficient way to control both the evolution of alternative energy supply and the network of distribution and transmission development. For instance, auctions have been very successful when it comes to wind power projects, competing with gas-fired power projects on an unsubsidised cost basis.

Nowadays, 75,5% of energy production is renewable in Brazil. However, hydroelectric power plants still are the most important source of electricity, since hydraulic sources account for 58,4% of Brazilian energy production in 2015.[42]

At the same time, wind power, biomass and solar assets are increasing. Wind power and biomass combined with hydraulic potential would provide bigger stability to energy production, since the moment when hydro levels are low is exactly when wind power and bagasse (product from sugar cultivation, the most important source of biomass in Brazil) are in their highest peak of production.

According to ANEEL, 377 wind power assets were operating in 2016 (corresponding to 3,5% of Brazilian energy production), 125 were in construction and 259 were planned to be constructed. When it comes to biomass, 523 assets were operating in 2016 (corresponding to 0,6% of Brazilian energy production), 10 were in construction and 41 were planned to be executed.

Additionally, photovoltaic plants are still an inexpressive source of energy in Brazil, mainly because of the barrier of converting photovoltaics cells of solar energy. Consequently, there were only 39 assets operating in 2016 and 98 were in construction. But this reality is expected to be changed. According to the Research Energy Enterprise (EPE), it is estimated a solar energy generation of 219. MW in 2022[43]. There are few government

---

[41] "[...]This system provides a contrast with the operation of power markets in many OECD countries (and the initial attempt at power sector reform in Brazil), where competition between suppliers is based on short-run marginal costs. In the Brazilian context, an emphasis on short-run marginal costs turned out to be too volatile, primarily because of the large share of hydro in the system (which is either available at very low marginal cost or, in the event of a shortfall, potentially unavailable in very large volumes), hence the preference for a system that provides more stable cash flows over time, easing project financing and investment". International Energy Agency, *World Outlook Energy*, [2013]. Available at: http://www.iea.org/publications/freepublications/publication/WEO2013.pdf. Last visited on July 14, 2016.

[42] According to the Ministry of Mines and Energy.

[43] D. G. Oliveira, Análise do impacto regulatório da medida provisória 579 de 2012 no mercado de energia elétrica nacional e na competitividade das fontes alternativas de energia, Minas Gerais, [2014].

incentives such as Normative Resolution 482/2012, which allowed consumers to install small energy generators (such as solar panels and wind micro turbines) and exchange energy with the local distributor in order to reduce the price of the electricity bill.

Furthermore, there is a Bill (PLS 167/2013) following the Congress procedure to be enacted that would exempt taxes on the import of photovoltaic modules, encouraging international market, but at the same time, inhibiting the development of a strong national industry in this area.

In conclusion, it is important to highlight that Brazil has committed itself to reduce its gas emissions in 43% by 2030 and 37% by 2025, as well as to increase the share of sustainable bioenergy to approximately 18% in 2030 and restore and reforest 12 million hectares of forests, reducing environmental impacts, when the Federal Government signed the Paris Agreement in 2016.[44]

In order to do so, the role of the State to achieve these bold goals is essential, because of its responsibility for controlling auctions and contracts established with concessionaires that explore energy sources in Brazil.

It seems that keeping up with the growth in electricity demand will be a challenge for Brazil. Projections estimate that it will have to double its power system in only two decades.[45]

On the other hand, wind power and solar energy potential in Brazil are enormous due to its geography, and they remain unexplored. For example, wind potential is estimated at 140,000 MW.[46] Only the Northeast, one of the poorest regions in Brazil, has a capacity of 75,000 MW. As for solar energy, Brazil has one of the biggest solar incidences in the world.

Thus, there are many clean options for Brazil to achieve its goals and to meet with the country's energy necessity, but how rapidly these resources can be explored is where the doubt remains.

In this matter, an expansion on hydroelectric power plants should not be among Brazilian priorities on energy sector right now, because they are environmentally questioned. The execution of new hydroelectric projects would be politically and socially controversial, especially because remaining hydropower plants are situated in the Amazon region. To

---

[44] According to the Ministry of the Environment. Available in: http://www.mma.gov.br/clima/convencao-das-nacoes-unidas/acordo-de-paris. Last visited on July 14, 2016.
[45] International Energy Agency, *World Outlook Energy*, [2013], p.335. Available at: http://www.iea.org/publications/freepublications/publication/WEO2013.pdf. Last visited on July 14, 2016.
[46] According to the Ministry of Mines and Energy.

execute such an impactful project there, with the alternative of other environmentally friendly resources to be explored, such as wind power and solar energy, is not socially easily accepted anymore. Brazilian society is claiming for its fundamental right of a balanced environment, not to mention the inconsistency of that these acts would have before the international community.

3. CONCLUSION

The Mexican and Brazilian experience, although very different in their legislative process, demonstrate an effort to take advantage of the very important resources both countries enjoy. It seems there is still a long way to conclude whether this regulatory framework will help comply with the commitments made in terms of the Kyoto Protocol, so both countries can reduce their dependency fossil fuels.

Distributed generation and the energy transition

ELOY ÁLVAREZ PELEGRY

Director of the Energy Chair. Orkestra. Deusto University.
Member of the Spanish Royal Academy of Engineering (RAI)

JUAN LUIS LÓPEZ CARDENETE

Profesor Extraordinario de Dirección Estratégica
del IESE Business School, Spain

1. PURPOSE

The purpose of this work is to examine the issue of distributed generation in the context of energy transitions. We shall begin with a historical review, in order to bring some perspective to the subject, and an examination of several concepts we believe to be relevant, such as economies of scale.

These days, we tend to think of distributed generation solely in terms of photovoltaic facilities in the residential and tertiary sectors and dispersed/distributed or "embedded" renewables in medium voltage networks.

We will look at ways of extending this concept, examining distributed generation in terms of the type of grid or network and fundamentally its degree of development. This issue is addressed in the section entitled 'Distributed Generation in New Times'.

One cannot properly understand the issue of distributed generation without first identifying the various elements that have led to the current situation. We shall therefore begin our analysis with a short historical review and go on to look at the currents of strategic change that are transforming the industry, which we call the intellectual, economic, technological and political currents.

Throughout the text, the term "distributed generation" is used in the broadest terms.[1]

---

[1] For a review of several definitions of distributed generation (and active demand management), see "Redes de Distribución Eléctrica del Futuro. Un Análisis para su

2. A HISTORICAL REVIEW. POWER TRANSMISSION

We shall start with a short historical review, in order to place the subject of energy transition in a sufficiently wide time period. We shall also briefly look at how transmission has developed to provide some context for the issues facing networks and distribution.

2.1 A historical review

The following notes are intended to explain the historical context of some topical issues related to distributed generation (DG) and energy transitions. As we shall see, there are certain parallels between today's technological and economic issues and development and a series of aspects and debates related to the industry from a century ago.

The power industry first developed in the last three decades of the nineteenth century, when the technology was not yet available to allow power to be transmitted over significant distances. This issue, which has been widely discussed, is associated with the "War of Currents" (see Munson (2005)[2])

Low voltages and direct current meant that electricity had to be consumed close to where it was produced –in other words, that it had to be produced close to the final customers. These early consumers initially came from the upper middle classes and in many cities, the first thermoelectric power stations were built close to wealthier districts. The absence of logistics, due to a lack of suitable technology, forced close geographical matching of supply and demand, and limited the use of electricity to a small group of consumers.

In the 1890s, development of the first high-voltage alternating-current transmission systems led to a substantial reduction in costs, because of the economies of scale and economies of location that the new freedom of site offered, and also because of a narrowing of margins as the supply areas of competing generators began to overlap. The new geographical make-up of the electrical industry led to radical changes with major advantages for incipient consumers.

Like so many other times in human history, networks emerged as drivers of social progress. Decisive and abundant network externalities allowed almost complete freedom of entry on both the supply and demand sides. Networks became the meeting place for supply and demand. And

---

Desarrollo". Álvarez Pelegry, E. et al. (2013). Orkestra. Cuadernos de Energía.
[2]   Munson (2005) From Edison to ENRON. The business of power and what it means for the future of electricity". Praeger Publisher.

so, the virtuous circle of the industry began to turn ever faster; reduced costs meant that a service that had previously been limited to a privileged few could now be afforded by an emerging middle class. The increase in aggregate demand made it possible to upsize power stations, thus reducing costs.

The captains of industry understood the importance of electricity as a powerful vector of strategic projection. One the one hand, the networks, with their ever larger power stations enjoying economies of scale, constituted natural monopolies, forming an effective barrier to new entrants. The need for ever larger volumes of capital to finance larger and larger generating stations, and the long pay-off periods of the investments, meant that required vertical integration was essential both upstream, to give access to the mining resources that all forms of thermoelectric generation required, and downstream, where without integration there would be no access to the income flows needed to fund such a capital-intensive industry.

All of these factors helped concentrate the financial –and thus the political– power required, leading to a complicit relationship between the leaders of industry and politics. In some cases, this unsteady balance worked in industry's favour. In others, it tipped towards politics and the industry began to be used as an instrument for channelling industrial, social, fiscal and even territorial policy. The result was to make electricity –an essential and universal service– more expensive.

Prices that had been set by market conditions gave way to regulated tariffs, which rarely reflected the real costs[3] incurred. From the start, subsidies and tariffs have been an essential part of industry practice.[4] In general small consumers pay more than the costs they incur and bear nearly all the other costs which, although unrelated to the industry, are recouped via charges for power consumption. Large consumers, on the other hand, tend to be subsidised and generally do not pay all the costs, except those that can be strictly attributed to the quantity, transmission and distribution of power.

2.2 The development of power transmission

According to David E Nye (1992),[5] in the United States "Power grids covered the nation in a period of just sixty years, starting with the cities

---

[3] This is no insignificant matter, given that it is difficult to know how to distribute costs that are known *ex ante* (because they are fixed), while those that are easy to allocate, such as generating costs, are only known *ex post*.
[4] Domestic demand normally subsidises industry. In populist regimes, however, the opposite occurs.
[5] Nye D.E (1992) Electrifying America, Social Meanings of a New Technology, 1880-1940.

in 1880s. The first places to get electricity were the homes of the wealthy, hotels, theatres, large stores and clubs. The new technology was a synonym of wealth, power and privilege. The first managers of power companies saw that the city with its compact size, provided more customers for a given investment, and found that it also favoured a good balance between daytime and night-time demand. (...) As the power lines spread, people could live far from the city and still enjoy all its advantages".

Thomas Hughes (1993) studied the development of power networks and systems over a fifty-year period (1880-1930), particularly in the United States, Germany and England. He found that some systems were planned with a sense of complete globality, while others grew more gradually through confluence with other systems.[6] Here we can see a parallel with two current concepts – Europe-wide market design and integration and local individualised and community development.

According to Hughes, from 1890 until World War I, power utilities in the United States, Germany and England concentrated on supplying the most heavily-populated and industrialised urban centres, where decisions were shaped by the load factor.

Another key element was geographical diversity, often related to the size of an area or region. Developing systems to cover a larger area was not simply a question of size but also of seeking load diversity to balance the generating equipment.

The economic mix also enhanced system expansion. This, according to the author, explains the spread of the high-voltage transmission lines of RWE, the Ruhr-based utility, into the lignite fields around Cologne and the water-power regions of the Alps. The decisions that were made to improve load factor and economic mix shaped the way supply systems developed.

According to Hughes, only rarely were these principles violated. London was a notable exception; local government and the forces it represented managed to contain electric utilities within the boundaries of local-government jurisdiction, thereby restricting them to small-scale technology and limited diversity. This was the price that Londoners had to pay for prioritising the power of local government over the lower cost of electric power.

The MIT Press.
[6] See description in Álvarez Pelegry "Economia Industrial del Sector Eléctrico, (1997) Ed. Civitas.

Luciano Segreto (2006)[7] identifies two clearly differentiated periods in the history of electricity: from the beginnings of the industry to the Second World War; and the period since the end of the Second World War (the "second sixty years"). In the first period, he describes the penetration of power, first in the "electrical city", then in electrification of the railways and new urban transport, later in industry, and finally in household electrification. Segreto examines the great electrical issues: construction of large distribution networks and rural electrification. While it is not our intention to offer a detailed study of these issues here, it is worth noting the importance and timing of the development of distribution networks and rural electrification schemes; in a modern context, this could be likened to cases of distributed generation in places where no networks exist.

Although this report is intended to be as broad and global in scope as possible, it nonetheless seems fitting to refer specifically – albeit briefly– to the Spanish case here. In their description of the early power connections and the origins of transmission in Spain, Álvarez Isasi et al. (2001)[8] identify a number of separate periods: the origins of the power industry (1880-1918); national power grid projects (1919-1943); creation of UNESA (1944-1984) and Red Eléctrica de España (1985-1999).[9]

Gregorio Nuñez (1994)[10] describes in detail the development of the networks and generation in Andalusia and Badajoz, in what we would now call distributed generation (given the relatively small capacity of those early twentieth-century plants compared to today's ones). At the risk of simplifying Nuñez's description, he traces the development of the local into the regional and the progressive penetration into new uses for electricity and new markets, not always with favourable economic outcomes.

3. ECONOMIES OF SCALE, KEY MARKETS AND MICROGRIDS

We shall start this section by reviewing the concept of economy of scale, looking at a number of examples and results. The second sub-section offers

---

[7] Segreto L. (2016). "Ciento veinte años de electricidad. Dos mundos diferentes y parecidos". In "Un siglo de luz". Historia empresarial de Ibedrola.

[8] Álvarez Isasi, R and Zorrozúa Arrieta, M (2011). "La evolución histórica de la red eléctrica en alta tension". In "Historia de la tecnología en España". Vol.I, ed. Francisco Javier Ayala Carcedo. Valtenea.

[9] For further information on developments in the 1920s, see Maluquer de Motes J. (2006) "Panorama eléctrico español hasta 1944. "En un siglo de luz. Historia empresarial Iberdrola". For the period 1913-1936 see also Sudria i Triay C. (1990). "La industria eléctrica y el desarrollo económico de España. En electricidad y desarrollo económico. Perspectiva histórica de un siglo". Hidroeléctrica del Cantábrico 75 Anniversary.

[10] Nuñez, G. (1994). "Origen e integración de la industria eléctrica en Andalucía y Badajoz". In Compañía Sevillana de Electricidad. Cien años de historia.

some notes on the subject of microgrids, identifying their role in reliable developed power grids and in distributed generation in places not served by a power grid.

3.1. Economy of scale and relevant markets

Technology and economics have always been closely related; developments in large coal-powered or nuclear stations made it possible to cut costs, by producing more electricity on the same site at a lower cost. It is perhaps only in the case of combined cycles that this relationship between size and economy has begun to change. In CCGTs, the aim is not to create larger plants; indeed, they tend to have a capacity of around 400 MW, as compared to 600-700 MW for coal-powered stations and 1.000 MW for nuclear plants. Rather, the goal in this case, as with wind farms, is to achieve economies of location, with several units operating on the same site.

The clearest example of this reversal of economies of scale can be seen in individual home-based PV installations. In a recent study, Cliff Rochlin (2016)[11] compares the cost of PV facilities with a capacity of over 1 MW ("utility scale") and residential-scale PV (less than 10 KW).[12] Depending on the components, he estimates a total of $1.80/W for the larger facility as against $3.05/W for residential; although the modules cost the same, the rest of the system is more expensive in the case of residential-size installations.[13][14]

Nonetheless, this does not mean that photovoltaic power is not subject to economies of scale. This is the case with the so-called "utility-scale" PV facilities, a term used to describe on-shore installations with capacities ranging from over 1 MW to hundreds of MW. Here too, economies of scale play a decisive role, making incentives, grants (tax credits or subsidies on investment or feed-in tariffs (FiTs)) unnecessary.

The advantage of solar power plants over rooftop installations has been shown in a study by the Brattle Group which concluded that a 300 MW solar photovoltaic plant has approximately half the cost per kWh of having 300 MW divided among 5-kW home installations (in Xcel Energy Colorado

---

[11] Rochlin Cliff. "The Electrical Journal". (January/February 2016)

[12] The range of capacities covered by the term "utility scale" is unclear. Figures range from 1 Mw to over 4 Mw, as in the case of Wiki-Solar. One key characteristic of all such facilities is that they feed power into the distribution network, sometimes with a power purchase agreement.

[13] These figures are taken from the MIT's study "The future of Solar Energy; An Interdisciplinary MIT Study"

[14] Recent cost figures show a reduction in the total CAPEX of PV giving an axis of up to $1/W when the scale is greater than 30 MW and all other conditions are favourable. Source: Gransolar

System) and consistently performed better in cost terms in all the scenarios considered in the study.

At "utility scale" the cost ranges from $66/MWh to $117/MWh; whereas for residential-scale it is in a range of $123/MWh to $193/MWh.[15] These differences may be attributed to economies of scale, and to the fact that in technical terms it is possible to make better use of the possibilities of panel orientation and control.

Utility-scale facilities are part of the reason India now has 13,602 MW in operation or under development (7,586 MW in operation),[16] albeit new factors appear to be conditioning development.[17]

The possibility may also be considered of cooperatively-developed PV (or wind) power generation at an optimum scale and in an optimum location (i.e. at utility scale), with output allocated to each of the consumers/developers thanks to the backbone role of transmission and distribution networks. Such a system would satisfy calls by certain quarters to democratise energy –in this case renewables– without harming production competitiveness.[18]

To conclude this discussion of the economic factors, it is important to remember that economies of scale[19] have to be seen in the context of their respective markets. In reliable, highly-developed grids, the relevant market will not be confined to one country, but will progressively spread to others, covering supra-national regions or areas. It will therefore be necessary to shed the autarchic nature that has characterised incipient renewables and this means considering the geostrategy of renewables, with all the advantages arising from such conceptual leaps. The opposite extreme is the case of domestic production by small consumers, whose relevant market will be self-consumption if the installation is not grid connected. However, for grid-connected facilities, a novel situation would arise; for own production and consumption, the relevant market would be the residential consumer, whereas for the portion bought back from the grid, the relevant market would be the power system to which it is connected.

---

[15] International tenders were recently (2016) awarded for "utility scale" PV plants in Peru and Mexico at $48/MWh and $67/MWh respectively.
[16] Of this total, 488.5 MW is solar thermoelectric, which also suggests that economics play a major role in both technologies.
[17] See for example, "Too much, too fast?" PV Magazine 6/2016
[18] This would make it necessary to rethink the cost items recovered through existing tariff systems and the nature of the collection structure.
[19] Although we are speaking of economies of scale, we should not forget the economics of coordination, with integration of the load diversity discussed in the historical review.

3.2. Some notes on microgrids

We shall now discuss the issue of microgrids in developed networks (the subject of microgrids in isolated rural areas will be dealt with in Section 5.2).

So what is the modern concept of microgrids? For Chris Marnay (2016),[20] a microgrid has two distinguishing characteristics: it is a locally controlled power system that can function either grid-connected or as an electrical island.

Marnay also distinguishes between two kinds of microgrid. The first is what he calls a "milligrid", which lies downstream of a substation and can function as an island. He gives the example of "Borrego Springs" in the San Diego Gas and Electric system, a project which was developed to mitigate the unreliability of supply in an area that lies at the end of a 32 km, 28 MW feeder line. Two 1.8 MW mobile generator sets and a 1.5 MWh, 0.5 MW Lithium-ion battery were installed, as well as two photovoltaic arrays of 26 MW and 5 MW.

The second type includes what are known as true microgrids. Here he cites the case of one built in Sendai, Japan, to improve supply quality in the University of Tohoku Fukushi campus, and nearby municipal facilities, a school and a water treatment plant. The set-up consists of 50 kW of photovoltaic panels, a 350 kW gas engine genset, molten carbonate fuel cells (250 kW), as well as the necessary switchgear and power electronics.

Marnay also discusses some other ideas we believe to be relevant. He says that the great interest of microgrids lies in the search for solutions for resilience and reliability. In the first case the aim is to ensure rapid recovery from a sudden change in conditions (this includes military microgrids) or greater network resilience to natural disasters. The second is associated with an improvement in reliability, where, for example, the United States has fairly low SAIDI and SAIFI values[21].

Two other examples may help focus the issue of microgrids. The first is the case of the Illinois Institute of Technology, which, to address issues of both resilience and reliability, built a microgrid at its campus with two 4 MW gas turbines, 8 kW of mini-wind installations and 160 kW of photovoltaic, with the idea of extending it to 1.3 MW and installing 500

[20] Marnay C. (2016) Microgrids: Finally Finding Their Place. in "Future of Utilities- Utilities of the Future". ed. Fereidoon P. Sioshansi. Academic Press
[21] SAIDI. System Average Interruption Duration Index; SAIFI. System Average Interruption Frequency Index

kWh in ZBB batteries (Shahidehpour M. et al (2012)[22]). The second is a 5 MW installation in Fort Collins (Colorado, US) to mitigate power spikes. Panwar M. et al (2012).[23]

4. CURRENTS OF STRATEGIC CHANGE THAT ARE TRANSFORMING INDUSTRY

Since the end of the 1960s, a number of profound currents of thought have had major strategic implications for the industry. Here we shall discuss four of these, which we call the intellectual, economic, technological and political currents. Ultimately they all influence the issues discussed here by establishing new game rules.

4.1. Current of intellectual change

The globalisation of western values has implanted in many minds principles such as the scarcity of natural resources, environmental sustainability and the need to combat climate change. It should also be said that there is still some mistrust among large corporations, private and public alike, and a certain lack of concern, typical of affluent societies, over the cost of certain options or policies.

A deep level of support has built up for the notion of the "democratisation of the economy"; in this case, this is seen as equating with proximity (the "plural sector"), smallness ("small is beautiful") and ecology, as well as a move away from what might be termed "economistic" approaches. There is a tendency to believe that if the issues on the table are important enough, then we should not be concerned with the cost of resolving them.

We can identify a number of pivotal milestones that have shaped this intellectual current of strategic change and can help explain how we have reached this situation. They include the movements of May 1968; the formation of the Club of Rome by Peccei and King in 1968; Donella Meadows' "The Limits to Growth", an MIT report commissioned by the Club of Rome in 1972; the 1973 OPEC oil embargo; the 1987 UN Brundtland Report on sustainability; successive reports by the United Nations IPCC and subsequent climate summits; the intellectual influence of Rifkin and Mintzberg; and Pope Francis's "Laudato Si" encyclical of 2015.[24]

---

[22] Shahidehpour M. & Clair J.F. A Functional Microgrid for Enhancing Reliability, Sustainability and Energy Efficiency. Electricity Journal (2012). October
[23] Panwar M. et al (2012). Electricity Journal (2012). October
[24] The encyclical centres on the Earth as the place in which humans live, and defends nature, animal life and energy reforms. The title of the encyclical is taken from St. Francis of Assisi's Canticle of the Sun, one of whose stanzas reads: "Praise be to you, my Lord, through our Sister, Mother Earth, who sustains and governs us".

It is within this intellectual framework that we must see the calls for each unit of consumption to have its own source of power production, in other words distributed –or rather "fragmented"– generation. In affluent societies, this model has little to do with that of the early years of the electricity industry.

4.2 Current of economic change

Paralleling this intellectual current of change, there has also been a successful current of new economic thinking which lays the emphasis on supply, managed by private companies subject to intense competition[25]. One of the clearest advocates of this model is Milton Friedman and the so-called "Washington consensus". President Reagan and British premier Thatcher were both strong exponents. The model of conversion and deregulation of the power industry in England and Wales in the 1980s grew out of that way of thinking and its essential features were replicated elsewhere.[26]

In a typical deregulated model, generation and marketing are split off, as activities that can compete freely in a regimen of free enterprise. Distribution, on the other hand, is viewed as a natural monopoly. This does not mean it cannot be privately owned, under the oversight of an independent regulator who ensures that the game rules apply to all agents involved. Finally, as part of the institutional architecture, there is a technical operator and an economic operator, whose respective missions are to facilitate and optimise physical and economic flows in the power system.

Margaret Thatcher undertook a profound transformation in the United Kingdom, while at the same time looking to achieve other ambitious aims, particularly in the coal industry where her goal was to increase economic competitiveness by reducing the power of the trade unions. She also sought to reduce the electrical industry's dependency on coal, by tapping the then abundant North Sea gas reserves; and to "democratise the economy", through "popular capitalism" and by giving ownership of large corporations to a large middle class with savings and private pensions. This radical transformation was given a further boost by the poor condition of state-owned companies, with power companies and mines functionally integrated or "quasi-integrated".

---

[25] We do not explore here, other currents of economic thinking that have considerable influence. Namely, the "Austrian Economics" and the Schumpeter concept of "creative destruction", that may be relevant in the future of the electricity industry.

[26] Chile was a successful model, imitated throughout practically all of Latin America

The new structural make-up of the resulting power industry has since been tightened up through the incorporation of environmental, safety and energy-related policies.

4.3 Current of technological change

The current of technological change has helped facilitate the other changes. One can identify four successful changes in generation and a fifth – potentially revolutionary– change in power storage.

4.3.i.-Combined-cycle gas turbines

Power generation using combined cycle gas turbines –CCGTs– marks a major step forward. It incorporates the technology behind aeronautical jet engines into a fully reconfigured conventional thermal power station. When these power plants are gas-burning, they can achieve primary energy usage levels well of over 50%, a very substantial improvement on conventional techniques (38% coal). That improved efficiency, combined with the use of a more hydrogenated type of hydrocarbon, natural gas, reduces specific CO_2 emissions by 60% compared to coal. This twin advantage is particularly useful in achieving environmental goals as well are more traditional ones related to competitiveness. It also offers advantages that modify the competitive structure. It reduces the intensity of capital costs to less than a third of those of a coal-burning station and much less than a sixth of those of a nuclear plant. Construction time is less than half that of a coal-burning station and less than a fifth that of a nuclear plant. These advantages, combined with those offered by a new and very different fuel supply chain are considerably reducing the input barriers for new investors, which in turn boosts competition. In addition, the developers can sell their output to free-access wholesale markets without needing to have their own end customers and with no possibility for "common carrier" networks to discriminate between new and existing agents. These developments have shaken up the structure of the industry.

4.3.ii.- Onshore wind energy and photovoltaic

Onshore wind energy and Photovoltaics (PV) are two successful technologies that can now be seen as being full members of the 'conventionals' club; indeed, despite their recent emergence, it would be no surprise to see them classed as 'traditional', in the same group as high-power hydro, in the near future. These new technologies can be rolled out on a mass scale at very competitive prices provided four requirements are met: optimally-scaled projects; the existence of a good wind or solar resource; a sufficient and assured income flow; and, last but by no means least, the fact that ownership is objectivised through competitive auction. When any of these requirements is lacking, the cost increases, delaying decarbonisation of the energy model and wasting scarce resources which could be used to address other social needs, a situation which is all too common.

4.3.iii.- Electricity storage

The greatest hope for technological change lies with advances in storage systems. Competitive solutions already exist for storing electricity in centralised pump-storage hydroelectric facilities. However, the topography and water resources required for this type of solution are not always in place. A battery would allow distributed storage to be combined geographically with distributed generation. A suitable solution would allow intermittent renewable technologies to be incorporated into the power system, facilitating synchronicity between consumer needs and the availability (in this case delayed) of production.

There are at present no enough solutions with sufficient storage density or with a suitable level of cost. The advances are important but the hopes placed in them are even greater. A suitable solution that would make the batteries technically and economically viable and competitive would allow for road transport of electricity. This would have an enormous impact on the decarbonisation of energy.

However, unlike the viable and competitive options available in the area of onshore wind and PV, in the case of energy storage, the technical and economic viability required for major deployment is still not here.

In any case, although the distributed power storage, which has yet to attain the better levels of technical and economic functionality that will make it more viable, will bring further changes.

4.3.iv.- Digitisation and ICT

Power distribution requires reducing high-voltage transmission levels (normally 400-220 and 132 kV) to the levels at which the electricity us used in companies and distribution networks (66-45-20 and 15 kV). This operation is performed in facilities known as substations, with infrastructures and operations that are characteristic of power distribution. Over the last decade in particular, there has been a major upgrading of the architecture and topology of distribution networks and substations.

Telecommunications and digitisation have been backed by electrical technology, improving the service quality and reducing average interruption time of distribution,[27] to offer a more efficient service with fewer power

---

[27]   Reduced from 9.8 hrs in 1987 to 1 hour in recent years. UNESA, "Contribución de las compañías que integran unesa al desarrollo de la sociedad española" (2013) y Guerra, A. and

cuts. Sensors, automation, remote control and operating systems all help facilitate remote monitoring of installations and improvements in supply.

This progressive transformation of the distribution networks has been driven by service quality, security of operation and operational efficiency. The process has also been affected, to a greater or lesser extent, by regulation.

Supervision and automation –which we may be classed together as remote management systems– are not new concepts or applications at distribution level; however their deployment at transformer and low-voltage levels *is* new. This development reinforces remote management in medium voltage and transfers it from medium to low voltage, deploying concepts and technologies common in substations to the ambit of transformer centres.

Moreover, the deployment of meters[28,] is changing distribution and will change it even further; once communication technologies are habilitated, it will be possible to exchange data in both directions between the meter and the remote management system.[29]

As information and management capacity is extended, there will be greater potential for aggregating demand in order to flatten load curves and reduce demand, with all the associated effects on investments in transport, distribution and conventional generation.

Business models have arisen linked to the deployment of smart meters and advanced measuring systems, which might be classed as energy services models, as well as smart solutions for the home and demand-responsive services, with several companies offering solutions in the different segments.[30] Here, active demand management is particularly

Hurtado, J., UF Distribución 1999-2008. (2009)

[28] Which in Spain is mandatory, whereby the end of 2014 figures of 42%-36% deployment had been achieved, with 11.9 million metering units fitted with capacity for remote measurement and remote management, and 10.19 effectively integrated in the corresponding systems. Maqueda Hernando, L. "La Regulación de las Redes del Futuro". Jornada Redes Eléctricas. Tecnología, Competitividad, Regulación y Nuevos Modelos de Negocio. Organizado por la Cátedra de Energía de Orkestra y Tecnalia. (2015). Hereafter referred to as "Jornadas 2015";

[29] Royal Decree 1110/2007 concerning points of measurement, imposes the following basic requirements: a) Active and reactive energy, b) Maximum power demanded, c) Six tariff periods, d) Storage of three months of hourly load curves, e) Quality parameters, f) Incorporation of power control switch, g) Remote reading, h) Remote parameterisation, i) Remote supply disconnection and reconnection, j) Capacity for load management. Royal Decree 216/2014, published in March 2014 established the method for calculating retail prices for small consumers. It imposes new requirements not initially planned for remote management system. Revuelta, J.M., "Jornadas 2015".

[30] Abella, A., et al. "Smart Energy: New Applications and Business Models" Cuadernos de Orkestra (2015)

important, with a variety of instruments and possibilities, one of the best-known being the role that could be played by the large-scale development of electric vehicles.

4.4. Current of political change

Politics operates somewhere between the art of the possible and the Quixotic wish to achieve the impossible. It stands at a crossroads between all kinds of interests, with the most noble of aspirations, against a backdrop of confusion, with public opinion decisively conditioning political action. In the area of energy, this is manifested in exhaustive, abundant and changing legislation, designed (not always successfully) to distinguish between regulatory and political independence.

It is here, in the political framework, that the intellectual, economic and technological currents converge. The energy transition is a truly political issue and will have political consequences.

One reason why the term "energy transition" has entered common parlance is climate change. Rising temperatures and their effects are measured in a scale of decades; indeed one-hundred-year horizons are even employed, for example when discussing the possibility of zero-carbon energy systems.

Vaclav Smil (2010)[31] has analysed several energy transitions, looking at the way the supply structures of certain primary energies are transformed. He finds that the unit in which transformation periods are measured is the decade and even the century.

One of the most striking of modern transitions is the German case (the *Energiewende*). In a recent analysis, Álvarez et al (2016) found that the origins of this transition can be traced back to the 1970s, when the growing influence of the Green Party played an essential role in its political conception and development; also important were new intellectual orientations, including a wish to develop local communities, and technological and economic changes linked to wind power and PV and economic factors such as premiums for renewables (Feed-in Tariffs).

No less important in this framework of energy transitions has been the role of the European Commission and the European Union, for two reasons. Firstly, because it has translated the fight against climate change, focusing on the development of renewables and energy efficiency, into concrete targets for 2020 and 2030 (indeed, many sources now include

---

[31] Smil, V. (2010). Energy Transitions: History, Requirements, Prospects. Santa Barbara, California: Praeger.

forecasts or targets for carbon reduction in energy and transport aimed at 2050).[32]

The second reason is related to the Energy Union. Even the motivations for this initiative (which must be seen as being political in origin) are related to one of the central issues of this work, specifically, the "empowerment" of citizens and consumers, which has been much discussed in recent years with proposals for a decentralised movement.

The European Commission (2015)[33] has said that the Energy Union will place consumers at its core, taking ownership of the energy transition, benefitting from new technologies to reduce their bills and participating actively in the market.

The Commission recognises that the emerging model of self-consumption offers energy consumers opportunities to cut their costs, particularly SMEs facing high electricity prices. It adds that new patterns of behaviour are emerging, particularly rooftop PV panels, whether they are owned by consumers, by third-parties or are cooperatively run. This reduction in costs will not result from greater competitiveness than that achieved at "utility scale" but from the costs that would no longer be paid to the electrical system and which are currently collected through payment for consumption. This would force regulators to consider other ways in which these costs could be recovered or the possible breach of previous commitments backed by those costs.

Moreover, the EU distributed generation roadmap very much factors in the penetration of renewables in final use.

Distributed generation is therefore a key issue in the debate on the future of energy. We all believe that our energy supply will change, and change radically; however, even having identified the elements or factors of change, we cannot say for certain what final direction energy systems are going to take nor with what intensity they are going to evolve.

5. DISTRIBUTED GENERATION IN NEW TIMES

We shall now examine two cases – one in which there are strong, highly-reliable developed power grids, capable of performing their required function; and another in which such networks are dysfunctional or non-existent and part of the population lacks access to electricity. These are

---

[32] Such as for example, in the document "EU Energy, Transport and GHG Emissions Trends to 2050 - Reference Scenario 2013(2014)".
[33] European Commission (2015). Commission Staff Working Document "Best Practices on Renewable Energy Self Consumption. COM (2015) 339 Final.

conceptually different situations and we believe they should be addressed separately.

The situation of dysfunctional or ineffective networks can be seen as combining some of the parameters or situations from the two cases examined here. It is not infrequent, even in developed countries, to find weak networks that suffer frequent power cuts. We call such networks dysfunctional or ineffective. In these cases, the purpose of distributed generation is to make up for the dysfunctionality in the grid. Given that battery-based power storage is not yet technically competitive, renewable power is less than ideal for dealing with this type of deficiencies, and most solutions use gas-powered arrangements or combustion engines.

5.1. Distributed generation in developed and reliable power grids

In examining this group, we believe it is helpful to draw a distinction between three situations.

In the first, distributed generation caters to large or medium[34] generators/consumers (typical examples might include CHP in industry with sizes ranging from one to several tens of megawatts).

The second situation involves medium-voltage power levels and scattered facilities in the networks. These might include wind farms and utility-scale PV arrays and the category covers a very wide range of power capacities.

The third case is that of distributed generation physically coupled to small and medium-sized consumers.

The reasons and incentives for distributed generation vary. In the case of CHP, its very *raison d'être* lies in maximising use of the primary fossil energy used, with all the environmental and economic advantages this entails. In the case of renewable generation, coupled with residential or tertiary consumption, both ideological and economic motivations are at play. In the latter case, this is due to the inappropriate signals given off by the uneven regulatory or fiscal playing field that has been created.[35]

---

[34] The purpose in this section and the next is to reflect on certain concepts and ideas. The terms "large", "medium" and "small" do not reflect exact amounts, but instead are intended to reflect general orders of magnitude.
[35] A separate issue are the reasons for the geographical configuration of large-scale renewable generation, which cannot be considered to be either concentrated or distributed generation.

5.1. i.- Large and medium-sized generators/consumers

Combined Heat and Power (CHP) involves the simultaneous cogeneration of electricity and steam. It massively improves energy efficiency, more than doubling the usage of the primary energy. In addition to the environmental advantages of such thermoelectric efficiency, there is also an improvement in competitiveness, when compared with the option of producing electricity and steam separately. Nonetheless, CHP has certain constraints which reduce its economic advantage, such as the need to match geographically the place of production with the place of consumption, and the limitation on the size of the plant which depends on steam requirements, rather than harnessing an optimum scale that would maximise the economy of the plant. In this case, the site is determined by the location of the host business and may not necessarily be the best in terms of the supply of fossil energy used. This is another case of distributed generation, but for very different reasons to those of the early days of the electricity industry.

CHP has a precedent in "District Heating" (DH), widely used in cities with harsh winters and a strong community culture or municipal influence. DH uses the heat from thermal power stations to provide heating and hot water to homes and other services in the urban area. This is a form of distributed power generation at an urban scale that does not seek to allocate its production to each consumption unit. The electricity is fed into the grid like any other power source.

There might also be a place for CHP in small units of residential or tertiary consumption. Micro CHP with gas turbines could nearly replicate the thermoelectric efficiency of larger-scale CHP.

The first CHP projects were created to make their developers self-sufficient in electricity and steam. From the outset, they were encouraged to feed their surpluses into the grid, for which they were paid higher-than-average prices. Maximization was achieved if the entire production was sold at a premium, and they bought all the power they consumed from the system. In general the regulators accepted a change in economic flows from "net balance" to what was called "all-for-all".[36]

5.1.ii.-Medium-power and dispersed generation in the grids

Countries in southern Europe, with the partial exception of Portugal, committed prematurely and on a large scale to immature renewable technologies (such as solar power ten years ago), thus paying for the

---

[36] If the way was to be opened to small-scale microcogeneration using gas as an energy vector, then it would create an incentive scheme diametrically opposed to that enjoyed by large consumers.

"learning curve" for the rest of the world, without the mediation of market mechanisms or effective control over deployment. In some cases, they were supported by groups that did not believe in the market's ability to capture efficiency and by investors specialising in attracting public income. Such generation is neither distributed nor centralised in nature. Geographically, it was introduced on the basis of criteria such as land price or administrative ease of obtaining licenses. Plants were not always built on sites with sufficient wind or solar resources, nor did they take into account the location of consumption. At the same time, an "autarchic" approach was encouraged at a national level. This tactic led to a wasting of resources; in some countries this has put a brake on the introduction of renewables in the present, when competitive technologies *are* available.

At this point, it may be helpful to discuss the difference between "grid parity cost" and "pool parity cost". At the beginning, the new renewables –still at an early stage of the learning curve– were naturally incapable of competing either in terms of cost of access to the grid –the "grid parity cost"– or (of course) in terms of the wholesale market cost, i.e. the "pool parity cost". In the first case, this was the retail cost paid by consumers. In the second case, it was the income obtained by generators for the electricity they produced. The retail price should only incorporate the costs of the product, the logistics and associated taxes. In practice, other costs of public policies, which are not always advisable or equitable, are also charged. There are also legal exceptions under which consumers in some cases are freed from bearing part of the previous costs.[37] Thus, the greater the charges deriving from public policies and the revenue raised through tax on consumption, the more competitive any production option will be.

5.1.iii.-Distributed generation physically coupled to small and medium consumers

The major reduction in costs in photovoltaic and wind technologies makes it possible (especially in the case of PV) to support a unit production cost which is lower than the "grid cost" even when the location and scale of the facility are suboptimal for competing with the "pool price". This is not yet the case with micro-generation.

These consumers pay higher costs to the electrical system than those they cause. They tend to subsidise large consumers. The most common tariff systems tend to recoup these costs through consumption charges, even in the case of fixed costs, which are not avoided by self-production. This is why the cost of self-production, which is normally greater than

---

[37] One example is the German case in which consuming companies with significant electricity costs are exempt from paying the costs of developing energy renewable. The remainder of consumers foot the bill for everyone.

that of production using economies of scale and location, can prove competitive when compared to the revenue avoided to the system. This income captured by the small self-producer, together with the associated tax benefits can make a distributed generation that is more expensive than the centralised generation it is replacing –and whose costs are met by other consumers– economically viable.

In the case of small consumers, we could call this "fragmented" generation. It is difficult to see how such generation makes sense, either from an economic point of view or for the system as a whole, in developed and reliable networks; in some cases political and intellectual motives clearly take precedence over economic factors. This might well mean that those most affected by these options would be the lowest-income segments of the population, clearly making it a socially regressive policy.

5.2 Distributed generation in areas with no grids

In a rural environment with a scattered population and no grid, distributed generation is the best way of ensuring a viable supply. The spectacular reduction in costs of PV and wind production have created a wonderful opportunity for boosting social development among these tiers of the population. Even in these cases, it is necessary to look for the best scale and the ideal location for the generation plants, where they can be coupled to microgrids distributing the electricity produced.

Distributed generation in off-grid areas can form part of a policy of universal access to energy, which might be defined as "access to clean, reliable and affordable energy services for use in cooking, heating, lighting, healthcare, communication and production". Level One of basic human energy requirements includes between 50-100 kWh of electricity per person per year for lighting, healthcare, education, communication and community services, as well as fuel and biomass for heating and cooking.

In this context, it should also be noted that the absence of power distribution networks occurs in what are called 'Isolated Rural Communities'.[38] A key economic issue is "affordability" which means that the cost of the energy must be compatible with income levels.[39]

Access to a home electricity supply is essential for human development since it allows lighting, telecommunications, cooling, facilitates education

---

[38] For a definition of these and their implications, see "Las Comunidades Rurales Aisladas". J.M. Arraiza. Tecnología para el Desarrollo Humano de las Comunidades Rurales Aisladas. Editors J.I. Perez Arraga and Ana Moreno Romero. Real Academia de Ingeniería (2011)
[39] Interestingly, the same is true in more affluent societies, where the level of investment, for example in PV in the residential sector, depends on available income.

and the use of household appliances. A universal electricity service is therefore a basic feature of any policy for combatting poverty;[40] most countries include a universal electricity service among their goals, and rural electrification schemes are being designed, often with good results.[41]

Most such schemes have until now viewed the enlargement of supply grids as being the only strategy for electrifying rural areas; the result is that large sections of the population, living in the most isolated rural areas are still without access.

Here, the case of China may be illustrative. Initially, extension or enlargement of the power grids was practically the only option and even in isolated cases where decentralised generation was introduced, it was considered not to be very reliable. However, given the difficulties of extending the power grid to all locations and the economic improvements seen in decentralised generation, the Chinese government now targets bringing a further 10 million people on line by 2020 using decentralised generation.

Closer to home, another example can be seen in Morocco. The general rural electrification scheme was launched in 1996 with the aim of extending access to electricity. Over the last eighteen years, more than two million homes in rural areas have been connected to a power supply, giving a rural electrification rate of 98%. On the basis of economic criteria, ONE (*L'Office National de l'Électricité*), introduced systems of off-grid renewable generation in isolated rural communities. More than 3,600 towns, with 5,800 rural homes were given access to photovoltaic systems. (Amegroud T. (2015)[42]).

Seen in overall or global terms, supplying electricity to this very large scattered population group, estimated at around 1.2 billion people requiring 571 TWh[43] of power, would mean designing distributed generation systems in areas with no power grid or where it is technically and economically unviable to extend the grid. The investment required would come to over 441 billion dollars in the next 20 years.[44] This type of distributed generation takes the form of home generation and micro networks; parallels could be

---

[40] Here one should also include power needs for basic uses in arable farming, for example, pumping for irrigation, which results in increased agricultural production, as in the case of the Jawaharlal Nehru National Solar Mission programme. See Comparative study on rural electrification policies in emerging economies. IEA (2010)
[41] A paradigmatic example is the case of Union Fenosa in Guatemala in the last decade.
[42] Amegroud, T. (2015). "Morocco's Power Sector Transition: Achievements and Potential. IAI working papers 15/05 February 2015. Amegroud, T. The author cites the ONEE Rapport dactivitès 2012, 2013
[43] Assuming a level of consumption of 475 KWh/year per person
[44] RAI (2011)

drawn with normalised access to mobile telephony, which does not require access to terrestrial networks or any extension to that network.

These "centralised" systems, similar to microgrids, not only include PV, but also wind and mini-hydro with viable back-up from gensets wherever possible. Important economic factors here include not only the cost of generation but also the cost of storage.

Existing projects, developed by Energy Without Borders, Microenergy Acciona, Iberdrola and the Endesa Foundation, highlight not only the importance of economic cost, but also the need to plan rural electrification and to have professional development and/ or business models, with the right incentives to ensure continuity, that are compatible with the culture and country in which they are introduced.

Implementation of those systems and experiences in cost management and reduction in distributed systems have shown that there is a huge potential for development, which could accelerate exponentially, especially at a time when electricity storage is at a breakthrough point –in economic more than in technological terms. Nonetheless, just because this is distributed energy, it does not mean that it does not require analysis and preliminary study. Proper planning, efficient financial mechanisms and cultural adaptation are all key to successful implementation.

Mohn, T. (2012)[45] compares microgrids in the developed world and in regions in which a significant proportion of the population does not have access to electricity. In particular, he discusses the UN's initiative launched in May 2011, and by the United Nations and the Energy Access Practitioner Network, emphasising the importance of an integrated approach to energy access. Comparing the potential of the power systems in the two cases, he suggests that the point of intersection between the two "worlds" lies in microgrids; albeit in developed world networks, they are promoted by subsidies and technological sophistication whereas in the off-grid world, the motivation is to provide access to electricity.

It is, therefore, in this very large potential field of areas of the world without access to electricity that we should concentrate our efforts. In the future the most important developments in distributed generation are likely to take place in this area.

---

[45] Mohn, T. (2012). In the Wider World, Microgrids will Flourish. The Electricity Journal. October (2012)

6. FINAL CONSIDERATIONS

- In the development of power systems over the last 120 years, power transmission and distribution networks have played a key role[46], benefitting both domestic and industrial consumers.

- The present currents of strategic change - intellectual, economic, technological and political-lead us to the concept of energy transition, where there has been a certain reappraisal of the role of distribution networks and distributed generation, in the broadest sense of the term.

- It is essential to draw a distinction between the role of networks and distributed generation in developed, reliable networks and in places or regions with no grids or dysfunctional networks.

- In distributed generation and in the power networks of the future, it is particularly important to take into account economies of scale, which facilitate or benefit the electrical system as a whole – and by extension all consumers.

- Social and political moves towards greater freedom and autonomy, sometimes linked to fragmented power generation, must be built on a level regulatory and fiscal playing field. Such aspirations must not be realised to the detriment of consumers who do not have access to these options. Once that is ensured, they should facilitate free entrepreneurial initiative.

- In places where there are no networks or only dysfunctional ones, the energy transition should reinforce distributed generation since technological and economic development will continue to enable a broad range of possibilities to be developed, favouring the most deprived members of society. The emergence of innovating business models will enable new areas to be electrified via distributed generation. A reduction in the cost of photovoltaic electricity is already helping to drive these changes.

---

[46] Economic advantages in some cases denominated "network externalities" or "network effects"

The regulation of demand side resources to support the energy transition

ANDREAS FORMOSA

Legal Counsel Energy Markets & Regulation
Tempus Energy, United Kingdom

1. INTRODUCTION

This chapter aims to set out the legal and regulatory framework underpinning the participation of the 'demand side' sector in energy markets across various jurisdictions. Demand side resources ('DS resources') is an umbrella term used to define essentially any electricity capacity that is not classified as electricity generation, i.e. neither large scale power stations nor even decentralised energy resources such as photovoltaic and CHP units (although with the latter there is an overlap in that they are both so called 'behind-the-meter' resources). These technologies include various forms of energy storage such as the in-demand lithium-ion batteries as well as 'demand response', i.e. electricity consumers responding to price signals by increasing or lowering their electricity demand[1].

This chapter will firstly give an introduction as to which technologies are considered to be DS resources and how they offer value to both energy markets and to the energy transition- in summary by more effectively integrating variable renewable energy ('VRE') onto the grid. Next the chapter will delve into the essential regulatory and legal 'ingredients' needed to provide for an active market for DS resources. Thirdly, the chapter will provide for certain case studies, through a comparative analysis of market structures as found in the United Kingdom, California and Chile. Finally, the chapter shall briefly touch upon some recommendations for improving the regulatory frameworks governing energy markets in order to adequately incentivise these key technologies to support the energy transition.

---

[1] This chapter has not included energy efficiency in the above definition

2. AN INTRODUCTION TO DEMAND SIDE RESOURCES

Setting the scene- a brief overview of electricity grid management

Unlike other forms of energy, electricity cannot be easily and cheaply stored. This means that the grid needs to be balanced in real time so that demand for electricity matches the supply of electricity. A failure to do so would result in outages of power, leading to large economic losses and a lack of grid security and stability[2]. For that reason, grid operators, mainly Transmission System Operators ('TSOs') invest heavily in market (e.g. forecasting) and technology (metering and monitoring) solutions to balance the grid to ensure the right level of frequency is maintained and that demand is always met.

Historically the above was fairly easy to predict as in most markets the generation portfolio was mainly made up of large, centralised fossil fuel or hydroelectric power plant, with a dispatchable schedule, and the only 'instability' was predicting consumers' electricity consumption patterns. Since the large scale incentivization of renewable energy, in the EU following the Climate & energy Packages of 2007 and in the US following the American Recovery and Reinvestment Act of 2009, the amount of electricity generated from renewable energy in both markets has increased impressively. In the EU for example the share of electricity generation from renewables has increased from 14.9% in 2005 to 27.5%[3] in 2015[4] with some countries in the EEA boasting shares of over 50%[5]. Despite the fact that the majority of renewables derive from non-VRE sources (hydro and biomass), the impact of a large amount of VRE generation, i.e. non-dispatchable generation, has lead to more actions being taken by the grid operator to ensure that the grid remains balanced[6]. In most cases this has lead to an increase in network balancing costs[7], as the grid operator must now take more actions and call upon a larger pool of dispatchable generation that

---

[2] In the USA, power outages caused by weather amount to between $20-55 billion annually in economic losses, 'Weather-Related Power Outages and Electric System Resiliency', Campbell, Congressional Research Service, 2012.
[3] Eurostat: Share of electricity from renewable sources in gross electricity consumption
[4] About 10% of that is variable RE - http://europa.eu/rapid/press-release_MEMO-15-5181_en.htm
[5] Ibid n.1, Latvia (51.1%); Portugal (52.1%); Austria (70%); Sweden (63.3%); Iceland (97.1%); Norway (109.6%)
[6] For a more detailed discussion, please see 'System Costs of Variable Renewable Energy in the European Union,' Thibault ROY, BEEP no 37.
[7] In GB balancing costs have already risen from £803m in 2012-13, or approximately £10 on a household electricity bill, to £1.08bn in 2015-16. This is expected to rise further. Source: National Grid.

also participates less in energy markets and must increase their prices in balancing markets to make up for the shortfall[8].

The above situation is one of the drivers we have seen that can be attributed to the rise in the need for DS technologies. These technologies, as described in more detail below, compete with traditional forms of generation to provide capacity for balancing, energy, and capacity markets, thereby lowering the grid impact of VRE. Other drivers are more cost-reflective tariff structures (both for energy and demand) that penalise users for using electricity during peak hours as well as significant advances in technology, from both smart metering to data analytics and impressive advances in software capability.

Following the COP21 Paris Agreement in 2015, as well as numerous pre-existing national climate targets, the electricity sector (accounting for 25% of global emissions[9]) will have to be almost completely decarbonised in order for the international community to be able to meet its goals. This will inevitably mean a significant increase in VRE, such as wind and solar. Maintaining grid stability and security, while ensuring balancing costs do not overburden consumers, means that DS resources are and will become even more critical to achieving decarbonised energy systems, both in centralised and decentralised formats.

What Technologies are we talking about?

There is no official definition or classification of DS technologies and they consist of a large number of varied technologies, old and new, but their commonality is that they allow electricity customers to actively engage in the energy market. For the present purposes this chapter shall focus on the below two categories.

Demand Response

Demand Response ('DR') refers to numerous techniques and methods of actively changing one's electricity consumption patterns in response to an external signal, that can be market driven or regulated as part of the electricity supply agreement[10]. DR is not a new concept and has existed for

---

[8] For a more detailed discussion on how variable renewable energy impacts balancing costs please see '*System LCOE: What are the costs of variable renewables?*', F. Ueckerdt, L. Hirth, G. Luderer, O. Edenhofer , 'Energy, Vol. 63'

[9] Source: IPCC (2014); based on global emissions from 2010

[10] The US Department of Energy has defined Demand Response as: "Changes in electric usage by end-use customers from their normal consumption patterns in response to changes in the price of electricity over time, or to incentive payments designed to induce lower electricity use at times of high wholesale market prices or when system reliability is jeopardized."

decades, however this was always within the narrow confines of system emergencies, typically through a contract with large industrial users for interruptible load programmes. DR has however, in certain jurisdictions moved beyond the traditional model of DR into a market and technology driven model that is already providing large benefits to the energy system[11].

The basic premise of DR is that it is cheaper in certain locations and at certain points in time to pay a customer (either directly or indirectly) to increase or decrease their electricity demand rather than to pay a generator to produce or stop producing electricity. This has, in a market context, a knock-on effect in that it saves the grid operator (and by extension all customers on socialised grid fees), the participating customer and the whole system, money, by lowering the energy and/or capacity market price. DR is deployed through certain hardware and software installations that are able to control the flexible energy consumption of a building or industrial complex and to communicate remotely with the grid operator for when the flexible load should and can be activated. Common examples of DR include[12]:

- Reducing or interrupting consumption temporarily with no change in consumption in other periods

- Shifting consumption to other time periods when the price is lower

- Temporarily utilising onsite generation in place of energy form the grid

As technology has developed and as smart meters have been rolled out beyond traditional industrial customers, it has been possible to replicate DR programmes with a much larger range of customers. DR can be carried out using industrial processes, heating and cooling appliances in commercial buildings, residential water heaters and supermarket refrigerators and lighting. This has created ever more sophisticated legal and regulatory frameworks, predominantly in certain parts of the US, Europe and Australasia where customers are rewarded for changing their electricity consumption patterns.

Energy Storage

Energy Storage is also not a new concept and encompasses a wide range of technologies. Grid operators have for decades used pumped hydro storage ('PHS'), where available, to balance the grid in a cost-effective manner.

---

[11] Demand Response provides 9.1% of peak demand in the PJM market in the USA- PJM Auction Results (2016)
[12] page 15, 'Demand Response as a Power System Resource', D. Hurley, P. Peterson and M. Whited, 2013

Dams would be filled up during the night when demand was low and discharged in the peak hours while also regulating grid frequency. This chapter will however focus on non-PHS technologies, which are much newer to energy markets and operate on a decentralised model. They include flywheel, compressed air, hydrogen and battery storage (which is further sub divided). All of these technologies are distinct and offer different advantages, but their main premise is the same, that they can convert and store electric energy from the grid and then re-convert and discharge that energy back onto the grid at a later point in time.

As costs for non-PHS storage technologies have been rapidly declining, but also due to the need to find cost-effective solutions to balance the grid in an era of decarbonisation targets; storage has increasingly become a popular technology to address several market issues. Storage can not only provide the same services and benefits as DR, but certain types of storage, such as batteries can also provide cost-effective and reliable frequency response services that historically were the sole responsibility of power generators. In addition, as storage is a physical asset, it may be the case that grid operators, being risk-averse organizations, prefer handling an asset that they can see, rather than relying on customers to change their consumption patterns.

However, as we shall see in more detail below, as storage is such a unique concept, its place in regulatory frameworks is often hard to identify. For example, under EU law, energy storage has not been explicitly classified, neither in the Electricity Directive nor in the EU Network Codes. Storage thus has had to rely on pre-existing regulations[13] in each EU Member State to operate. In some markets, storage must choose whether it is classified as a generator or a consumer. As it shall be highlighted below, as we come to understand more about this technology it becomes imperative for laws and regulations to catch up and provide a legal classification for this technology.[14]

How do DS Technologies offer value to the energy market and energy transition?

As briefly outlined above, DS technologies can offer advantages on three fronts. Firstly on an economic basis, peak energy and peak capacity demand, i.e. both network infrastructure and the marginal cost of producing electricity, is often more cost-effectively met through DS technologies, especially considering that there are 'peak generators' that are built only to

---

[13]   With the exception of a few Member States such as Italy that have specifically legislated on energy storage

[14]   For example, the EU funded stoRE project has called for the European Commission to define electricity storage in relation to the EU Electricity Directive, in its 2013 report *'European*

generate for limited hours per year[15]. Where markets allow for costs to be accurately reflected in tariffs and prices, DS technologies can outcompete power plants to meet peak demand[16]. These cost savings can be passed on to consumers through lower wholesale prices as well as lower network and balancing costs as network operators need to spend less on building infrastructure and procuring grid balancing and regulation services.

Secondly, to tackle the variability problem of certain renewable energy technologies (that are largely supported through subsidies), many energy systems procure (often through further subsidies) back-up fossil-fuel generation to operate when the weather conditions become unfavourable for renewable generation. One can thus see how many countries are not only subsidising renewables for their low carbon qualities but at the same time are also subsidizing fossil fuels to act as back-up when renewables are not available. A key method of tackling this problem in an economically rational way is by incentivising[17] and deploying DS technologies to manage grid stability. For example, wind power operators can install batteries to function when the wind is not blowing, or customers can be incentivised to shift their consumption to low or even negatively priced power periods (which are in any case mainly driven by an oversupply of renewable energy).

Thirdly, DS technologies, just like with distributed energy, allow for the so called 'democratisation' of energy, i.e. allowing individuals and companies to have control over their consumption and production of energy at a local level. While PVs have allowed communities to procure their own power from cleaner sources, the problem of variability of such resources means that they still need to be connected to the public grid for energy security reasons. If such individuals and communities adopted DS technologies to balance their generation output, whether in countries with a sophisticated grid system or countries with low levels of electrification, they can truly become fully self-sufficient.

3. REGULATORY AND LEGAL INGREDIENTS REQUIRED FOR THE COMMERCIAL ROLL-OUT OF DS TECHNOLOGIES

As new technologies trying to fit into a market structure that was designed in another century for a very different type of market actor, it

---

Regulatory and Market Framework for Electricity Storage Infrastructure'

[15]   Page 88, *'Demand Response and Market Power'*, B.R. Huber, 100 Iowa L. Rev. Bull. 87 2014-2015

[16]   DR providers have consistently won contracts in yearly capacity market auctions in PJM, and in 2016 received 9.1% of the capacity contracts (PJM).

[17]   For example by mandating that renewable generators be 'balance responsible parties', thereby being responsible for any imbalances caused due to their variability- this could act as an economic incentive for such generators to invest in DS resources

is clear that DS technologies can only enter the market (subsidy free) if the right conditions are present. Evidence showing their value has nudged regulators and law makers to at least create the foundations of a market that equally rewards capacity and participation, regardless of whether it is a generator or a customer. Evidence has also shown that such technologies do not even need subsidies to deliver value[18]. This section will outline the key regulatory and legal ingredients that are required to bring forward demand side capabilities[19].

(i) A genuine understanding of the characteristics of DS Resources

In many ways this is the most key ingredient of all and can be used to build the basis of a well functioning market in demand side resources. Storage and DR have unique characteristics (both between themselves and in relation to generation) and cannot simply be expected to participate in markets explicitly designed for large scale, centralised power stations. For this reason, before designing the future energy market, regulators and policy makers need to identify both the unique characteristics of DR and storage and appreciate the ways in which these technologies can significantly support their aims.

One pertinent example highlighting the need to fully comprehend how demand side resources operate is in relation to cultural changes, both in a business and domestic setting. For example, in terms of DR, business customers, whose primary responsibility is running their business, need to invest time and money to change their operational business practices, install equipment and train staff. While not easy to quantify into a capital expense the same way a power generator does, the same level of stability and security is needed for customers providing DR. Discounting this barrier may lead to a lack of investment in DR especially in a capacity market setting where contract lengths vary depending on a strict application of upfront capital investment[20].

(ii) A Level Playing Field

Once policy makers and regulators have understood the unique characteristics and opportunities of DS resources, they need to establish a market that a) actually allows DS resources to participate and b) offers a

---

[18] Page 10, 'Smart Power', National Infrastructure Commission 2016
[19] It is important to highlight that this chapter will focus on regulatory designs and recommendations for markets that have liberalized their electricity sectors for participation of market actors in various electricity markets. The benefits of DS technologies can still be realized in monopoly/closed markets (e.g. China and India) but would be incentivized through different mechanisms, mainly through State-owned utilities.
[20] The UK's capacity market has opted for this approach, where DR cannot receive the same contract lengths as other technologies as policy makers assumed there were negligible

level playing field between technologies. In relation to the first point, most jurisdictions still do not allow for any form of participation of demand side resources in either all or some of the following: wholesale electricity markets, balancing markets, ancillary services and capacity markets. For the most part, this is simply a factor of the fact that when designing market rules decades ago, legislators did not have DS resources in mind as a resource that could provide steady and secure capacity. Opening up the market to these technologies will thus require an in-depth analysis into, for example, the characteristics of these technologies, as well as things such as establishing baselines upon which to assess whether a customer has indeed changed its consumption pattern[21].

In terms of a level playing field, this criterion is inextricably linked with understanding the operational characteristics of DS resources. By simply changing a rule or regulation to technically allow DS resources to compete, this will very likely not be sufficient to incentivise these resources. A clear example is that, especially in relation to DR where customers are foregoing their normal business activity to provide flexibility, the ability of such resources to provide capacity is restricted to a few hours at a time, mainly to cover peak demand. If rules oblige a certain period of availability that is too long, then this can restrict their access to the market. Another example is that these resources are normally small in size, often even less than 500 KW, and if rules are imposed that they must meet a certain threshold size this can also foreclose the market.

An example in relation to battery storage is that, in some markets, such as in the UK, where all actors must fall into either one of 'generation' or 'demand' (and must pay the relative grid fees), operating storage will incur double grid fees and levies, i.e. fees when both charging and when discharging, even though it is discharging the same electricity it drew from the grid. One can easily argue that this arrangement is unfair and unnecessarily raises the costs to deploying battery storage, but at the same time it is certainly understandable how these rules came into being. For this reason, both in relation to DR and storage, markets need to be designed with the unique characteristics of DS resources in mind to avoid a good market design simply on paper.

It is worth bearing in mind that DS resources directly compete with power generators and at times distribution and/or transmission network operators and there is a natural and inherent tension between these

capital costs for DR unlike for new power stations, for more please see *'Incapacitated: Why the capacity market for electricity generation is not working, and how to reform it'*, 2016

[21] For more on baselines please see: 'Demand response in U.S. electricity markets: Empirical evidence'; Elsevier 2010; Cappers, Goldman & Kathan.

various interests. Understanding these natural tensions and the interests of all stakeholders will be key to regulators and policy makers in order to create markets that work for consumers rather than perhaps protecting the incumbent industries.

(iii) Cost-Reflectivity

Cost-reflectivity of both network tariffs and energy prices is a vital ingredient to encouraging DS resources to participate in markets. If prices and tariffs are socialised and their true value to the system is not adequately reflected to the end user, this does not encourage demand flexibility on behalf of the customer. As explained above, prices, even if they are socialised, are not equal at every point in time and location[22]. Peak hours naturally incur the highest costs to the system, when both the networks reach full capacity and the most expensive forms of generation enter wholesale markets to cover the gap in supply. As described above, DS resources are only cost-effective at certain points in time and at certain locations, and investors must be able to see price signals in order to amortise their investments, in the absence of a Government subsidy.

Cost-reflectivity should be encouraged in distribution and transmission network tariffs, in terms of time of use and/or location. An example of the former includes the UK's RIIO system[23] that has encouraged a triple band system, with a red (very high), amber (relatively high) and green (low) price period. The effect of this new charging methodology has been to incentivise both DR and battery storage deployment to avoid peak charges during the red periods. In terms of location, several energy markets (most notably the 'ISOs' in the USA) have wholesale market prices unique to specific zones or 'nodes' in their jurisdiction to reflect that the cost of delivering electricity to an end consumer differs depending on where they are, and this is a factor of high demand, adequate transmission capacity and type of generation. This acts as a transparent mechanism through which investors can identify financially optimal locations to deploy their DS technologies.

In energy markets, cost-reflectivity can be achieved in a number of ways. A very economically effective way of doing so in wholesale markets is to adopt a 'scarcity pricing' approach. Scarcity pricing is a simple concept that dictates that prices should reflect actual demand and supply. In the periods when demand is very high, prices are reflected to that effect to encourage

---

[22] Even in markets where customers are not explicitly exposed to price differentials, the electricity system is still more costly to run at certain points in time and certain locations, and this cost is passed on to end-users.

[23] For more information please see https://www.ofgem.gov.uk/network-regulation-riio-model

rational economic behaviour[24]. This, among other things suggests that price caps are not cost-effective, and even though policy makers may be reticent about allowing prices to reach over $1,000/MWh, in reality these events only occur in limited 15-minute periods throughout an entire year. Importantly, scarcity pricing needs to be applied to what is known as the 'imbalance market'. This is the period of time after all the final (and binding) financial positions of each market actor have been notified to the system operator, otherwise known as after 'gate closure'[25]. Once gate closure occurs, the system operator quickly analyses whether, over granular periods (ranging from 5 minutes to 60 minutes) demand equals supply. If there is a mismatch, a formula is used to either penalise or reward market actors that have helped or endangered the grid stability. These prices are known as 'imbalance prices'. For rational economic behaviour these prices need to reflect actual demand and supply as far as possible[26], and only then will companies invest in DS resources to avoid prices when they are predicted to be high[27].

As highlighted above, DS resources cannot be called upon on a continuous basis and have their specific time and place in the market. For example, battery storage can now be deployed for as low as $321/MWh as peaker replacement and $211/MWh as frequency regulation (levelized cost of storage comparison)[28]. That means there are currently (based on battery costs) limited price periods where it makes sense to use one's battery instead of drawing power from the grid. But these price signals need to be reflected to the end consumer in order to give them the choice of opting for a storage option when prices are very high, thereby doing both themselves and the whole system a service and getting rewarded for it.

(iv) Smart Metering and 'Real-Time' Financial Settlement

A smart grid, which is a loose term to define a grid that is digitised, can foster flows of electricity from all directions, and is thus cleaner and more

---

[24] For a more detailed discussion on electricity market design and scarcity pricing in particular, please see 'On an "Energy Only" Electricity Market Design for Resource Adequacy', William W. Hogan, 2005

[25] For more on 'gate closure' please see Chapter 7. Carlos Batlle. 2014. Electricity Generation and Wholesale Markets. In: Ignacio. J. Pérez-Arriaga ed. Regulation of the Power Sector. 2014

[26] Both Germany and Switzerland for example are currently looking to reform their imbalance prices to do just this.

[27] This chapter is of course assuming that liberalised market based electricity systems are optimal and that States are willing to completely commoditize what is seen by many as still a public good. It is still in many countries politically difficult to fully expose consumers to scarcity pricing and that is why many retail tariffs are still regulated. This chapter however assumes that liberalisation is the most efficient way of achieving the objectives of the energy trilemma.

[28] p.10, 'Lazard's Levelized Cost of Storage Analysis- V 1.0', 2015

efficient, needs a smart infrastructure. To create a smart grid, one needs smart meters, i.e. meters that can measure the consumption of electricity in almost real-time and transmit that data through mediums such as wireless internet or mobile networks to the bodies responsible for the settlement of electricity balances. Why is this important for DS resources? If DS resources are to be deployed across a large volume of energy consumers, there needs to be the infrastructure to record when such technologies are being used in order to gain from the price incentives (assuming there is cost-reflectivity).

An example of the above is a customer installing a battery to avoid peak distribution and/or transmission charges, which occur for limited minutes/ hours at a time. However, if there is no meter capable of recording exactly when electricity was consumed (or worse there is a smart meter but no ability to use that data in settlement), and the customer has to rely on their meter to be read manually, then it is clear that this opportunity is wasted. In addition to having a meter that can record consumption in a granular fashion, customers' electricity usage needs to be 'settled' on a very granular basis, ideally in tandem with the meter's recording capabilities. By doing so, and assuming that there is at least a limited amount of cost-reflectivity in prices, a natural incentive is created for customers to invest in demand response and/or storage to take advantage of price differentials throughout the day and be able to be 'settled' or billed on what they actually consumed at a specific point in time. If this is not possible, then customers have no economic incentive to change their consumption patterns.

While this is a very logical step, in practice it has not occurred as fast as it should have. Incumbent interests, slow moving regulation and 'technical difficulties' have all held up transitioning to a system where all customers both have a smart meter and are billed on what they actually use for every settlement period[29]. For example in the UK, it took seven years from when the policy was proposed for smaller industrial and commercial customers to be mandatorily billed on their actual consumption in half-hourly settlement periods.

On the other hand, if the market decides to move ahead with rolling out smart meters ahead of the official State rollout this can create problems of harmonisation and sunk capital costs. Countries usually agree on technical specifications of smart meters before a rollout begins, and this is partly what causes much of the delay. If companies install 'unofficial' meters this may create a harmonisation problem in the market once 'official' meters are rolled out. A fragmentation of this critical infrastructure may hamper

---

[29] Settlement periods vary- quarterly, half-hourly and hourly are the most common

cost efficiencies that are normally associated with harmonisation and may push costs up.

(v) General Legal Issues

This section seeks to draw attention to certain legal questions and issues that have arisen since the commercial deployment of DS resources in order to have an awareness of the legal complexities that are being created and will continue to grow in the future.

The issue of remuneration of DR has gained much attention following the US Supreme Court decision[30] (and preceding deliberations) in January 2016 on the Federal Energy Regulatory Commission ('FERC') Order 745. While the case focused on a jurisdictional matter in relation to whether FERC, under the Federal Power Act[31], could regulate DR, the case became very much a battleground between DR and generators.

The case emerged from the FERC decision to reward DR with the same market price as generators. The argument against this decision was rooted in the fact that customers providing DR never paid for the initial electricity costs they were then offering to forgo at the wholesale market price, and thus received a double benefit. The generators through their trade association EPSA argued that DR providers should receive a lower price that accounts for their retail tariff rate. While the case was won on a jurisdictional ground[32], there remains a legal question whether it is fair for market actors to resell a product that they initially did not pay for. On the other side of the Atlantic, at the EU level there is currently a discussion as part of the draft Network Code[33] on Electricity Balancing[34] on this very point, as to how to remunerate DR resources.

Another legal issue relates to the unbundling regime in the EU. The EU embarked on a gradual unbundling of the energy sector starting in 1999 and culminating in the Third Energy Package in 2009. This process aimed to separate out the various functions of the market while introducing or further promoting competition in both wholesale and retail markets. The Electricity Directive made it illegal for network operators[35] to own and

---

[30] 14-840 FERC v Electric Power Supply Association 2016
[31] the Act gives FERC jurisdiction over wholesale inter-state markets
[32] It was held that demand response relates to wholesale rather than retail markets and thus falls within FERC's jurisdiction
[33] For a longer discussion of Network Codes vis-à-vis demand response please see page 19 of 'In need of a clearer legal & regulatory framework for demand-response and smart consumption?', Chamoy and Musialski, OGEL 2012
[34] https://www.entsoe.eu/major-projects/network-code-development/electricity-balancing /Pages/default.aspx
[35] Both transmission and distribution

operate their own generation assets (subject to a de minimis level) for obvious reasons of competition.

As energy storage was never defined explicitly in the Directive, it would most likely fall into the category of a generator. This would mean that regulated entities such as DSOs and TSOs could not own and operate storage assets. This would of course create competition problems, as DSOs could be the ultimate procurer of DR and storage services that it itself also competes to provide against market participants, raising conflict of interest issues. Going forward, regulators in liberalized, unbundled markets should carefully consider the ownership of such resources in relation to network companies.

4. CASE STUDIES-A COMPARATIVE ANALYSIS

Great Britain

Great Britain[36] ('GB') has developed a range of regulatory frameworks with the aim of promoting both DR and storage, with some being more advanced and successful than others. Most of the incentives available have however so far only been taken up by large industrial and commercial ('I&C') customers.

Being a Member of the EU[37], GB has adopted provisions found in the EU Electricity Directive, the Energy Efficiency Directive and several Network Codes, that all aim to create a level playing field between DS resources and generation in providing electricity capacity. However, perhaps the strongest incentive that GB has offered the market has been the cost-reflectivity in network tariffs that offer significant opportunities to those wishing to avoid peak charges.

Network charging on the transmission grid in GB is split into both an energy and a capacity component. However the way costs are recovered for capacity (the larger share) for most I&C customers are through a cost-reflective 'Triad' system[38]. This system takes the three highest half-hourly settlement periods in the winter period[39] with the highest system demand and then bills customers for the entire year based on their usage within these three half-hourly periods. These periods see demand charges

---

[36] This chapter refers to Great Britain rather than the United Kingdom due to the fact that the energy system only covers England, Wales and Scotland, as Northern Ireland is part of the Irish energy system.
[37] At the date of publishing the UK is still a full member of the EU
[38] http://www2.nationalgrid.com/UK/Industry-information/System-charges/Electricity-transmission/Transmission-Network-Use-of-System-Charges/Transmission-Charges-Triad-Data/
[39] The Triad period runs from November to February (inclusive)

skyrocketing into the tens of thousands of GBP per MW[40] and act as a huge incentive for customers to invest in DR and storage to reduce their use of the transmission grid during these peak events.

Network charging on the distribution grid, through Ofgem's RIIO framework[41] is also very cost-reflective. Depending on the region within GB, tariffs are set up on a green, amber and red time basis. The red zone is typically 2-3 hours in the evening when charges can be several times those in the green zone. On Western Power Distribution's network[42], the difference between the red and green zones for half-hourly settled customers is over 200 times[43]. Yet again this charging regime offers an excellent opportunity for DS resources to enter the market in order to help customers avoid such peak charges.

Apart from the above 'implicit incentives', i.e. those based on price that incentivizes rational economic behaviour, there are other frameworks in GB that allow for the participation of DS resources in various markets. For example, National Grid, the UK designated System Operator, has the power through its licence to organise and set the rules for the balancing market. The balancing market comprises of a number of tenders for specific services in order to maintain grid stability, such as for frequency response or for when a large power station has a blackout. DR providers have for years now been providing services through products such as STOR, DSBR and Frequency Response. According to NG data, DR capacity in its products now amounts to 2634 MW[44] (3.6% of peak demand). However, a word of caution is needed here, as in GB the vast majority of what is termed 'demand response' is not a customer turn down but rather the use of an onsite generator to cover its energy needs during peak events. These generators can be climate friendly gas or biomass CHP units or also highly polluting diesel generators.

One of the most successful tenders internationally for battery storage was the 2016 Enhanced Frequency Response[45] tender organized by National Grid, which saw battery storage providers take up most of the available capacity. This tender has been hailed worldwide as a breakthrough as battery storage outcompeted other technologies to be awarded a four-year guaranteed return on investment.

---

[40]   National Grid Triad Data for the period 2015/16 show that the three highest periods were at £47,601, £47,982 and £50,596 per MW
[41]   https://www.ofgem.gov.uk/network-regulation-riio-model
[42]   This is the Distribution Network Operator for the South-West of England
[43]   Western Power Distribution (West Midlands) plc Use of System Charging Statement NOTICE OF CHARGES Effective from 1st April 2016 to 31st March 2017
[44]   National Grid, Non-BM Balancing Services Volumes and Expenditure 2015
[45]   http://www2.nationalgrid.com/Enhanced-Frequency-Response.aspx

Following the Electricity Market Reform process that was started in 2010 which aimed to drive investment into GB's ageing generation capacity, Parliament passed the Energy Act 2013, that included the creation of a capacity market. The capacity market is a form of subsidy gained through a competitive auction that provides payments for capacity rather than energy sold on the wholesale electricity market[46]. The Energy Act, as well as subsequent secondary legislation, provides for the participation of DS resources. On the face of it the capacity market was an ideal route to market for such technologies, as evidenced from the capacity market in the PJM market in the USA. However, the capacity market in the UK has come under intense scrutiny[47] for basically failing to meet the legal and regulatory ingredients as outlined in section 3. The capacity market has for example been criticised for not ensuring a level playing field through the imposition of criteria that do not allow DS resources to adequately participate[48].

California

The USA is not a single electricity market and there is jurisdictional division between State and Federal powers. States have been free to couple their wholesale markets and system operation responsibilities into single entities however. This has resulted in the formation of several large wholesale electricity markets across the USA (and Canada). California operates its own wholesale electricity market under the auspices of the California Independent System Operator ('CAISO')[49]. At State level, California (and all States) largely have flexibility to legislate on State related energy targets, such as renewable targets, while the Federal Energy Regulatory Commission passes orders in relation to the functioning of wholesale electricity markets.

California has long been viewed as a leader in technology innovation and this has also extended to the legal and regulatory frameworks that govern DS resources. California has a very ambitious target of meeting 33% of its electricity generation needs form renewable energies by 2025[50].

---

[46] For a more in-depth discussion on capacity markets and the interaction with demand response please see 'Peak Energy Demand and Demand Side Response', *Jacopo Torriti, Routledge, 2015*

[47] The demand response sector, many academics and NGOs have been very vocal about their opposition ot many of the design features; In addition the capacity market is subject to an ongoing legal challenge at the General Court of the EU.

[48] For more information please see n.17

[49] However California has coupled its balancing market with several other Western US States.

[50] AB 32, 'Global Warming Solutions Act of 2006'

Californian policy makers quickly realised the need to incentivise the deployment of energy storage solutions in order to be able to operate an energy system with a large amount of variable renewable resources. In 2010, a new State law was passed[51] mandating the State Regulator ('CPUC') to impose targets on the utilities. In 2012 the CPUC imposed a target of 1.325 GW for energy storage by 2024 on the three large investor-owned utilities ('IOUs'). The targets were technology neutral and left it up to the utilities to procure the most cost-efficient technologies depending on the service they were procuring. The proceeding auctions held by the various IOUs attracted a lot of interest from storage providers. For example Southern California Edison launched an auction[52] in 2015 for the provision of capacity in the West LA basin for almost 1.9 GW of which almost 27% was won by DS resources[53], outcompeting traditional forms of generation. One possible reason for the success in attracting so many DS resources may have been due to the certainty provided to the financial community through the 10-year capacity contracts.

In terms of demand response, California had previously been lagging behind other markets within the USA. Commentators have claimed that this was due to the fact that California did not operate a capacity market, a mechanism that many have argued, if designed correctly, can quickly create a booming demand response market due to the certainty and positive revenue stream provided. However, in 2014 the CPUC issued a mandate requiring the three large IOUs to hold auctions for a specific capacity of demand response, under what is known as the Demand Response Auction Mechanism Pilot ('DRAM')[54][55]. The DRAM uniquely further distinguishes between residential and commercial targets. This will enable residential DR, a sector that has so far not been active in DR markets mainly due to high opportunity and equipment costs relative to electric load, to start to become more active in the energy market.

Chile

Chile has in recent years demonstrated its commitment to cost-effective renewable energy deployment and as of this year has surpassed 1 GW[56]

---

[51]   AB2514
[52]   https://www.sce.com/wps/portal/home/procurement/solicitation/lcr/!ut/p/b0/04_Sj9CPykssy0xPLMnMz0vMAfGjzOK9PF0cDd1NjDz9nQxdDRyDPS1cXD1cDYL9zfQLsh-0VAQ4EJ6E!/
[53]   Including energy efficiency, demand response and storage
[54]   Order Instituting Rulemaking to Enhance the Role of Demand Response in Meeting the State's Resource Planning Needs and Operational Requirements- Rulemaking (R.) 13-09-011
[55]   Following the launch of 'DRAM' the three IOUs have procured 120 MW of Demand Response over two auctions in 2016, but must procure at least 1 GW per year.
[56]   Out of around 16 GW in total installed capacity

in installed solar capacity with another 2.2 GW in the pipeline[57]. Chile also has an ambitious renewable electricity target of 70% by 2050. By expanding so rapidly in solar power, it became apparent that the energy system required cost-effective balancing solutions to support the high amount of solar energy penetration.

In 2015, the Chilean Parliament passed the Electricity Transmission Act that had the primary aim of creating a unified transmission grid and independent system operator. Until now Chile was broken into 3 separate transmission grids due to the enormous distance between regions. The Act will hopefully allow the large solar reserves in the country's North to be utilized by sending electricity to where most of the country's demand is- in the centre. This will end the unnecessary curtailment of solar energy production currently going to waste.

The Act however, is one of the few legislative frameworks worldwide to explicitly mention and formally regulate energy storage. It remains to be seen how the future ISO will incentivize storage specifically, but just with the recognition of the technology in the Act, Chile has already moved in a very positive and forward-looking direction in recognising the benefits this technology can offer.

Even prior to the Act, there had already been investments in both energy storage and demand response in Chile. Utilities have been procuring demand response services[58] (primarily from the energy-intensive mining industry) and many solar energy producers, particularly in the Northern Atacama region, have been complimenting their installations with various storage technologies. One such example, the Copiapó project in Atacama, operates a Concentrated Solar Power (CSP) installation with thermal storage, which avoids the plant needing back up power. The CSP can therefore operate 24 hours a day. This is essentially the ideal form of asset we should be seeking in a decarbonized energy world, where renewable energy generators can rely on flexibility options such as storage to cover periods when they do not produce, thereby reducing any need for fossil fuel generation.

The Chilean example demonstrates that DS resources are not only available or commercially viable in developed markets, but that they can

---

[57] http://www.pv-magazine-latam.com/noticias/detalles/articulo/chile-instala-ms-de-1-gw-fotovoltaico-y-exporta-energa-solar_100022070/
[58] For an in depth discussion on demand response in the Chilean electricity market please see http://power.sitios.ing.uc.cl/alumno16/dresponse/mercados.html

be vital for the cost-effective energy transition or even electrification[59] of many emerging markets.

5. THOUGHTS ON THE WAY FORWARD

Technology will always move faster than regulation and legislation, and this is what is at the heart of the difficulties DS resources are facing when trying to enter the energy market. Many regulatory and legal frameworks were built on a foundation of another era, where large-scale, centralized generation was the only option, and where consumers were not allowed to participate.

In addition to the above, it is widely agreed among the energy community that we need to strive to solve the energy 'trilemma', of creating an energy system that is sustainable, secure and cost-effective. To achieve this second objective all technology at our disposal should be used; and results have already shown how DS resources are an ideal technology and commercial partner to VRE. For this reason, energy legislation will need to adapt. To do so it is advisable to create rules that fully embody the triple objectives set out by the energy 'trilemma'. Principles embodying the 'ingredients' set out in Section 3 can be used in principles-based rather than prescriptive regulations that can properly incentivize the deployment of DS resources. For example, an understanding of new technologies is needed to create a genuine level playing field, as opposed to a theoretical one, where all technologies, however small or large are allowed to compete in transparent and fair auctions for capacity or grid services.

By creating principles-based and technology-neutral laws and regulations we are ensuring a framework that can hopefully stand the test of time. While we know the innovative technologies in the market today, who knows what shape or size they will be in a decade or two.

[59] Many regions within emerging markets lack complete access to electricity, such as in sub-Saharan Africa and India, but DS resources can allow the constant operation of off-grid renewable energy systems.

The Role of Power Purchase Agreements (PPAs) in the Renewable Energy Markets - Are Corporate Renewable PPAs the Future of Power Supply?

DR. ECE GÜRSOY

Chief Legal Officer of Lightsource, United Kingdom

LUCILLE DE SILVA

Partner of Dentons, United Kingdom

ANDREW MEADEN

Associate of Dentons, United Kingdom

1. INTRODUCTION

A power purchase agreement (**PPA**) is, in part, a product of the particular regulatory regime which dictates the terms under which the power is sold. For example, some countries, including Vietnam and Nigeria, retain a monopolistic system under which a generator may only sell its power to a single state-owned supplier, who in turn sells the electricity to the ultimate consumer. In these circumstances, the generator is prohibited from selling its power to independent suppliers or other corporate entities and thus PPAs tend to follow a predictable structure, with limited scope for negotiation. By contrast, countries such as the United Kingdom (**UK**) and Germany are examples of highly liberalised electricity markets in which generators have a variety of potential customers and where the ultimate consumer has a wide choice of suppliers. In such markets there is currently far more opportunity for novel PPA structuring and innovation. For this reason, this chapter focuses predominantly on PPAs within liberalised electricity markets and in particular the UK, using examples to illustrate the possible market practices.

Securing a commercially acceptable long-term PPA with a creditworthy offtaker is crucial to a power project's financial viability, especially if the project is dependent on project finance, as revenues gained by the generator under the PPA usually comprise the project's main source of revenue. Furthermore, the trend towards a reduction in renewable subsidies has heightened the importance of PPA revenues. However, recent developments in the UK electricity market (such as low wholesale electricity prices, the erosion of renewable subsidies and regulatory uncertainty) have led some experts to question the extent to which commercially attractive long-term PPAs with traditional utility offtakers will remain available to renewable generators in the future.

Nevertheless, in the face of these challenges to the current long-term PPA market, this chapter will contend that the corporate renewable PPA has the potential to breathe new life into the UK PPA market. A crucial reason behind this contention is the large numbers of global companies (including Goldman Sachs, Johnson & Johnson, NIKE, Inc., Procter & Gamble, Starbucks and Walmart) that have, in light of the COP21, committed to source 100% of their electricity from renewable energy. Such commitments, if fulfilled, present an exciting opportunity for renewable generators in the UK and globally.

In view of these developments in the renewable electricity markets, this chapter explores:

- The PPAs in general and the types of PPA;

- Key provisions of a PPA;

- Key challenges for the availability of long-term renewable PPAs; and

- The potential for corporate PPAs.

2. THE VARIOUS TYPES OF PPAS

As stated above, the UK electricity market is highly liberalised. This provides the opportunity for a number of different PPA structures to be offered on the market, including:

- **Long-term PPAs** enable investors in large-scale renewable projects to secure their long-term investment and recoup the high capital expenditure associated with renewable projects which need to be amortised over the longest possible periods to ensure affordability. Long term PPAs often form the basis for project financing.

- **Short-term PPAs** are suitable for energy trading purposes (e.g. trading on the spot market) and are often simpler to negotiate than their long-term counterparts.

- **Private Wire PPAs** involve a direct electrical connection between the generating plant and the offtaker, for example a solar farm located next to an industrial factory. To the extent that the renewable generation does not meet the organisation's electricity demand, the shortfall is sourced via traditional utilities. There are various reasons why pursuing a private wire structure may be attractive to both the generator and the offtaker, including the potential to share the value of avoided grid charges and additional regulatory costs that are applied to electricity imported from the grid. However, as well as the benefits, private wire structures also impose additional costs when compared to grid connected projects, such as in relation to the installation and maintenance of the private wire infrastructure, which are reflected in the power purchase price.

- **Standard Corporate PPAs** offer organisations with a large electricity demand (for example, an industrial customer) the opportunity to directly enter into a PPA with the owner of a renewable generator as a way of notionally meeting its demand. As with private wire PPAs, to the extent that the renewable generation does not meet the organisation's demand, a traditional utility will typically provide the balance of the power requirements. Section 5 of this chapter will focus in more detail on the significant growth opportunities presented by corporate PPAs.

- **Virtual/Synthetic PPAs** are essentially hedges that avoid physical delivery of power. Where the standard form of corporate PPAs is not permitted due to regulatory reasons or where the offtaker has facilities on different locations, organisations may prefer synthetic/ virtual PPAs rather than standard PPAs. A company enters into a contract to pay a renewable energy project on an agreed power price. The renewable energy project sells the generated power into the wholesale market on a merchant basis or to a utility. The project pays the company if the electricity is sold into the market above the agreed contract price, and the company pays the project the difference if the electricity falls below the agreed price.

3. KEY PROVISIONS OF A PPA

The terms of a PPA vary depending on issues such as the type of generation facility, structure and features of the electricity market in a particular country. However, the majority of renewable PPAs include some or all of the following provisions:

Conditions Precedent: A PPA is likely to contain a number of conditions precedents which need to be satisfied before the offtaker is obligated to purchase power from a renewable generator. Failure to comply with the required CPs before the long stop date may entitle the non-defaulting party to terminate the PPA. Examples of CPs typically included in renewable PPAs include:

(a) receipt of all consents and permits necessary for the plant to be constructed and operated;

(b) grant of occupation rights in relation to the site on which the plant is located;

(c) financial closing (if the project is being financed).

There may also be some conditions precedent to the buyer's obligations, although this list is likely to be much shorter.

Term: The PPA will specify the term of the agreement. PPAs can be either short or long-term with long term PPAs typically having a life span of about 15-20 years. Short-term PPAs are suitable for energy trading purposes (e.g. trading on the spot market) and are often simpler to negotiate than their long-term counterparts. Long-term PPAs enable investors in large-scale renewable projects to secure their long-term investment and recoup the high capital expenditure associated with these projects which need to be amortised over the longest possible periods to ensure affordability. These PPAs often form the basis for project financing or refinancing.

Tariff: For many projects it is essential that the PPA offers a degree of revenue certainty. In this regard, provisions relating to tariffs are essential to ensure that the cost of operating the facility, repayment of debt and provision of reasonable return on equity is covered. Depending on the term of the PPA (if long term), there is an argument in favour of "price review" clauses; however, having these clauses brings uncertainty to the long-term pricing mechanism and results in an increase in the price. Tariff reopeners can either be: (i) time-based: a reopener after a certain length of time; or (ii) incident-based: a reopener upon the occurrence of a certain event.

Tariffs can be either two-part (capacity and energy) or single part (energy only). Capacity charge deals with the price for the available capacity of the facility whether or not the utility actually purchases any of the power. While the energy charge provides for the actual power delivered. Typically, in (non- fuel based) renewable projects, availability is not remunerated, other than if storage is deployed.

Metering: To calculate the energy charges payable by the buyer, the dispatched energy needs to be metered. It is usually the generator's responsibility to install and maintain the meters, but the PPA will give the buyer various rights to validate the meter readings.

Payment Security: The type of payment security required will depend on the creditworthiness of the offtaker. Types of security include: sovereign guarantee (more common in developing jurisdictions), letter of credit, parent company guarantee, offtake diversification and prepayment.

Representation and Warranties: Typically a PPA will include basic representations and warranties by both the generator and the buyer, of the type usually found in commercial agreements, addressing key issues such as the due execution and enforceability of the project documents.

However, the warranties may also cover more specific issues. For example, the generator may be required to warrant that it has applied for all permits, consents and exemptions required for the construction and operation of the plant, and that it has no reason to believe that such consents and permits will not be granted or such exemptions will not be available.

Interconnection/Delivery Point/Transmission: The PPA should stipulate which party is responsible for connecting the facility to the power grid (if it is grid connected) and transmitting power generated to the nearest substation. Lenders will in most cases prefer the offtaker to bear the bulk of the transmission or interconnection risk. Transmission is a critical issue for projects which are often far from "load" centres.

Termination: It is essential that the termination events in a PPA are clearly drafted and should be for only significant events. The generator, usually operating through a special purpose vehicle (SPV), will seek to limit the offtaker's rights to terminate the PPA. It is also advisable for the generator to ensure that grace periods and cure rights are provided for. Lender's will usually want step-in rights to cure any defaults so as to avoid the risk of stranded assets, particularly in emerging markets.

Typically the PPA will provide for termination by the buyer in the following circumstances:

(a) failure by the generator to commence commercial operation of the plant by a specified long stop date;

(b) abandonment of the project by the generator;

(c) termination of any of the other principal project documents, such as the fuel supply agreement (if any) or connection agreement, resulting from a default by the generator;

(d) the generator becoming insolvent;

(e) other material breaches of the PPA by the generator.

The PPA may also specify other specific breaches of the PPA which entitle the buyer to terminate the PPA. For example, the PPA may provide for termination where testing reveals that, for a specified number of times, the actual capacity of the plant was in fact a specified percentage below the capacity declared by the generator.

The PPA will also provide for the generator to have the right to terminate the PPA in various circumstances, including the following:

(i) failure by the buyer to observe its payment obligations or maintain any security for payment which it may be required to provide to the generator under the PPA;

(ii) insolvency or dissolution of the buyer;

(iii) other material breaches of the PPA by the buyer;

(iv) expropriation by the host government, or similar events which make it impossible or impractical to continue commercial operations;

(v) whilst not typical, there are PPAs pursuant to which the generator agrees to forsake the right to terminate the PPA in exchange for other remedies, such as the exercise of rights pursuant to a host government guarantee;

(vi) in addition to the rights of termination described above, the parties will generally have the right to terminate the PPA if a force majeure event prevents performance of a party's obligations under the PPA for a specified period of time (e.g. six months). However, some PPAs do not provide for automatic termination rights upon prolonged force majeure, but rather seek to deal with force majeure through other means, such as an obligation for the parties to meet and determine a way to overcome the force majeure event.

Assignment: The PPA will usually restrict assignment by the parties so that a party may only transfer its rights and obligations with the consent of the other party. There are, however, some exceptions such as assignment by the generator to the lenders via security and assignment to the government by the offtaker if there is a restructuring of the electricity industry.

Change in Law, Change in Tax: These are risks associated with power projects. PPAs, particularly if long term, contain provisions aimed at protecting the project company against the effect of such change. To deal with such circumstances, the change in law clause in the PPA may provide for the parties to agree to change the scope of the obligations under the agreement – for example, changes required to take account of the change in the regulatory regime.

Force majeure: The PPA should excuse the generator from performing its obligations if a force majeure event occurs (an event beyond the reasonable control of either party) and prevents performance of its obligations. The allocation of cost and risk associated with force majeure events will depend on the availability of insurance and in some instances the available political risk in the particular jurisdiction. Furthermore, long-term force majeure events may lead to the termination of the PPA as discussed above.

Governing Law and Dispute Resolution: The governing law is usually the law of the host country. The PPA should provide for the dispute resolution mechanism to be utilised in the event of disputes. In most cases arbitration in a neutral location under generally acceptable rules (such as the LCIA, UNCITRAL or ICC arbitration).

4. KEY CHALLENGES FOR THE AVAILABILITY OF LONG-TERM RENEWABLE PPAS

With evolving energy markets, distributed, low-carbon energy generation is fast replacing the declining capacity of centralised, fossil-fuel based power stations that once dominated the electricity market. From regulatory uncertainty to removal of subsidies and low fossil fuel prices, the renewable energy industry is challenged on various fronts. In addition, in recent years, several factors have contributed to the deterioration in the availability of bankable long-term PPAs for renewable generators. These factors include:

Price Risk: Over the last five years or so there has been a growing reluctance from traditional utilities to take price risk in their long-term PPAs. Some renewable generators have reported that while indexed 15 year floors of £28-30/MWh were generally available until around 2010, there has been a progressive reduction in the number of PPA providers willing and capable of providing floors at this level and tenor. This reluctance can be explained, in part, by the greater penetration of renewables in the UK electricity market. It has been demonstrated that greater volumes of wind and solar generation have a downward effect on wholesale electricity prices and has led to a greater probability of periods of low or even negative prices (for example, in the German market during peak renewable generation periods).

Removal of long-term subsidies: The role of subsidies in the renewable energy sector was crucial in the development of renewable energy sources. However, in recent years, many governments have started to introduce sudden cuts to renewable subsidies to force bills as low as possible, often to reflect falling supply chain costs. For example, in the UK with the closure of the Renewable Obligation scheme to new projects in 2017, the appetite of traditional utilities to enter into long-term contracts for renewable obligation certificates (ROCs) appears to have reduced. Suppliers are increasingly able to satisfy their renewable obligations from their own assets or under existing PPAs. Furthermore, a significant pipeline of large traditional utility-owned renewable projects have come online in the last few years. This has resulted in fewer suppliers left in the ROC market and a growing trend for these remaining suppliers to manage the year-on-year fluctuations in the level of their obligation (driven by churn in the retail customer base) through short-term ROC trading.

Impact on balance sheet: Ratings agencies have been adopting a more stringent approach to the long-term liabilities incurred by traditional utilities under PPAs. In the UK this has materially affected the ability of traditional utilities to enter into long-term PPAs.

Regulatory uncertainty: PPA providers are increasingly looking to impose a level of change in law risk on renewable generators that is unacceptable to lenders. This has been driven by factors including uncertainty as to the long-term impact of Electricity Market Reform and Ofgem's Electricity Balancing Significant Code Review.

5. CORPORATE PPAS – A NEW DRIVER FOR RENEWABLE SECTOR

Coupled with the key challenges stated in the previous section, uncertainty across the markets, particularly in view of UK Brexit, volatile wholesale prices, rising non-commodity costs and a drive in consumer demand for green credentials, more and more corporations with intensive electricity needs are being driven to seek options to reduce their electricity costs through corporate PPAs.

What are corporate PPAs?

The old mindset – that a company can only future-proof its electricity costs for 12 or 18 months – is now obsolete. Instead of pursuing the traditional approach of buying power direct from utilities, often on fluctuating price terms, a number of businesses across the world are now purchasing electricity under long-term PPAs, with increased price certainty, directly from independent renewable energy generators.

While the corporate renewable PPA market typically started in the US, evolving energy markets globally, including the UK, indicate that corporations are now seriously exploring the purchase of electricity through corporate renewable PPAs.

Corporate PPAs can offer enhanced financial certainty for renewable generators, thereby removing a significant roadblock to both debt and equity financing, thus unlocking investment in the building of such new renewable facilities. In a world where many countries are reducing or withdrawing subsidies for renewable energy, a corporate PPA with a financially strong, creditworthy counterparty is seen by many developers, equity investors and funders as an income stream which is comparable to the traditional utility PPA. Such a robust income stream is an essential component for achieving a "bankable" project. Accordingly, it is expected that corporate PPAs will become increasingly important in the continued growth of renewables, especially non-subsidised renewables, in the UK.

From a corporate buyer's perspective, there are many advantages of corporate PPAs. In view of COP21, green and low carbon sustainability goals play a particularly important role in this rising trend. However, even in cases where the corporate's main driver is not its carbon footprint, there are other obvious key drivers. For example, from an economic perspective, the primary incentive behind corporate PPAs must be the ability to negotiate a lower and fixed inflation indexed price for the electricity, and to have price predictability over a longer time horizon. In the UK market, there appear to be only a few utilities that will contract on a long-term basis with a corporate buyer at fixed prices acceptable to a corporate buyer, notwithstanding the current drop in wholesale electricity prices today.

In contrast, a renewable generator under a corporate PPA can potentially undercut market prices for electricity offered by utilities by a significant percentage. More importantly, however, the renewable generator is often able to offer the certainty of inflation-indexed fixed pricing, which gives the generator revenue certainty and, at the same time, removes the risks that the generator might otherwise face if it were to sell its power into the wholesale market, or indeed to a utility on half hourly or other volatile pricing.

Does the renewable generator have other options for the sale of its electricity? Potentially not, as utilities may be wary of offering fixed price, or floor price, mechanisms for the sale of their renewable generation – unless such mechanisms are linked to the current market price. This often results in a willingness only to offer fixed pricing which is lower than the wholesale market price at the time of entry into the PPA, and only for a short duration. Compared with a creditworthy, long-term fixed PPA at optimum pricing, renewable generators may be incentivised to move away from traditional utility sales.

While the price and revenue certainty in a corporate PPA provides financing security and bankability for the project to the renewable generator, it also provides a supply and price guarantee to the corporate and thus the corporate PPA works for both parties. Put differently, corporate PPAs can limit both a seller's and buyer's respective exposure to the volatility of market prices for electricity in the long-term.

It is important to note that one of the key elements of the price predictability provided by the renewable generator in the corporate PPA flows from the potential removal of fuel price risk for the generator as well as grid charges, additional regulatory costs, levies or taxes from the price depending on the nature of the generator. Thus the cost base of the renewable generator is based on predictable capex, and an element of predictable operating costs. This is in contrast with non-renewable generators, such as gas and even fuel-based renewable generators (such as biomass or waste to energy generators), who are exposed to fluctuations in feedstock pricing for the lifetime of their project. The "commodity" element of the price is subject to supply, demand and geopolitical influences which could cause such costs to rise or fall often in short time periods. In contrast, for the renewable generator with no fuel cost exposure, its capital and operating costs are arguably more predictable. Obviously, all generators could be subject to regulatory changes – e.g. to the extent that its cost base comprises charges, levies or taxes which are forecasted to, or could, change as a result of government interventions and changes in law and policy. For example, in the UK, those that are anticipated flowing from the government's review of transmission and distribution costs.

In addition to the absence of fuel risk, corporate PPAs can be cash flow positive from the start, which means that the price payable for renewable power is actually less than the price payable for traditional electricity from the utility. The consequence of such changes to the customer/end user is one of being forced into short-term planning of their energy strategy. In this respect, renewable energy generation, for example by way of procuring solar electricity, is a perfect hedging strategy against market uncertainties as it provides a direct, reliable and independent source of locally generated power.

In simple terms, through corporate renewable PPAs, a renewable generator can provide businesses with their own, exclusive renewable power station and, better still, with potentially significant lower costs than forecasted grid supplied electricity.

The graph set out below is an illustration of the costs reflected in a typical electricity price, which also compares the typical electricity price including all applicable charges and levies for a large electricity user against the price offered by a corporate renewable PPA:

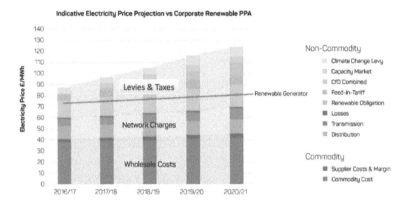

Regulatory factors and buyers' preferences determine what type of PPA is used in any given transaction. Corporate PPAs can generally be grouped into two categories:

(i) Standard or Physical PPAs, which provide for the physical delivery of electricity (whether or not via a private wire or a traded electricity system); and

(ii) Virtual or Synthetic PPAs, which are based on the concept of financially setting differences between floating prices in the local electricity market and contracted prices under the PPAs based on a volume of electricity.

Standard PPAs

The standard corporate PPA model requires that renewable energy be physically delivered to buyers. This includes private wire or behind the meter generation where the generation and the offtaker are either on the same site or within close proximity.

Standard PPAs guarantee the owner of the generator a revenue stream by selling electricity at a fixed, inflation-indexed price to a creditworthy purchaser. These forms of PPAs are the optimum solutions for corporations with large electricity needs (requiring for example more than 5,000MWh/year of electricity) with, for example, manufacturing facilities. Solar plants offer one of the most efficient solutions, as they can often be constructed in close proximity to the buyer's offtake point and the offsite generator can deliver energy at the buyer's facilities, at which point title and risk to the electricity is transferred from the generator to the buyer. The generator can also transfer relevant renewable energy associated benefits to the buyer (depending on the underlying regulatory regime).

Typically such standard PPAs are for 15-20 years and during this term the buyer is required to purchase a fixed percentage of electricity generated by the solar plant under a take or pay structure. The solar generator owns, operates and maintains the plant, often for a period in excess of 15-20 years.

In addition to market price risk, credit risk is another key element in structuring corporate PPAs as both seller and buyer should provide security to guarantee their respective obligations, especially the corporate buyer's obligation to pay. The corporate buyer's credit risk and the provision of an adequate security package are key requirements in the financing of corporate renewable PPA projects.

From the perspective of the renewable seller's security, a corporate PPA buyer usually requires credit support from the seller for failure to perform – for example, to cover risks such as the seller's failure to generate/deliver the electricity to the buyer, which would cause the buyer to source electricity from a third party (potentially at a higher price and additional costs). Depending on the creditworthiness of the parent, parent company guarantees are often the typical form of security, as opposed to letters of credit. In such parent company guarantees, important issues to be considered are the creditworthiness of the parent, the cap on the guarantee and waiver of certain surety defences.

Buyer security and the buyer's creditworthiness are important considerations in determining the bankability and financing of the renewable project. In this respect, the funder of the project will run strict creditworthiness checks on the buyer and both the funder and the seller will often require some form of credit support (for example, in the form of a letter of credit or a guarantee) from the parent company of the corporate buyer.

As part of the financing of the renewable energy projects with corporate PPAs, funders seek a first ranking charge on specific project collateral under facility documentation supporting the corporate PPAs as well as step-in rights to the PPA documentation, via direct agreements.

"Synthetic" or "Virtual" PPAs

Direct sales by a generator to a non-utility purchaser, such as industrial and commercial customers, are not permitted in a number of jurisdictions. In these jurisdictions renewable generators and customers may adopt a "sleeving" structure to work around restrictions on the direct retail regulations. In this case, sellers and buyers with a third party entity licensed to be the retail entity (or the utility) enter into a tri-partite arrangement under which the third party entity purchases power directly from the non-utility generator and sells to the corporate buyer. The concept of such "Virtual" PPAs include structures such as "contracts for differences" and as part of the contractual structure involved in more complex "sleeving" arrangements.

Essentially, whatever they are called, "Virtual" or "Synthetic", these type of arrangements are hedges that do not involve physical delivery of power. The customer enters into a contract to pay the renewable generator an agreed power price. The renewable energy project sells the generated power into the wholesale market either on a merchant basis (eg via a power pool) or to a utility offtaker. The generator pays the customer if the electricity is sold into the market above the agreed contract, or "strike" price, and the customer pays the generator the difference if the electricity market price falls below the agreed "strike" price.

In more complex arrangements, the utility may acquire all the renewable generation of the generator which it then sells into the wholesale market. Simultaneously, the generator will enter to a "virtual" PPA with the customer (as described above), with the customer buying its physical power from the utility and effectively hedging its pricing with the generator party. It should be noted that entities other than generators, eg financial institutions, also often act as the hedging counterparties in such transactions. The tripartite nature of the arrangement is that all three parties structure the arrangements to be back to back. The advantages are that the utility gets the benefit of a volume of predictable green power which it can sell into the market. The customer and the generator get price certainty – around an agreed reference strike price. The arrangement may also be structured such that the customer is "deemed" to be buying low "carbon green" power.

Generally, the characteristics of a "virtual" PPA include:

- from a volume perspective, a virtual PPA can be structured so as to hedge against market price volatility by providing pricing certainty for a negotiated quantity of electricity (based either on actual output of the generator/demand of the customer, or a fixed amount per year);

- the customer provides a price floor below which the electricity price may not fall – therefore the generator is not exposed to the risk of the market price falling below the floor price, as this risk is absorbed by the corporate buyer;

- conversely, the hedging mechanism also works in the opposite direction to the benefit of the corporate buyer, in that if the electricity price is above a pre-agreed reference price the generator pays the corporate buyer the difference between the actual price and the reference price.

As long as it is properly structured, and the arrangements are with creditworthy entities, these hedging arrangements can be used to stabilise projected revenues to enable the renewable generator to attract project financing. It is important to note that although we have set out one of the most common virtual PPA structures, as discussed above virtual PPAs can be structured in a variety of ways (and with a variety of different names and counterparties), including, contract for differences, options – put options, call options and commodity hedges.

Since the large corporates today lack the necessary in-house skills to put the complex arrangements to agree and document the virtual PPAs, corporations tend to approach them with more scepticism. In addition, the regulatory base for the virtual PPAs is not clear in every jurisdiction and therefore respective regulators are required to clarify the extent to which the parties will be subject to commodity market regulations, particularly from the financial obligations associated with the swap and hedging transactions and energy market regulatory licensing requirements.

6. CONCLUSION

Evolving electricity markets, the continued growth of decentralised energy solutions coupled with sustainability goals and volatile pricing risks is pushing businesses to control and manage the supply and price of their electricity.

As explained, the main drivers behind corporate renewable PPAs are economic benefit and sustainability. However, in developing markets with less developed transmission and distribution infrastructure, and less installed generation capacity of any nature, there is also a rising trend to enter into private wire/on-site corporate renewable PPAs.

In this respect, while corporate renewable PPAs have been surging in the US, the signs clearly show the rising profile of corporate renewable PPAs in other developed electricity markets, such as the UK and also in emerging markets, through experienced and creditworthy renewable generators and operators.

As discussed, the price security provided over the long term is available through indexed-based fixed prices as a result of the removal of any regulatory or additional charges and levies. Regardless of the PPA model chosen, this gives rise to mutual benefits to the generator and corporate customer. From the perspective of the generator, long-term secured revenues backed up by robust credit support provides bankability for the projects and removes the exposure to price volatility arising from wholesale electricity prices. From the perspective of the customer, there is the guarantee for the renewable generation at a predictable price.

Put differently, through corporate renewable PPAs, a renewable generator can notionally provide businesses with their own, exclusive renewable power station but, better still, at a potentially significantly lower cost than if purchased under conventional utility model supply arrangements.

While corporate renewable PPAs offer advantages to both the seller and buyer of electricity, they can also be complex arrangements to agree and document, especially so for virtual PPA arrangements, due to the hedging mechanism or setting an escalation factor for the strike prices.

This complexity explains why, with their in-house capabilities of negotiating and documenting such complex PPAs, the initial entrants to the corporate renewable PPA market are some of the large US businesses, for example, Google, Facebook and Amazon. However, given their advantages, there is also a rising demand from small to mid-sized companies towards the standard renewable PPAs. We believe that the education phase and the transaction completion timeline will get shorter with the current rise in demand for these PPAs, as familiarity with corporate renewable PPA structures increases across the market and their increased usage in the energy markets will grow. Through corporate renewable PPAs, renewable generation will continue to develop as a viable alternative to traditional retail electricity supply.

Renewable energies in the Argentine Republic: Special reference to the legal regime of the electric sector

EZEQUIEL CASSAGNE

Partner CASSAGNE – Abogados, Argentina

1. THE ELECTRIC ENERGY MARKET

1.1 Electric Energy Generation

In our country, the generation of electric energy is not a public service, though they are, its transportation and distribution. Generation, on the other hand, is considered by Law No. 24,065, which regulates the electricity market, as an activity of general interest[1]. This characterization of general interest has not had a doctrinal precision as the public service does, although it is recognized that it is a highly regulated commercial activity, precisely because it has a general interest in the proper functioning of the Electricity market, necessary not only for the subsequent distribution of electricity to all households in the country, but also for industrial development, which requires constant electricity supply[2].

Well, taking into account the different activities that are present in putting into operation the electricity market (generation, transportation, distribution, and consumption of large and small users), there exists in our country, at a national level, the Electric Wholesale Market commonly known as CAMMESA), formed in the singular form of a non-profit corporation, whose main function is to manage the wholesale electricity market, optimizing the physical resources of the market, and liquidating economic transactions among market agents. The capital of this company is divided into five classes of representative shares, each of 20% of the total, whose rights owners are the National State, and the four civil associations that represent the agents: generators, distributors, transporters and large

---

[1] Cf. art. 1 of the Law 24065 of 1992.
[2] Cf. FONROUGE, Máximo (2003): "Guidelines of the legal regime of electricity", in VV.AA., Public Service, Police and Development (Buenos Aires, Rap Publishers), p. 551.

users. The president of CAMMESA is the Secretary of Energy of the Nation, whose vote is necessary to have a quorum in the Directory[3].

Both CAMMESA and the Energy Secretariat play a preponderant role in any public energy generation program, as was the case of GENREN ("Renewable Energy Generation Program"), which was implemented until December 2015, and the RENOVAR program, which was established in 2016, and is currently in force. Both GENREN and RENOVAR signify an intervention in the Energy Policy, which can make a significant contribution to a greater sustainability of development in all its dimensions: social, productive, economic and financial.

Under the GENREN program, the main player has been the state-owned ENARSA, created under the legal form of a state-owned private company, with the declared purpose of the State becoming a major player in the development of the energy market. This company was the one that carried out the biddings, awarded the projects and acquired the energy. In fact, it acted as an intermediary between the generating companies and the final purchaser, CAMMESA. However, based on the new management model established in RENOVAR, the company ENARSA has been set aside as an intermediary between generating companies and CAMMESA, and as will be explained below, the new renewable energy supply contracts are signed directly with CAMMESA.

The great infrastructure works that every country needs to increase its production of electric power require the need to have suitable tools to obtain its financing, in these times in which the investment does not abound.

They are, in these cases, real infrastructures, because they support the activity of electricity generation, connecting in turn to the energy network, which are part of the transport and distribution services[4].

In Argentina, electricity generation is mainly based on the thermal source, the hydroelectric source, and the nuclear source, respectively. According to CAMMESA's annual report for 2016, 60% of the installed power corresponds to the thermal source, the hydraulic energy 36% and the nuclear power 3%.

---

[3] Cf. Sobre Casas, Roberto (2003): *Contracts in the electric market (Buenos Aires, Abaco), p. 129.*.
[4] Aguilar Valdéz argues that every infrastructure supports a network or is linked to a network. See AGUILAR VALDEZ, Oscar Rafael (2005): "Legal Principles Applicable to Public Infrastructures", in VV.AA., Administrative Organization, Public Function and Public Domain (Buenos Aires, RAP Publishers), p. 377.

In this scenario, renewable energy sources, such as wind energy, small hydroelectric projects, solar energy, thermal energy from biofuels, biomass and geothermal energy are pointed out.

1.2 Towards Renewable Energy

The renewable energy sector is an example of the need to define public-private partnerships, since without public aid this industry could not be developed, as its subsequent exploitation is not cost-effective, whose Market is currently low.

On the other hand, it is part of a true global energy policy, which implies a shift towards a sustainable energy matrix in those countries with an environmental conscience, many of which have other more pressing infrastructure needs, which determines the importance of collaboration of the private sector for the development of this type of renewable energies.

The renewable energies are tools capable of achieving a truly sustainable development, a concept that has been defined by the doctrine as *"a process of economic, social, ecological and cultural transformations designed to meet the needs of all social groups while preserving the productivity of resources and the integrity of ecological systems, considering the dynamic nature of social coexistence and technology, both productive as well as the one focused in reducing or eliminating environmental damage"* [5].

In the path of this sustainable development, our country possesses exceptional geo-climatic characteristics, characterized for having, for example, quantities and qualities of winds usable for the Aeolian generation. In fact, 70% of the country has strong and constant winds necessary for this type of production[6]. On the other hand, Argentina is condemned to become a world-wide power in generation of wind energy, if the public policies accompany. On the other hand, biomass is a very attractive bet, as it may have different origins in the different geographies of the country, such as sugar cane bagasse, charcoal, residues from afforestation or any agro industrial production. With regard to biofuels, Argentina, given the well-known fertility of its land, is a major producer of soybeans, the main raw material for biodiesel production.

It is important to bear in mind that energy policy must be a long-term sectoral policy, embedded in global development policy, which requires a

---

[5] Badeni, Gregorio (2006): Treaty of Constitutional Law (Buenos Aires, Law, Volume I), p. 591.
[6] Cf. *Chamber of Project Industries and Engineering of Capital Assets of the Argentine Republic* (2012): "Presentation of the Argentine wind cluster", available at http://www.clustereolico. com.ar/docs/presentacion-del-cluster-eolico -argentino.pdf (last accessed: 07/21/2014), p. 11.

well-established institutional and legal basis for it to be systematically and harmoniously developed within a pre-established planning.

There are at least 60 countries in the world that have policies to promote renewable energy for electricity generation, as in the United States, Australia, Brazil, Uruguay and, later, Argentina. In many countries, such as Argentina, the development of green energy generation plans are required, as energy imports have grown considerably in recent times, mainly due to the purchase of liquid fuels and natural gas, and this will not change in the short term, not even as a result of the auspicious projects of shale gas and shale oil that have been detected in the Argentine basins, since their eventual production will not be immediate, in addition to the fact, not less important, that they require large sums of money to realize them, beyond the logical enthusiasm shown by provincial and national officials with these unconventional reservoirs. Likewise, it is not necessary to exclude the resistance that this modality of extraction has in the environmentalists, who have come to obtain the prohibition by law of this activity in countries like France.

While with different methods, all renewable energy projects are based on a guiding principle: they need extra financial incentives for their realization. Without this, it is almost impossible to establish it in the era of fossil fuels. As we have said, the great problem with the generation of electricity through renewable sources in Argentina is that it is an expensive energy due to its cost of production compared to other sources such as hydroelectric or thermal. For this reason, it is essential that any incentive program for the generation of green energy allows or subsidizes the final price of the same, so that it can be sold at the market prices of other energies, or that the purchase is guaranteed at the price of this type of energies.

In this understanding, public aid is essential to realize this sustainable challenge. De la Riva, who has studied in depth the development institute, explains that the distinctive element of public aid or promotion is the coincidence of public and private interests, being possible *"that the individual acts voluntarily in the expected direction, and that pursuing its own benefit will contribute to the general interest ", whereas" the legal core of the relationship between the granting authority and the beneficiary receiving it is due to the allocation of the assets granted to the activity in view of which are conferred"* [7].

---

[7]   See DE LA RIVA, Ignacio (2003): "The figure of Development: need to face a conceptual review", in VV.AA., Public Service, Police and Development (Buenos Aires, Ediciones Rap), p. 417.

Strictly speaking, these are development activities, although the use of the term development must be carried out in its broad sense, that is to say, equivalent to encouragement, since it covers promotion and protection techniques, as was for example provided in the law of industrial development No. 21,608. In this sense, among these promotional measures we can find several favoring techniques, such as tax exemptions, tax deferrals or any other fiscal benefit, direct and indirect subsidies, grants, preferential loans, exemptions from legal obligations, regulatory or contractual, etc.

However, much has been written about the principle of subsidiarity, as a guiding principle that justifies, in certain cases, the interference of the State in the economic and social community. Such a model recognizes non-delegable functions of the State (justice, security, defense, foreign relations, legislation) and others that fulfill a complementary mission of private activity (education, health, public services)[8].

State subsidiarity can be formulated in the following terms: *"it is not lawful to remove individuals and transfer to the community what they can do with their own effort and initiative"*[9].

This principle posits two great directives for the State that complement each other: the positive one, by virtue of which the State must come to the aid of individuals when they are insufficient to fully develop an activity necessary for the common good, and a negative postulate, which indicates that the State should not substitute individuals when they can carry out those activities[10].

The principle of subsidiarity takes on its full dimension in the field of renewable energies, and its positive mandate, that is to say, is the aid to promote this activity aimed at transforming the energy matrix of a country - and of the world when the circumstances determine that private individuals cannot fully develop them.

It should also be noted that the general environmental law itself enshrines the principle of subsidiarity as the guiding principle of public

[8]   Cf. CASSAGNE, Juan Carlos (2006): Administrative Law (Buenos Aires, Abeledo Perrot, volume I, eighth edition), pp. 61-63, with quotes from Drs. Barra, Cassagne, Messner, Soto Kloss, Massini, and Sagües; Cf. MESSNER, Johannes (1967): Social, Political and Economic Ethics in the light of Natural Law (Madrid, Rialp), p. 949 and ff.
[9]   Ariño Ortiz, Gaspar (2004): Principles of Public Economic Law (Granada, Comares, third enlarged edition), with special reference to Pius XI (1931): Quadragesimo Anno (Rome), pp. 111-112.
[10]   See UTZ, Arthur (1961): Social Ethics (translated by Carlos Latorre Marín, Barcelona, Herder, volume), p. 312 ff.

behavior in order to ensure the preservation, conservation, recovery and improvement of the quality of natural environmental resources.

In fact, art. 4 of Law No. 25,675 requires that *"The national State, through the various instances of public administration, has the obligation to collaborate and, if necessary, to participate in a complementary way in the actions of individuals in the preservation and environmental protection"*.

At the same time, the main concern of any public procurement scheme for the development of large infrastructure projects, such as the works needed to develop renewable energy generation, is to obtain financing. It is clear that the State alone cannot cope with major infrastructure works, such as hydroelectric power plants, nuclear power plants, road works, railway transport, improvement and expansion of public service networks such as gas and water, oil and gas production, ports, airports, hospitals, waste processing plants, etc.

It is a clear fact that the scarcity of public resources in the face of growing social demands must lead governments to seek and develop innovative financing alternatives, with increasing private participation[11].

2. THE RENEWABLE ENERGY DEVELOPMENT PROGRAMS IN ARGENTINA

2.1 The normative framework in force until October 2015

It is important to keep in mind that in 1998 the Argentine National Congress had enacted a law - No. 25,019, which declared wind and solar energy generation to be of national interest, establishing benefits for its development, such as fiscal stability for the term of fifteen years and the deferral of taxes, creating in turn a Renewable Energy Trust Fund intended to encourage the generation of this type of energy, through a system of premium per MW (currently, approximately 10 dollars per MW).

Then, in 2006, Congress passed Law No. 26,190, which declared the generation of electric energy from the use of renewable energy sources for the provision of public service, as well as research for development Technological and manufacturing of equipment for this purpose, and

---

[11] En nuestro país, las Provincias presentan un cuadro de situación mucho más desalentador que el Estado Nacional. Es así que muchas obras provinciales son en realidad financiadas por el Estado. Como destaca Gorostegui, *"estas contrataciones se estructuran habitualmente a través de acuerdos (que van desde leyes que los determinan a simples convenios) entre las jurisdicciones, a través de organismos pertinentes, donde se establecen los lineamientos generales de las contrataciones (...) virtualmente trilaterales"*. Ver Gorostegui Beltrán (2012): "Régimen de Obras Públicas Financiadas por el Estado", *La Ley*, 2012-C, pp. 642.

established as objective to achieve that renewable energy sources reach 8% of the national electricity consumption by 2016.

To this end, new tax benefits were established, such as accelerated depreciation of investments and exemption from the minimum presumed income tax, while the system of premiums - payments - per KW generated was updated. Regrettably, the law was only regulated in 2009, thus losing three valuable years. Equally, the premium set in these laws, to compensate the generation, for example, wind, does not even cover 50% of the costs of this type of generation[12].

For this reason, GENREN programs were implemented in 2009, which we will analyze in detail in the next section, in order to achieve the goal of reaching 8% of the electricity matrix. According to sources from the Argentine Energy Secretariat itself, 2,500 MW of renewable energy generation would be installed as a consequence of these public policies.

It is interesting to note that in 2011, the Energy Secretariat itself issued a general resolution (Res. SE 108/2011), through which it replicated the GENREN scheme for future projects, regarding the establishment of a fixed purchase price of Renewable energy for the term of fifteen years, but in this case without the granting of guarantees nor the endorsement by the National State, which helps to obtain financing.

On the other hand, in the specific case of biofuels, the State has enacted several laws tending to promote its production and sustainable use in the Argentine territory[13]. The most important measure in this regard was the order to cut with biofuels the mineral fuels used in the domestic market, in a proportion of 5%, a share that increased to 7% in the middle of 2010. Also, this promotional legislation generated important Tax benefits for biofuel producers.

At the end of May 2014, a law was approved exempting biodiesel from the tax to help this industry which, since November 2013, has suffered from the obstacles imposed by the European Union to the exports of this fuel.

This new law reformed Law No. 26,028, which determines the additional tax on gas oil, establishing that the aliquot of 22% is not to be

---

[12] Cf. Giralt, op, cit., p. 68. En España, en cambio, el esquema de primas ha funcionado. Como explica Ariño Ortiz, *"el sistema de primas como complemento al precio de la energía entregada al sistema ha demostrado su eficacia, dando lugar, como hemos visto, a un extraordinario desarrollo de algunas energías renovables (especialmente la eólica)"*, en Ariño Ortiz, Gaspar, DE LA CUETARA, Juan Miguel y DEL GUAYO CASTIELLA, Iñigo (2012): "Las energías renovables: marco normativo y problemas que plantean", en *Regulación Económica, lecturas escogidas* (Madrid, Thomson Reuters), pp. 864.

[13] See Law No. 26093 from 2006 and Law No. 26334 from 2008.

applied to biodiesel intended for electricity generation. It also exempts from the aliquot of 19% of the tax on liquid fuels, retrofitting the situation to November 2011.

Despite the efforts made to achieve the 8% objective outlined by the law, the installed capacity in Argentina in 2016 from renewable sources - excluding large hydroelectric projects - is approximately 1.8% of total energy generation[14].

Wind energy is the renewable energy with the most projection in Argentina, given the climatic conditions of its territory, being a recognized world power, forming a group led by countries such as Russia, Canada, the United States and Australia. Since 1994 wind farms have been installed in Argentina. However, at present only a power of 215 MW has been achieved. It is a reduced power when compared to the theoretical wind potential of Argentina, which impresses, as it could reach more than 2,000 GW, a value equivalent to twice the current generation capacity in the United States. In 2012, the Argentine Wind Cluster was formally formed by several national companies, which predict that in eight years a production of 1,000 MW per year will be achieved, developing 500 suppliers and four brands of national wind turbines. Its main focus was the GENREN projects, and now the RENOVAR programs.

Although Argentina has advanced significantly faster than its neighbors in the implementation of its first wind farms financed by the State, its limited access to financial credit has hardened the conditions for its granting, mainly in new projects such as those related to wind farms of production of electrical energy, we must follow in this matter the examples of our neighboring countries, Uruguay and Brazil.

In fact, the program of incentive to alternative sources of electric energy in Brazil, "PROINFA", that started in 2002, is now a tangible reality. The objective of the program is to increase the participation of Renewable Energy in order to diversify the energy matrix through the installation of thousands of MW, equally divided between wind turbines, small hydroelectric power stations and power plants that use biomass energy.

The program promotes the participation of Independent Private Producers, who are guaranteed the purchase of electricity delivered to the National Interconnected System through Electrobrás, over a period of 20 years, at a rate established by the Ministry of Mines and Energy. The

---

[14] Cf. Di Paola, op., cit, p. 7, The annual report of CAMMESA prepared in 2015 on 2011, and the report of the Renew Program, dated July 2016 issued by the Undersecretary of Renewable Energies of the Argentine Republic.

Energy Development Account has been created to guarantee the necessary funds, apportioned among all consumers, with the exception of the low-income population. And as it could not be otherwise, the BNDES is the main source of financing of the PROINFA projects. After several initial setbacks, the Brazilian wind market grew to over 7,000 MW today.

For their part, the Wind Energy Program in Uruguay (PEEU), a joint initiative of the National Government with the United Nations Development Program, implemented by the Ministry of Industry, Energy and Mining through the Directorate of Energy, And funded by the Global Environment Facility, is also a tangible reality.

The history of wind farms for large-scale electric power generation in Uruguay is recent, since 2006, when the country's first wind farm was launched. Since 2009, with the installation of the Cerro de los Caracoles Wind Farm, Uruguay has a state-of-the-art wind farm capable of responding to the difficult demands of electrical systems for the integration of large wind power. But its expansion does not stop, and the construction and inauguration of parks continues, and it is not difficult to predict that installed wind power in Uruguay will reach high levels by 2020, surpassing all expectations.

Renewable energies are a reality that prevails in today's world, and will impose itself even more in the future, since they solve the problem of energy, but taking care of the environment, so that they are sustained over time, generating the development of contemporary humanity in a sustainable way, as well as the care of future generations.

By protecting the environment as well as being clean energies, they prevent energy generation from contaminating the air, degrading the soil and its resources, importing an environmental hazard in its different stages of production, transportation and marketing, etc.

In short, renewable energies prevent environmental risks and damages, which is why it is necessary that their promotion be included in precautionary energy public policies. Strictly speaking, the principle of *"precaution is the one that most clearly expresses the essence of environmental administrative law,"* and productive activities must meet present needs without compromising those of future generations[15].

Indeed, these public policies must ultimately be imposed given the mandate that contains the constitutional right to a healthy environment.

---

[15]   Cfr. Cassagne, Juan Carlos (2004): "El daño ambiental colectivo", en VV.AA., *Lecturas sobre Derecho del Medio Ambiente* (Colombia, Universidad Externado), p. 166.

In effect, as of the constitutional reform of 1994, article 41 has been incorporated into our constitution, which prescribes the following:

Art. 41 CN: All inhabitants enjoy the right to a healthy, balanced environment, suitable for human development and for productive activities to meet present needs without compromising those of future generations; and have a duty to preserve it. The environmental damage will generate as a priority the obligation to recompose, as established by law.

The authorities shall provide for the protection of this right, the rational use of natural resources, the preservation of natural and cultural heritage and biological diversity, and environmental information and education.

It corresponds to the Nation dictating the regulations containing the minimal protection budgets, and to the provinces, those that are necessary to complement them, without those altering the local jurisdictions.

The entry to national territory of currently or potentially dangerous or radioactive waste is prohibited.

Notice that, apart from recognizing the right to a healthy environment, the National Constitution establishes a clear mandate to national, provincial and local authorities, demanding to furnish the protection of this right, the rational use of the natural resources, the preservation of natural and cultural heritage and biological diversity, and the environmental information and education.

LORENZETTI sees it this way, he believes *"it is not, otherwise, mere theoretical statements, but operation regulations, which effectively oblige the State; and expose it to claims – even of the judicial type- in case of non compliance"*[16].

On the other hand, the General Law on Environment, which establishes minimum budgets for environmental protection in the Republic of Argentina Territory, determines with precision that the national environmental policy must meet the following objectives, among others:

1) Ensuring the preservation, conservation, recovery and improvement of the quality of the environmental resources, both natural and cultural, and the performance of different anthropogenic activities;

2) Promoting the improvement of the quality of life of the present and future generations, as a priority;

3) Promoting the rational and sustainable use of the natural resources;

---

[16] Lorenzetti, Ricardo Luis (2008): *Teoría del Derecho Ambiental* (Buenos Aires, La Ley), p. 48.

4) Keeping balance and dynamics of the ecological systems;

5) Ensuring the conservation of the biological diversity;

6) Preventing the harmful or dangerous effects that the anthropogenic activities generate on the environment to enable the ecological, economic and social sustainability of the development;

7) Promoting changes in the social values and behaviors that enable the sustainable development, through environmental education, both in the formal and non-formal systems;

8) Organizing and integrating the environmental information and ensuring population's free access to it;

9) Establishing adequate procedures and mechanisms for the minimization of environmental risks, for the prevention and mitigation of environmental emergencies and for the reconstruction of the harms caused due to environmental pollution[17].

Understanding this, Bernard Frank Macera states that "*as people in charge of protecting the assets of the community from any kind of aggressions and, also, as greater interpreters of the general feeling of the collective, the Public Powers have the mission of tutoring the general interests through the exercise of the powers inherent to their supremacy, which means, in the subject we are right now speaking of, they have the task of looking out for the protection of the environment against any polluting source*"[18].

In the end, to obtain sustainable development in the energy sector, Bellorio Clabot argued that "*it is necessary to eliminate barriers and to incorporate elements favoring the technological options, and the effective inclusion of the theme in the agenda of the municipalities and other decentralized entities ... also, it is indispensable establishing technology encouragement and energy market creation policies, as well as a rational policy in terms of the exploitation of fossil resources*"[19].

2.2 GENREN program

GENREN program (as we said earlier, "Renewable Energies Generation Program") was implemented through ENARSA Company, who called a public bidding in 2009, in which different companies offered their renewable energy production projects, competing between them for the

---

[17] See. Art. 2 of Act Nº 25675 from 2002.
[18] Macera, Bernard-Frank (1998): *El deber industrial de respetar el ambiente* (Madrid, Marcial Pons), p. 153.
[19] Bellorio Clabot, Dino (1997): *Tratado de Derecho Ambiental* (Buenos Aires, Ad-Hoc, volume II), p. 305.

price of the megawatt (MW from now on) they offered ENARSA[20]. In this case, the methodology used was closer to a public auction process[21]. The awarded party, signed with ENARSA contracts for the construction and exploitation of those power plants, guaranteeing them the purchase of the said renewable energy during the next 15 years at the value proposed in the offers, which was around 120-130 dollars per MW.

The entry into effect of all these contracts was subject to the subscription of a Supply contract between ENARSA and CAMMESA, through which the latter was obliged to buy from ENARSA all the energy generated by the new power plants.

In the first GENREN bidding, ENARSA requested 1015 MW of renewable energies; and among them there were wind energies, thermal with biofuels, small hydroelectric projects, biogas, and solar. It is interesting to highlight that 754 MW were allocated in wind projects[22] (17 projects), 10.6 MW in small hydroelectric uses (5 projects), 20MW in solar energy (6 projects) and 110.4 MW in thermal energy projects using biofuels (4 projects).

The results of the auction displayed that solar energy is the most expensive, at an average Price of 570 USD/MW, followed by thermal energy using biofuels at 290 USD/MW, then small dams at 160 USD/MW, and finally the wind projects, with an average Price of 120 USD/MW[23].

Now, in this scheme, the private sector should –and shall- have obtained their own financing. In that sense, some companies opted for direct indebtedness, through, for example, the issue of negotiable obligations, and other companies chose the project finance modality, which guarantees the financers will collect their credit and that is why it is the fund flow of the current project[24].

The project finance schemes are fundamental in the structure of big projects financing, since these do not require direct indebtedness by the companies, nor the use of State resources.

In the project finance models, a Specific Purpose Company (SPC) is formed, which will have as a purpose the Project (in this case the long term

---

[20] National and International Public Bidding N° 1/2009.
[21] See Giralt, Cecilia (2011): "Energía Eólica en Argentina: un análisis económico del derecho", *Revista Letras Verdes*, N° 9, pp. 69.
[22] Cf.. Giralt, op. cit, ps. 64-86.
[23] Cf. Di Paola Di Paola, María Marta (2011): "El escenario de las energías renovables en Argentina", *The Environmental Supplement Law*,4/07/2011, p. 7.
[24] As appointed by Aguilar Valdéz, project finance is, truly, financing "the project" and not specific legal persons. See Several Authors. (Aguilar Valdez, 2005, p. 419).

energy sale contract), which constitutes the only source to repay the debt, which generally is around 60% and up to 80% of the requested inversion amount, and which is usually cancelled after a period of 10 to 15 years. For this reason, the structure of this type of financing takes longer than a traditional corporation loan, since the project must be analyzed in detail (income, costs, awarenesses it may have, etc.), how the risk allocation is performed (which follows the premise of allocating each part of the risks that are in better conditions to be assumed), structuring legally the guarantee schemes, etc[25].

The project finance model overcomes the classic direct corporative financing, since this last one has the limits imposed by the indebtedness restrictions of each company.

Taking into account that the infrastructure financing is similar to a puzzle in terms of the complexity of its generation and in terms of the negotiations that have to be carried out to obtain an effective set of lending agreements and guarantees, many of these finances take years until their structuration and closure, and it is common that they are affected by social, economic and politic contingencies, that force the introduction of modifications and successive amendments to the original contract projects[26].

Since obtaining financing is a decisive element for the development of the works, GENREN project considered, to give safety to the investments, the creation of a Guarantee Fund in order to guarantee the compliance of the obligations undertaken by ENARSA under the Provision Contracts.

Therefore, in order to comply that, ENARSA, CAMMESA and the Argentine Investment and Foreign-Trade Bank (BICE, from now on), signed a trust contract in order to guarantee the payment of the Price that ENARSA owes the contractors of all the supply contracts, and the payment that CAMMESA owes to ENARSA as a consequence of the *"Delivery Contracts"*.

In the trust contract, the granting of an Endorsement by the National State of a sum of up to two thousand million United States Dollars (USD 2,000,000,000) in favor of ENARSA was expected. At the same time, this

---

[25] Cf. Ariño Ortiz, op. cit., p. 700. In the chapter about public infrastructures, the well-known author holds that in project finance it is fundamental *"to proceed to a distribution of the risks between the entrepreneur and the financial entity (since not all of them are assumed by the latter)"*, and since this financing modality consists in that the only guarantees of the financial entity are the flows generated by the financed project, its particularity *"forces to perform an exhaustive analysis of these flows"*.

[26] Cf. Barbier, Eduardo Antonio (2007): "Project Financing Contract", in *Contratación Bancaria* (Buenos Aires, Astrea, volume II, second edition, updated and extended), pp. 253.

state Company, in the same contract, committed to transfer this guarantee to the trust in order to ensure the payment of the Price to the contractors. The recipients of the endorsement are the contractors or those who result to be transferees of the collection rights derived from the supply contracts.

It is clear that although the endorsement integrates the trust, this only had as a purpose ensuring the payment of the price owed by ENARSA derived from the supply contracts. Said in short, about the contracts that ENARSA signed with the private companies for the development of energy power plants through renewable sources, the trust contract and, specifically the endorse, are the means through which the investors are guaranteed that ENARSA will meet their obligations.

The constitution of that payment guarantee was extremely relevant for the companies at the time of finding financing, since the endorsement is a key element that lenders take into account to evaluate credit conditions (interests rates, term, risks, etc.).

Nevertheless, it is important to highlight that companies found difficulties to obtain private financing for this projects. In some cases, they tried to go to credit entities such as the Development Bank of Brazil (BNDES from now on), which demanded having an export insurance, and registering through the Agreement of Reciprocal Payments and Credits (CCR) of the Latin American Integration Association (Aladi)[27]. Also important is the fact that the loans offered by the said entity were required under the Buyers credit modality, which means, finance to Specific Purpose Societies (SPS) that must import the acquisition of goods from Brazil (such as wind turbines). These negotiations did not prosper because, also, BNDES required that the Central Bank of the Republic of Argentina (BCRA from no own) guaranteed irrevocably the payment to the Central Bank of Brazil, who at the same time was going to guarantee the payment to BNDES.

In other cases, financing operations under traditional schemes with the Bank of the Argentine Nation (BNA from now on) were closed, which means, loans from this institution to the societies developing the projects, expecting the said financings to be made through the creation of investment trusts, that issue Debt Securities (DSs), in which BNA invests, and the repayment would be guaranteed through the trust transfer of the

---

[27] CCR is basically a compensation mechanims between Central Banks, where every Central Bank established, with every other bank in the System, a reciprocal credit line established United States dollars and which varies, depending of the case, depending on the importance of the market currents established in the different countries. These credit lines allow channeling the payments between members, covering the daily balances produced between two Central Banks; as well as enabling the deferred payment of the balance of the debits of the accounts between them.

payment rights related to the Electric Energy Provision Contract celebrated between ENARSA and the private Company. In many of these schemes an important part of equity from the companies was demanded[28].

Also, several companies have tried to obtain financing from the Inter-American Development Bank (BID); from BICE; from Andean Development Corporation (CAF); and from different national and foreign private banks, that do not need to be mentioned in this document. Other companies could be financed issuing negotiable obligations.

2.3 The new legal framework regulating the development of renewable energies in Argentina

During October of 2015, Law 27191 was passed in Argentina, which modified the National Development Regime for the Use of Renewable Sources of Energy destined to the Production of Electric Energy. The said regulation was ruled through Decree 532/16

Its purpose is achieving that the 8% of the national matrix of electric energy comes from renewable energies in year 2017 and reaching 20% in year 2025.

Among the novelties, a trust fund (FODER) was conformed in order to support the financing of the inversion projects, and the following benefits are given for the entrepreneurships:

1. Accelerated repayment in the Gains Tax and in the early repayment of the Value Added Tax.

2. Disruption compensation with earning.

3. Minimum Presumed Income Tax exemption.

4. Deduction of the financial load of the financial liability.

5. Distribution of dividends or utilities tax exemption.

6. In case of crediting in the investment projects crediting faithfully sixty per cent (60%) of integration of national component in electromechanic facilities, excluding civil work, or the minor percentage credited inasmuch as it proofs effectively the non existence of the national production —which in no case could be under thirty per cent (30%)—, there will be the right to perceive as additional benefit a tax certificate to be applied to the payment of national taxes, for a value equivalent to the credited twenty

---

[28] After this article, BNA, together with BICE, gave financing for one of these projects, in this case a wind project: Parque Malaspina I.

per cent (20%) of the national component in the electromechanic facilities —civil work excluded—.

7. Exemption from the payment of the import duty and of every duty, special tax, correlative levy or statistics rate, excluding any other compensatory rates for services, for the introduction of capital goods, special equipment or parts or elements composing the said goods.

On the other hand, the Public Trust Fund called "Fund for the Development of Renewable Energies" (FODER) is formed by an administration and finance trust, which will regulate across the whole territory of the Republic of Argentina, which will have as a purpose the application of the trusted goods on the loan granting, the implementation of the capital contributions and acquisition of every other financial instrument destined to the execution and financing of eligible projects in order to make available the acquisition and installation of capital goods or the manufacturing of goods or infrastructure works, in the framework of electric energy production from renewable sources entrepreneurships according to the terms of act 26.190.

FODER has important economic resources coming from the following sources:

a) Resources coming from the National Treasure as assigned by the National State through the Authority of Application, which cannot be annually lower than fifty per cent (50%) of the annual saving in fossil fuels due to the incorporation of generation from renewable energies obtained in the previous year, according to what the regulations establish.

b) Specific charges on the demand of energy as established.

c) The recovery of the capital and interests from the granted financings.

d) The dividends or utilities received due to the ownership of stocks or shares in the eligible projects and the revenue produced due to their sale.

e) Whatever is produced due to the operations, the rent, the outcome and investment of the trusted goods.

f) The income obtained due to the issue of trust securities that the trustee issues on behalf of the Fund. To such effects, the Fund may request the endorsement from the National Treasure in the terms established by the regulations.

Among its responsibilities, FODER can:

a) Provide funds and give facilities through loans, acquisition of public or private trust securities, as long as these were issued with the exclusive purpose of obtaining financing for the projects explained hereby.

b) Give capital contributions in societies carrying out projects and subscribing any other financing instrument that determines the Application Authority, as long as these allow financing projects with the addresses provided in this act.

c) Crediting percentage points from the interest rate of credits and security titles granted or in which financial entities or other agents taking care of financial support intervene. In this case, the credit risk will be taken by the said entities, which would be in charge of the evaluation of the credit risk. Nonetheless, to grant the benefit they must have the approval of the prior eligibility of the project by the Executive Committee.

d) Giving endorsements and guarantees to support the electric energy sales contracts to be signed by CAMMESA or by the institution appointed by the Application Authority representing the National State.

Another extremely important aspect introduced in the new act refers to the contribution of the electric energy users to the compliance of the objectives of the renewable energies development regime.

With that purpose, the act establishes that all the electric energy users from the Republic of Argentina must contribute to the compliance of the objectives fixed in act 26190, and every obliged subject must reach the minimal incorporation of 8% of the total personal electric energy consumption, with energy from renewable sources, by the 31st of December of 2017, and of 20% by the 31st of December of 2025.

To reach this compliance degree, the normative itself establishes that it must be performed gradually, according to a Schedule that sets goals every two years.

Another key aspect would be establishing a penalized obligation on the big electric energy users –specifically those with consumption equal or higher than 300 kW– for the individual compliance of the renewable energies consumption goals that the law sets.

With this measure it is intended to contract energy volumes directly in the market, either with independent renewable energies generators, through marketers or through the execution of own projects.

About this subject, big consumers may use the "joint purchasing" model, which means, contracting their supply through CAMMESA, who will call biddings in order to acquire the energy. If they did this, they would not be penalized if they do not reach the renewable energy rates, since their incorporation to the Joint Purchase mechanism and the payment of the cost of the electric energy from renewable sources conveniently consumed by them would be enough to establish their compliance with the Development Regime.

Without prejudice of that, among the alternative that big consumers have, they can get renewable energy through three alternative mechanisms:

1) Individual contract with a renewable generator directly or through a marketer or distributor, to be negotiated freely between the parts.

2) Self-generation

Self-generator is that kind of consumer that generates electrical energy as a secondary product, being their main purpose producing goods and/or services. It must have an installed power that cannot be lower than 1 MW, with an annual average availability that is not lower than 50%. The available power, the product of the installed power by the informed availability, must be available of meeting the 50% or more than the informed annual energy demand. Self-generators can sell in MEM their energy surplus or buy the lacking.

As a variant, there is the role of the "distributed self-generator" (created through Resolution SE 269/08), being, apart from an energy consumer, an energy generation, with the particular feature that the consumption and generation points as linked to the Argentina Interconnection System (SADI) in different connection nodes.

3) Co-generation

The co-generator represents that entity that generates jointly electric energy and steam or any other form of energy with industrial, commercial, heating or cooling purposes.

Co-generators can sell in MEM the electric energy production necessary for the production of steam or any other kind of energy needed for their production process, but differently from the auto-generators, they cannot buy energy.

It is important to highlight that those who opt for any of the three alternatives commented above, must state their will before the Ministry of Energy and Mines in order to be excluded from the Joint Purchase mechanisms mentioned above, being therefore automatically included if they would fail to do this.

2.4 RENOVAR program

Parting from the new normative quoted above, a new stage has started in the field of the development of renewable energies in Argentina. And this was arranged through the new renewable energies development program called RENOVAR (Plan de Energías renovables RENOVAR). It is a well defined public policy that will stay over time, which will be arranged as long as there is legal security and a trust climate that allows the approach of investors betting for this type of projects.

RENOVAR program is inserted in the compliance of the purposes established by acts 26190 and 27191 and their regulatory decree 531/16, on renewable generation contribution.

The Ministry of Energy and Mines of the Nation issued Resolution 136/16, through which the conditions to bid the installation of the power of renewable energy with an objective of 1000 MW were established. The bidding, named "RENOVAR Round 1" set as a criteria allocating 600 MW on wind projects, 300 MW on solar projects, 65 MW on biomass projects, 20 MW on small hydroelectric projects and 15 MW on biogas offers.

Round 1 of Renovar was structured using a three guarantees system. In the first case, FODER, mentioned above, guarantees the payment that CAMMESA must be for the contracted energy, and as well in the case of contract termination. At the same time, there is a second level guarantee, assuming the National State as guarantor in case of termination of the contracts. Finally, in case it is necessary, as final guarantee there is the World Bank, also for this last scenario.

In the case of FODER, the energy generators could claim directly to FODER the payment of energy that would not have been paid in time and in the way asked by CAMESA. FODER must pay vendors directly, and then it will claim CAMMESA the corresponding repayment.

In the case of termination of a supply contract by CAMMESA, or sale of the project, and CAMMESA would fail to comply its payment obligations, the generator Company must present their claim before FODER, who at the same time will request funds from the Ministry of Energy and Mines, exchanging the guarantees given by the National State. In the case that the National State does not have the necessary funds to tackle the debt and in consequence FODER cannot pay the claim presented, the Company may claim directly to the World Bank, who must pay directly the defined amount and who will arrange their differences directly with Argentina.

The terms of Energy sales contracts (PPA) were extended from 15 to 20 years, and the new legal framework established in the current normative, granting the important public aids indicated before, generated the adequate framework that allowed the bidding process to be a true success, having really competitive prices. CAMMESA itself and the Ministry of Energy and Mines set in advance price caps for the offers with the following values: Wind Energy 82 USD/MW, Solar Energy 80 USD/MW, Biomass 110 USD/MW, Small Hydroelectrical Projects 110 USD/MW; and Biogas 160 USD/MW, and the adjudicated prices were for much lower amounts.

In Round 1, 123 offers were presented, for a total of 6343MW, and 105 offers were qualified to compete, for a total 5209MW. This competence allowed assigning 17 projects distributed as follows: 12 wind energy contracts for a total 708MW, four solar projects for 408MW, and one Biogas project for only 1MW.

In Round 1, average awarded prices for every type of project were the following: 59.4 USD/MWh for wind energy; 59.7 USD/MWh for solar energy; and 118 USD/MWh for energy derived from Biogas.

Success was so resounding that immediately a new contest was published, called "Round 1.5", in which only the projects already presented in Round 1 and were not awarded were allowed to compete. The new call indicated expressly the list of the projects that may state their interest to participate in this new call.

In "Round 1.5" 30 projects were awarded for a total 1281.6 MW, distributed as follows: 10 wind energy contracts for a total 765.4 MW and 20 solar energy contracts, for a total 516.2 MW.

In this Round, the average prices per type of project were the following: 53.34 USD/MWh for wind energy and 54.94 USD/MWh for solar energy.

2.5 Contract adequacy of some contracts celebrated under the previous regime of GENREN

As explained before, under the GENREN regime, the energy generation companies signed "Energy Supply" contracts with ENARSA, through which they sold generated energy to the state company, which later would sell it to CAMMESA.

This way, a system of mirror contracts was implemented, in which the contract conditions agreed between the production companies and

ENARSA –in the Energy Supply contracts– has to be reflected in the contracts between the latter and CAMMESA –in the Delivery Contracts–.

While the GENREN scheme was in force, ENARSA proceeded to the contract modification of the agreed conditions with some generator companies, and the corresponding addendums were performed. The main modifications consisted in a price reduction and in the extension of the terms to end the works.

So these modifications agreed between ENARSA and the generation companies could come into force it was necessary to reflect these conditions in the mirror Delivery contracts between ENARSA and CAMMESA.

Now, before the addendums of the *"Delivery Contracts"* between ENARSA and CAMMESA were signed, the change in the government took place and the new administration decided to suspend these addendums since they considered that the conditions agreed between ENARSA and the generation companies did not reflect the current market conditions.

In that sense, the Ministry of Energy and Mines of the Nation dictated Resolution 202/2016 through which the generator companies meeting some specific requirements were allowed to modify the structure of the contracts under the GENREN regime and adapting them to the new regime of the RENOVAR Program.

Energy storage: a clear key technology priority in the energy system

CARLOS VÁZQUEZ COBOS

Partner of Gómez-Acebo & Pombo, Spain

ALEXANDRE DÍEZ BAUMANN

Partner of Estudio Jurídico Internacional, Spain

MARÍA JOSÉ GÓMEZ SERRANO

Partner of Estudio Jurídico Internacional, Spain

VICENTE LÓPEZ-IBOR LOBATO

Lawyer of Gómez-Acebo & Pombo, Spain

1. INTRODUCTION

As mentioned by the European DG ENER in its *"Proposed Definition and Principles for Energy Storage"*, *"energy storage in the electricity system would be defined as the act of deferring an amount of the energy that was generated to the moment of use, either as final energy or converted into another energy carrier"*.

Energy Storage (ES) is expected to play a major role in Europe's future Smart Grid. The European Commission's 2012 Communication *"Renewable Energy: a Major Player in the European Energy Market"* states that *"electricity storage is a clear key technology priority for the development of the European power system of 2020 and beyond, in light of the increasing market share of renewable and distributed generation and the growing limitations of the energy grid"*.

The Commission's Working Paper "The future role and challenges of Energy Storage" more specifically states.

"Energy Storage can supply more flexibility and balancing to the grid, providing a back up to intermittent renewable energy. Locally, it can improve the management of distribution networks, reducing costs and improving efficiency. In this way, it can ease the market introduction of renewables, accelerate the decarbonisation of the electricity grid, improve the security and efficiency of electricity transmission and distribution, stabilise market prices for electricity, while also ensuring a higher security of energy supply".

The DG ENER explains that electricity storage was not considered a priority in the past for energy system development, partially because in a fossil fuel based electricity system the benefits of storage were limited.

Because the installed generating capacity of renewable energy, whose output cannot be controlled by the grid operators, in percentage of the total electricity mix is becoming important in many countries[1], the fluctuation in the output of renewable generation makes system frequency control difficult, and if the frequency deviation becomes too wide, system operation can deteriorate. Energy storage systems, alongside with the implementation of smarter grid distribution solutions that facilitate active network management, can mitigate the output fluctuation and avoid the temptation of installing renewable generation overcapacity with the purpose to secure enough power[2] and therefore will leads to much lower costs compare to the conventional fit-and-forget "business as usual" solution[3].

Therefore, energy storage solutions will be needed at different locations throughout the power system, to level the mismatch between renewable power generators and consumption and/or to store the surplus of power from renewable sources for later use during non-generation time periods, or low power generation time periods, and will result in a growing need for storage capacities in the mid to long-term.

Closely related to energy storage is energy efficiency. The 2012/27/EU Energy Efficiency Directive establishes a set of binding measures to help

---

[1] In June 2014, the International Renewable Energy Agency (IRENA) launched a global renewable energy roadmap called Remap 2030. The aim is to assess pathways to double the share of renewable energy in the global energy mix by 2030. According to IRENA "Renewable and Electricity Storage A Technology Roadmap for Remap 2030", June 2015, in 2030 the annual share of annual variable renewable power generation will be over 65% for Denmark, over 45% for Germany, over 40% for the UK, over 35% for Spain and over 25% for the United States

[2] International Electrotechnical Commission, Electrical Energy Storage White Paper, 2011

[3] "Utility of the Future" and MIT Energy Initiative response to an industry in transition. Massachusetts Institute of Technology in collaboration with Universidad Pontificia Comillas, Madrid, 2016.

the EU reach its 20% energy efficiency target by 2020. Under the Directive, all EU countries are required to use energy more efficiently at all stages of the energy chain, from its production to its final consumption.

On 30 November 2016, the European Commission presented a package of measures to keep the European Union competitive within the actual global energy market transition, commonly known as the "Clean Energy Package".

Such package includes, among others, a revised renewable energy Directive, new energy measures, a new electricity market design and new proposals for a regulation on the Governance of the Energy Union.

Within its six key areas of actions, the revised renewable energy Directive is concluding that the consumers are the drivers of the energy transition, that new technologies like smart grids, smart homes and battery storage solutions make it increasingly possible for energy consumers to become active players on the market, and therefore is focusing on empowering and informing them.

2. ENERGY STORAGE COMPLYING WITH THE LEGAL FRAMEWORK OF THE EUROPEAN UNION ENERGY POLICY

In the EU, Article 194 1st paragraph of Treaty for the Functioning of the European Union sets up the policy framework of the EU energy policy and states four objectives guiding its development[4]

Energy storage will help EU member states achieve the objectives and requirements established in the above-mentioned article. Indeed, energy storage will facilitate the introduction of more renewable energy generation capacity to the power system supplying greater flexibility and balance to the grid, providing a back-up to intermittent renewable energy.

European energy storage development requires new European rules to enable its speedy development, while avoiding distortion in competition and allowing cross-border trading.

Furthermore, and as mentioned by the DG ENER in its Working Paper *"The Future Role and Challenges of Energy Storage"*, locally, energy storage can

---

[4] Article 194 1st paragraph, Treaty for the Functioning of the European Union: "1. In the context of the establishment and functioning of the internal market and with regard for the need to preserve and improve the environment, Union policy on energy shall aim, in a spirit of solidarity between Member States, to ensure the functioning of the energy market;
a) ensure security of energy supply in the Union;
b) promote energy efficiency and energy saving and the development of new and renewable forms of energy; and c) promote the interconnection of energy networks [...]."

1) improve the management of the distribution networks by:

   a) reducing costs (avoiding costly grid reinforcement, for example),

   b) improving efficiency, and

   c) easing the introduction of renewables,

2) accelerate the decarbonisation of the electricity grid,

3) improve the security and efficiency of electricity transmission and distribution (reducing unplanned loop flows, grid congestion, voltage and frequency variations),

4) stabilise market prices for electricity, and

5) ensure a higher security of energy supply.

All the above are perfectly aligned with the objectives mentioned in Article 194 of the TFEU.

3. KEY QUESTIONS TO BE CONSIDERED IN POSSIBLE FUTURE ENERGY STORAGE REGULATION

Any new storage regulation should contemplate and/or answer the following points and questions[5]:

1) The regulatory framework needs to provide clear rules and responsibilities concerning the technical modalities and the financial conditions of energy storage, and should foresee the most suitable bidding format for an energy storage system, with adequate flexibility to obtain maximum efficiency.

2) Shall energy storage be subsidised or shall investments be based on market revenues? Storage in some cases, could be considered as reserve and shall be efficiently price as such.

3) Regarding grid energy storage, shall such energy storage be rewarded for the services provided on a peer basis with the alternative suppliers for those services?

4) Energy storage as a supporting mean for integrating variable renewable energy could be rewarded for the contribution to improving energy supply security and decarbonisation of the electricity grid or other economic sectors; thus, could the avoided

---

[5] Some of these points were mentioned by the DG ENER in its Working Paper *"The Future Role and Challenges of Energy Storage"*

costs of variable renewable energy curtailment and the carbon reductions of the backup capacities support a business-focused case for large scale energy storage?

5)   Enabling micro grids with energy storage solutions

6)   Avoiding distortion in competition, i.e. the framework should be technology neutral, ensuring fair competition between different technological solutions (not picking a winner).

7)   It should ensure fair and equal access to electricity storage independent of the size and location of the storage in the supply chain.

8)   It should ensure medium-term predictability in the investment and financial conditions (taxes, fees etc.), enabling favourable conditions for all kinds of storage, particularly micro-storage (home and district level).

9)   The grid tariff could be based on the principle of cost causality: if an energy storage system is systematically using the grid during off-peak periods and not during peak periods, it should not generate grid investment. Thus, the introduction of a time component in grid tariffs could take into account the portion of grid investment due to energy storage.

10) Should storage be charged for connecting to the local or national electricity networks in the same manner as electricity generation facilities? Could storage be charged less, or even nothing at all, for connection given that storage may reduce network operators' costs, in contrast to generating facilities?

Therefore, and in opinion of the DG ENER, *"there should be a stronger focus on storage in EU energy and climate policies, and improved coordination between the issue of storage and other key policy issues. Energy storage should be integrated into, and supported by, all relevant existing and future EU energy and climate measures and legislation, including strategies on energy infrastructure, including the Connecting Europe Facility; RES promotion; Smart Cities and Communities; completion of the Internal Market; Energy Efficiency Directive; Horizon 2020; 2050 Roadmap; as well as the forthcoming discussion on a 2030 Strategy"*[6].

---

[6]   DG ENER Working Paper The future role and challenges of Energy Storage

4. GERMANY

Germany is already experiencing strong interest for self-consumption with storage systems. Some figures for Germany suggest that 12% of solar PV systems are coupled to an energy storage system. The national subsidy program[7] has provided loans for 10,000 systems in 2013 and 2014. The demand for residential battery storage systems is partly due to the continuing feed-in tariff decline.

A German study has demonstrated that today, a one-hour error in the forecast of upcoming wind creates a need for anywhere from 5GW TO 7GW of electricity. These needs must be covered by electricity storage: gas fired power plants will be able to deliver the electricity within an hour or two; electricity storage must deliver during this gap time[8]. Energy storage systems are an integral part of **Germany's Energy Transition** (*Energiewende*).

4.1 Energy storage regulation in Germany

a) The Renewable Energy Sources Act or EEG (German: Erneuerbare-Energien-Gesetz or EEG)

The EEG, is a series of German laws that originally provided a feed-in tariff (FIT) scheme to encourage the generation of renewable electricity. The EEG (2014), the current version of the law, instead specifies the transition to an auction system for most technologies by 2017.

The EEG is also a key element in the implementation of EU Directive 2009/28/EC on the promotion of the use of energy from renewable source. This directive requires Germany to produce 18% of its gross final energy consumption (including heat and transport) from renewable energy sources by 2020. In this endeavour, the EEG is complemented by the Renewable Energies Heat Act (Erneuerbare-Energien-Wärmegesetz or EEWärmeG).

b) The Renewable Energy Sources Act (2014)

This revision took effect from 1 August 2014. The act required operators of new plant to market their electricity themselves. In turn they receive a market premium from the grid operator to compensate for the difference between the fixed EEG payment and the average spot price for electricity. The act also paved the way for a switch from specified feed-in tariffs to a system of tendering.

---

[7]   The battery storage subsidy scheme by the German Federal Ministry of Economic affairs and Energy (BMWi) is called 'KfW-Programm Erneuerbare Energien "Speicher" – 275 Kredit' and is administered by KfW

[8]   DG ENER Working Paper The Future Role and Challenges of Energy Storage

The purpose of the EEG (2014) is stated in Section 1:

"The purpose of this Act is to enable the energy supply to develop in a sustainable manner in particular in the interest of mitigating climate change and protecting the environment, to reduce the costs to the economy not least by including long-term external effects, to conserve fossil energy resources and to promote the further development of technologies to generate electricity from renewable energy sources."

The level of remuneration is still prescribed under the EEG until 2017. From 2014–2017 onwards, defined remuneration rates will be replaced by competitive bidding, also known as auctions or tenders. Those investors offering the lowest prices will then receive support. The new act does not specify the auction model in detail, but potential designs were piloted in 2015 using ground-mounted photovoltaic systems.

c) Renewable Energy Sources Act (2017)

With the soon coming new Act, the prescribed feed-in tariffs will disappear for most technologies. Specific deployment corridors are the ones which stipulate the extent to which renewable electricity is to be expanded in the future. From then onwards, the Government will not set the funding rates; instead they will be determined by auction.

4.2 Residential energy storage market

The federal government, via the German state-owned development bank KfW, provided a subsidy, originally created in May 2013, to encourage the uptake of solar-plus-storage, which has been instrumental in fuelling uptake of battery storage, from almost nothing three years ago.

Under the renewable energies program entitled "Storage", KfW Bankengruppe and the Federal Ministry for the Environment are supporting the increased use of energy storage in conjunction with solar photovoltaic systems linked to the electricity grid. The program aims to encourage further technical development of storage battery systems for solar PV installations and to increase their market penetration. Prices are expected to fall as the use of technology increases.

The program was initially started in May 2013[9] and ran until the end of 2015. It was then relaunched on 1st March 2016 and will run until the end of 2018. For the year 2013 alone, 25 million Euros was made available for the program.

The exact level of state funding applicable toward the purchase of a storage system is dependent on the costs of the battery system selected, as well as the size of the solar power system. System operators can apply for aid if their solar power systems were installed after January 2013 and have a maximum capacity of 30 kilowatts[10].

The newly launched battery storage funding program aims to ensure that connecting PV installations to the grid is expected to be even more beneficial to the overall system by limiting a PV installation's maximum feed-in to 50 per cent. Additionally, the new funding program is to be adapted to cost reductions in battery systems that have already taken place in the past or are expected to take place in future. The official funding announcement was published in the Federal Gazette on 29 February 2016[11] - official section of the Federal Gazette, 29 February 2016.[12].

Between 50% and 60% of German residential battery storage customers in Germany take advantage of the incentive, also known as KfW program 275, per GTAI[13].

Apart from this program, in Germany there are various incentives available for supporting storage facilities[14]

---

[9] The program is supervised by the Chair of Electrochemical Energy Conversion and Storage Systems, which is headed by Professor Dirk Uwe Sauer and part of the RWTH Institute for Power Electronics and Electrical Drives, ISEA, Aachen. The program aims to incentivize investment in decentralized battery storage systems and thus to help enhance the development of such systems and decrease their cost. With the help of the support program, a significant number of systems shall be developed and thus a commercially viable market created in the long run. As photovoltaic storage systems are often not as yet profitable without subsidies, incentives for operators of such systems include low interest rate loans and repayment subsidies.

[10] BSW-Solar Information paper, 15 May 2013

[11] www.bundesanzeiger.de/only in German. Official web-page of the German Federal Ministry for Economical Affaires and Energy (BMWI) http://www.bmwi.de/EN/root.html

[12] http://www.bmwi.de/EN/Topics/Energy/Storage/funding-initiative-for-energy-storage.html

[13] Germany Trade & Invest (GTAI), the economic development agency of the Federal Republic of Germany.

[14] Germany Trade & Invest (GTAI), the economic development agency of the Federal Republic of Germany.

Target group	Description	Conditions	Program ID
Private consumers	Investment grants up to 25% and low interest loans for PV-connected storage with grid connection and data management systems	Budget: €30 million until 2018	KfW 275
Private consumers	For Energy storage combined with renewable generators		KfW 207 & 274
Companies in Germany	For large-scale investments of large enterprises in the German Energiewende (energy supply, efficiency, storage and transmission)	Loans of €25 – 100	KfW 291
Companies in Germany	Investment grants up to 30% and low interest loans for large-scale pilot projects		KfW 230
Municipal utilities and PPPs	For extension and new construction of storage projects	€50 million loan limit	KfW 204
Municipalities	For extension and new construction of storage projects	Interest rate @ 0.6 – 1.3% up to 30 years	KfW 203

In addition, **Electricity storage facilities are exempt from grid tariffs,** EEG levies and, in the case of pumped hydro, also from electricity taxes.

Overall, as many as 25% of new residential PV installations in 2015 have battery storage, according to GTAI's November 2015 Market Status & Outlook on Batteries for Stationary Energy Storage in Germany.

4.3 Grid-supporting energy storage

Batteries or other kinds of energy storage should be able to be installed on strategic points of the grid network, which will also alleviate problems created by high levels of renewables penetration, via peak shaving and works deferral. There is no general funding or subsidies in the country for large power plants. This means grid-scale energy storage plants have to be able to stand on their own merits.

To be prequalified, a technical unit must demonstrate that it meets the transmission system operator's (TSO) reliability requirements for the secure supply of frequency response.

A number of technical requirements have to be met by the operators, some of which are international including those listed below:

– German requirements:

- IEC 62619 Secondary cells and batteries containing alkaline or other non-acid electrolytes - Safety requirements for secondary lithium cells and batteries, for use in industrial applications (IEC 21A/529/CD:2013-10)

- VDE-ST-Li-ESS-001:2013/03: Prüfbestimmung für Lithium-Speichersysteme

- Secondary cells and batteries containing alkaline or other non-acid electrolytes –

- Secondary lithium cells and batteries for portable applications (IEC 61960:2003); German version EN 61960:2004

Power generation systems connected to the low-voltage distribution network - Technical minimum requirements for the connection to and parallel operation with low-voltage distribution networks.

– International requirements:

- AENOR DIN EN 61010-1 VDE 0411-1:2011-07 Safety requirements for electrical equipment for measurement, control, and laboratory use -- Part 1: General requirements

- AENOR IEC 61000-3-2: Electromagnetic compatibility (EMC) - Part 3-3: Limits - Limitation of voltage changes, voltage fluctuations and flicker in public low-voltage supply systems, for equipment with rated current ≤16 A per phase and not subject to conditional connection

- AENOR IEC 61000-3-2: Electromagnetic compatibility (EMC) - Part 3-2: Limits - Limits for harmonic current emissions (equipment input current ≤ 16 A per phase)

- IEEE 1547: Standard for Interconnecting Distributed Resources with Electric Power Systems

- IEC/EN 62133: Secondary cells and batteries containing alkaline or other non-acid electrolytes - Safety requirements for portable sealed secondary cells, and for batteries made from them, for use in portable applications

- AENOR EN 62311:2008: Assessment of electronic and electrical equipment related to human exposure restrictions for electromagnetic fields (0 Hz - 300 GHz)

- European Parliament Directive 2006/95/EC OF THE EUROPEAN PARLIAMENT AND OF THE COUNCIL, 12TH December 2006 on the harmonisation of the laws of Member States relating to electrical equipment designed for use within certain voltage limits

- EMC Directive 2004/108/EG Electromagnetic compatibility OF THE EUROPEAN PARLIAMENT AND OF THE COUNCIL,15t December 2004 on the approximation of the laws of the Member States relating to electromagnetic compatibility and repealing Directive 89/336/EEC

- Electromagnetic compatibility (EMC) - Part 4-2: Testing and measurement techniques - EN 61000-4-2: Electrostatic discharge immunity test

- AENOR IEC 17065Conformity assessment - Requirements for bodies certifying products, processes and services (ISO/IEC 17065:2012)

One of the main issues in Germany is whether Energy storage will be considered, or dismissed, as a great additional value to the tool box of infrastructure assets, that distributed network operators (DNOs) have.

5. UK

The Government includes energy storage as one of eight great technologies in which the UK can become a global leader[15]

UK Power Networks (UKPN) suggests that storage should not be subject to certain green levies (such as the levelisation charge for the Government's feed-in-tariff scheme[16]) because storage is not an electricity end-user. UKPN proposes that charging these fees disincentives storage and end-users effectively pay the fee twice on electricity that reaches them via storage.

The UK's new enhanced frequency response market, overseen by grid operator National Grid, will benefit from energy storage's ability

[15] https://www.gov.uk/government/publications/eight-great-technologies-infographics
[16] http://www.endco.co.uk/market-information/industry-charges/, accessed 24th February 2015

to respond rapidly to grid signals. The addition to the National Grid's ancillary services market is attracting a mix of businesses, from Utilities to independent power producers, which have bid for contracts, many of which are proponents of the use of battery storage.

5.1 Energy storage regulation in UK

a) Energy storage is not a defined activity within the electricity sector

In the UK legal framework, energy storage is not explicitly recognised as a distinct activity or asset class (although within the gas market, gas storage is a distinct licensed activity).

In the absence of an alternative option, energy storage has been treated as a type of generation asset. In GB, large scale pumped storage hydro assets hold generation licences, while smaller scale facilities can qualify for exemption from the requirement to hold a generation licence.

Exemptions from the requirement to hold a generation licence can be granted to classes of generators or to particular generators in specific circumstances specified in 'The Electricity (Class Exemptions from the Requirement for a Licence) Order 2001[17]. A generator can be exemptible as a small generator if output to the total system (GB transmission system and all distribution systems) is less than 10MW, or if output to the total system is less than 50MW and the declared net capacity of the power station is less than 100MW. The definition of 'declared net capacity' in this context is as follows:

> *'The declared net capacity of a generating station which is driven by any means other than water, wind or solar power is the highest generation of electricity (at the main alternator terminals) which can be maintained indefinitely without causing damage to the plant less so much of that capacity as is consumed by the plant'.*

While larger scale assets which deliver energy on a comparable basis to conventional generation can operate under the 'generation' banner, it is more problematic for smaller scale resources that have different applications.

---

[17] 2001 No. 3270 ELECTRICITY The Electricity (Class Exemptions from the Requirement for a Licence) Order 2001 Made 28th September 2001. Laid before Parliament 28th September 2001 Coming into force - - 1st October 2001

b) GB generation definitions and applicability for storage

From a European context, 'generation' is defined as the production of electricity, while the definition in the Electricity Act 1989 simply links the activity to generating electricity for the purpose of giving or enabling supply of electricity to some premises. Both are relatively generic definitions. The Electricity (Class Exemptions from the Requirement for a Licence) Order 2001 develops the definition of *'generation'* further, highlighted as follows:

> **Electricity Act 1989, 4(1)(a):** Licence allows the licensee to generate electricity for giving a supply to any premises or enabling a supply to be give.

- **Order 2001, Interpretations paragraph 2(d):** A person shall be treated as generating electricity at any time if he is the operator of plant or equipment which at that time:

  (i)   is generating or capable of generating electricity;

  (ii) or (ii) is not capable of generating electricity only by reason of the maintenance, repair or testing of the plant or equipment.

- **Order 2001, Schedule 2, Class A**: Small Generators:

Persons (other than licensed generators) who do not at any time provide more electrical power from any one generating station than—

(1) 10 megawatts; or

(2) 50 megawatts in the case of a generating station with a declared net capacity of less than 100 megawatts; disregarding—

(a) power supplied to—

> (i) a single consumer who occupies premises which are on the same site as the premises where the generating station is situated and who consumes all the power provided to him from that generating station at those premises or supplies all or some of such power in circumstances specified in the description of Class B in Schedule 4, and consumes at those premises any of such power not so supplied by him; or

(ii) two or more consumers who form a qualifying group each of whom occupies premises which are on the same site as the premises where the generating station is situated and consumes all the power provided to him from that generating station at those premises or supplies all or some of such power in circumstances specified in the description of Class B in Schedule 4 and consumes at those premises any of such power not so supplied by him; and

(b) for the purposes of paragraph (2) above power temporarily provided in excess of 50 megawatts due to technical circumstances, outside the reasonable control of the person providing that power. (1) 10 megawatts; or

- **Order 2001, Schedule 2, Class A:** The definition of 'declared net capacity' includes the following:

"The declared net capacity of a generating station which is driven by any means other than water, wind or solar power is the highest generation of electricity (at the main alternator terminals) which can be maintained indefinitely without causing damage to the plant less so much of that capacity as is consumed by the plant."

This highlights two important messages in relation to the GB framework:

- first, that the definition of generation is unclear; and

- second, that storage does not sit comfortably within the definition of generation as its stands.

In the context of smaller-scale, distribution connected storage projects, the generation licence exemption conditions become important. Points to note are that exemption is granted:

- on a plant by plant basis (not across a portfolio); and

- to plants with output below 10MW or below 50MW if net declared capacity is below 100MW.

This allows small scale electricity storage facilities to fall under the 'Small Generator' class exemption, thereby obviating the requirement to hold a generation licence for such facilities. These thresholds are more than sufficient for most distribution constraint avoidance applications, for which assets of sub-10MW are required.

5.2 Limitation on the Role of Network Operators

Under the Electricity Act 1989 and the Electricity Directive 2009/72/EC, local and national electricity network operators are not permitted to control the sale of electricity to consumers. This is designed to prevent network operators from entering the electricity market and competing with private providers of storage, something which is considered undesirable given that network operators have the advantage of being regional monopolies. However, industry is concerned that the restriction makes it difficult for the financial benefit of avoiding network expansion. UK Power Networks (UKPN) is testing an approach where the network operator uses storage. In the trial, UKPN controls when storage discharges and charges for network purposes, while interaction with the electricity market is carried out by a private third party. It is not clear whether this approach, or any alternatives, could be used beyond this trial, without entailing a change to legislation[18]

5.3 Legislative, Regulatory and Commercial Barriers

There are interrelated legislative, regulatory and commercial barriers to grid-scale electricity storage. Legislation and regulation treat storage either as generation or as an electricity end-user (Electricity Act 1989 and EU Directives)[19] Industry suggests that this leads to private storage facilities being charged too much by the regulated network operators and energy suppliers and it makes it difficult for network operators to use storage to help avoid electricity network expansion and its associated costs. The latter might otherwise provide an earlier, economically viable route to market for grid-scale electricity storage.

The Government is supporting storage through the following policies.

- Electricity and Heat R&D and demonstration

Public bodies including the Engineering and Physical Sciences Research Council, Energy Technologies Institute, Ofgem, Department of Energy and Climate Change and Innovate UK, each have programs funding electricity and heat storage development with multi-year budgets ranging from millions to tens of millions of pounds. In 2013, public sector energy storage spending on R&D was £9m and on demonstration £5m. Research and development (R&D) spending aims to develop lower cost technologies, while demonstration spending is also looking to tackle regulatory and commercial barriers.

[18] Personal communication, Ofgem and UK Power Networks
[19] Poyry, July 2014, Smarter Network Storage Low Carbon Network Fund, Electricity Storage in GB: Interim Report on the Regulatory and Legal Framework

- Transport Sector Policy

Energy storage in transport is not directly supported, but there are policies to support lower carbon vehicles. EU regulation sets targets to reduce CO2 emissions from new UK passenger cars by 2020 by 26% from 2013 levels.[20] For the 2010-2015 period the Government committed to spending £500m more on low-emission vehicles over 2015-2020, of which £200m is on grants to increase vehicle uptake (including car and van grants of up to £5,000 and £8,000) and £100m on R&D. There are also regional policies offering benefits to low carbon vehicles such as free parking.

5.4 The Capacity Market

The 2013 Energy Act established the Capacity Market regulatory regime, which offers regular payment to organizations that can guarantee to supply electricity when required.[21]

Competition for the limited Capacity Market revenue is encouraged via an annual auction, which does not favour any particular technology. The first auction took place in December 2014. Existing electricity storage accounted for 5% of the total capacity awarded; no new storage projects received support.

The Electricity Storage Network says that it is unlikely that the additional auctions will incentivize new storage construction because of the short one-year contracts, and competition from small diesel-fuelled generation units.

6. SPAIN

6.1 Challenges for the development of renewable energies in Spain

In 2015 the final energy consumption in Spain grew by 0.5%. Renewable energy accounted for 14.8% of total final energy consumption, 0.8 points below the 15.6% achieved in 2014. Renewable energy in 2015 covered 36.9% of peninsular electricity demand, 5.9 percentage points lower than the 42.8% achieved in 2014. In terms of installed capacity, the total capacity of renewable energies in Spain stood at 33,138 MW in 2015.

Wind energy represents Spain's third largest power generation source, after nuclear and coal energy, with a production of 48.016 GWH in 20015,

---

[20] Calculated based on The Society of Motor Manufacturers and Traders Limited, 2014, New Car CO2 Report

44 European Commission, accessed 5th January 2015, Reducing CO2 emissions from Passenger Cars

[21] DECC, accessed 5th January 2015, Electricity Market Reform: Capacity Market

covering 19.1 % of the country's electricity demand. Wind energy was the renewable technology with a major contribution, followed by hydroelectric with an 11% contribution and solar photovoltaic with 3.1%.

Spain's energy and climate targets for 2020 (which require that more than 40% of the electricity generation come from Renewable Energy (RE), mainly wind energy)[22] are to be met pursuant to several national action plans (The National Energy Efficiency Action Plan or NEEAP, updated in 2014; and the National Renewable Energy Action Plan or NREAP, updated in 2011 as the Renewable Energies Plan)[23]

In a study developed by REE (Red Eléctrica, Spanish Electricity Operator -TSO- for the peninsular and non-peninsular systems), it was already pointed out that Spain could not use all the RE produced in 2014 and 2% of this energy will be wasted[24].

Consequently, one of the main challenges that the Spanish electricity system currently has is how to manage all the renewable energy produced, in order to cover those hours of the day where the sun doesn't shine or the wind doesn't blow. And in this context, energy storage becomes a key tool which could help to achieve this goal in an effective manner.

6.2 Energy storage regulation in Spain

a) General regulation: Law 24/2013

In recent years, the energy regulation in Spain has been mainly focused on the resolution of several issues including, among others, *security of supply, lack of interconnections, tariff deficit, overcapacity of the installed power due to the lack of control in the development of renewable energies, or the decrease in the premiums granted to renewable energies brining a new regulation since the entry into force of RDL 9/2013.* In this context and although the energy storage technology might be a solution for some of these problems, Spanish legislation did not evolve much with respect to the challenges stated on the Energy Storage Action List.

---

[22] Including:
• a 26.4% reduction of its primary energy consumption compared to the business as usual scenario;
• a 20.8% share of renewables in final energy consumption (20.8% being a national target; the EU target for Spain's renewables is 20%); and
• a 10% reduction of GHG emissions in the non-ETS sector and an 21% reduction of GHG emissions in the ETS sector.
As in UK and Germany, one of the key issues related to energy storage is the management of the energy storage when is delivered into the grid, and of its transportation.
[23] IDAE (2011) Plan de Energías Renovables 2011-2020
[24] Report on the integration of renewable generation in the mid-term for the 2009-2014 period (REE)

In previous legislation, the former Electric Law 54/1997, (currently repealed by Law 24/2013) included few references to energy storage, always linked to the electric vehicles infrastructure.

Law 24/2013, currently in force as the main regulation of the sector, includes, for the first time, a mention of energy storage facilities in its article 48.1 "energy recharge service" although only in relation to storage for electric vehicles *"The recharge energy service shall have as the main function the delivery of energy through the recharge services of electric vehicles and storage facilities under conditions that allow to load efficiently and at minimal cost to the consumers and to the electric system".*

b) Energy storage connected to generation facilities

The only regulation that simultaneously tackles energy storage connected to generation facilities is the recent Royal Decree 900/2015, 9th of October (hereinafter, RD 900/2015) regulating the administrative, technical and economic conditions for methods of electricity supply based on self-consumption and production with self-consumption connected to the distribution network[25].

Article 9 of Law 24/2013, December 26th, on the Electricity Sector, defines self-consumption as the consumption of electricity from generation plants connected within a consumer´s network or through an electric power direct line associated with a consumer and distinguishes various forms of self-consumption based on two types of self-consumption facilities: Type 1, for facilities with nominal power up to 100kW which may not sell the electricity generated and are forced to donate this electricity free to the grid without compensation and Type 2, with a nominal power above 100kW which must be register in order to sell electricity on the spot market for any excess produced.

The relation between self-consumption generation installations and energy storage facilities is included in its article 5.5 *"It would be possible to install storing elements in the self-consumption facilities regulated under this Royal Decree as long as they have protections as settled in the rule of safety and industrial quality applying to them and which are installed in such a way to share meter equipment recording the net generation or measuring equipment recording the hourly energy consumption".*

Therefore, according to RD 900/2015 there are two requirements to connect a storage facility to a generation installation: (i) that the installation

---

[25] RD 900/2015, of 9 October, which regulates the administrative, technical and economic conditions for the modalities of electric power supply with self-consumption and production with self-consumption.

provides protection measures set out in the rules of industrial safety and quality and (ii) the generation facility and electrical storage installation share measuring equipment.

However, RD 900/2015, only regulates storage services which are always tied to electric vehicle infrastructures including in its Second transitional provision the Complementary Technical Instruction (ITC-BT-52) meaning the technical procedures necessary to carry out and legalize the infrastructure for the recharge of electric vehicles.

In this sense, it seems that the adoption of specific ITC applicable to the energy storage services connected to generation facilities and electricity networks is currently pending. Nevertheless, while this specific ITC is not yet approved, any energy storage facility, whether it is connected to a generation facility or not, must meet the requirements of industrial safety and quality requirements specified in the Low Voltage Regulation (REBT) in particular, ITC-BT-40[26] and its Technical Guide, because even although it is not binding, it is the only technical reference that is currently available to carry out the energy storage facilities connected or not connected to low voltage installations.

In short, the RD of self-consumption regulates only those electric batteries or energy storage facilities that are linked to generation installations for self-consumption, not including, in its regulatory regime, independent storage facilities.

Consequently, those independent storage facilities do not need to adapt to the provisions of RD 900/2015, and therefore only need to fulfil the technical requirements established in the REBT, as industrial safety regulations of general application for all electrical installations, which expressly provides for the technical scheme applicable to this type of installation.

---

[26] Under REBT, the electrical storage facilities are comparable to generation facilities. This equalization is exclusively for the purposes of compliance with industrial safety regulations, but not to configure storage facilities as generation facilities for all purposes. In fact Article 6 of Law 24/2013, defines generators as "natural or legal persons who have the function of generating electricity, as well as of building, operating and maintaining production facilities". Therefore, neither the electrical storage facility can be considered a generation facility in the eyes of Law 24/2013 nor the holder of an electric storage facility can be understood to be an electricity producer under RD 900/2015.

This criteria was confirmed in the tenth Transitional Provision of RD 900/2015, where it states that "the accumulation elements will be installed in such a way that they will share measurement equipment and protections with the generation facility", thus differentiating, undoubtedly, between generation facilities and accumulation elements.

6.3 Financial economic regime for power storage connected to a generation facility

Law 24/2013 establishes the obligation of self-consumption facilities to contribute to the financing of costs and system services in the same amount as standard consumers[27] but RD 900/2015 goes even further and has been controversial as it includes an unpopular charge, commonly known as a "sun tax" defined as the charge to pay for the backup obtained from the whole electric system to enable self-consumption, which, far from encouraging self-consumption, contains a series of measures that will adversely affect people who produce and consume their own electricity while connected to the distribution network.

Effectively this "sun tax", apart from including administrative and economic requirements for self-consumption, introduces two new items (i) a 'support charge' with the aim of taxing individuals who consume self-generated electricity while being connected to the national power grid., as well as (ii) a charge due to the simple use of a storage facility associated to a generation installation for self-consumption.

The only cases which are exempted from the payment of these charges are installations that are smaller than 10 kW and all installations located in the Canary Islands and the cities of Ceuta and Melilla (these are Spanish territories in Africa). Furthermore, installations with co-generation will be exempt from this 'sun tax' until 2020. And the Balearic Islands of Mallorca and Menorca will pay a reduced price.

Off-grid installations are not within the regulatory scope of this Royal Decree and shall obviously not pay any grid tax whatsoever.

In this context, it is fair to affirm that the main problem with the new Royal Decree 900/2015, is that it taxes self-consumption for all the PV installations above 10kW even for the electricity they produce for their own use, and is not fed into the grid and it also charges the self-consumer for the simple use of a storage facility connected to his generation facility.

6.4 Energy storage connected to the electricity network

In this context and despite the limited legislation which currently exists in Spain, it seems clear that there is an awareness of the vitally important role that energy storage services will take on in the coming years. This has been reflected not only in the investments carried out by the private sector, both in and outside the Spanish borders, but also by the plans furthered and developed by the Spanish TSO, Red Eléctrica de Spain (REE).

---

[27] Explanatory Memorandum of Law 24/2013, December 26th, on the Electricity Sector

As previously stated, even if there is no specific regulation relating to energy storage connected to the electric network (including distribution or transmission services) REE, has launched the Project Almacena[28] with the aim of evaluating the results of storage systems connected to the transport network for future development. This is an important milestone for the storage sector, as it represents the first connection Project between the storage facilities with the transmission network, being funded by the European Regional Development Fund (ERDF).

The Project consist of a field installation located in Carmona (Sevilla) of a prismatic ion-lithium battery with a power of 1 MW and capacity of at least 3MW and provides important benefits such as the greater presence of renewable generation and its unpredictable nature, along with the need to manage large variations between the peak and valley of electricity demand and operating the system ensuring security and quality of supply.

6.5 Conclusions

Currently, there is no specific legal framework applicable to energy storage services in Spain. This lack of regulation increases the uncertainty to develop this technology in Spain which could prove very useful not only on a small-scale basis but also to help achieve the RE goals set for 2020.

Effectively, Law 24/2013 only makes a minor reference to energy storage services but neither defines it nor settles an administrative and legal procedure. Moreover, at regulatory level, RD 900/2015 includes the possibility to attach storage services to generation facilities as long as they comply with quality and security requirements and share the connection point, not providing further information.

In this context, the Low Voltage Regulation (REBT) currently becomes the unique rule which establishes a legal and technical procedure applicable to energy storage facilities. However, in a sector as regulated as the energy sector, a specific legal framework is needed which regulates both the energy storage services themselves as well as their connection with both electric generation facilities and transmission and distribution networks.

Currently if the installed power is less than 10 kW the installation established plus the storage facility shall not pay any extra charge in addition to the energy consumed from the network. However, if the installed power exceeds 10 kW, the so-called *"sun tax"* shall be charged, taking into account the power of the storage facility as the fixed quota and the self-consumed energy as the variable factor of the aforementioned quota.

---

[28] http://www.ree.es/es/red21/idi/proyectos-idi/proyecto-almacena

7. GENERAL CONCLUSION

From the all the above we believe one can conclude de following:

1. If each country currently has a different electricity power structure and mix, electricity storage is a clear key technology for the development of the power system considering the increasing market share of renewable and distributed generation and the growing limitation of the energy grid.

2. There is not one single storage solution or technology above others. Storage will be needed at different locations throughout the power grid and with different capacities.

3. Modifications of the existing regulation is needed to facilitate and support the storage deployment needed.

4. Today, no commonly recognized and agreed legal guidelines exist regarding energy storage. Such general regulation framework should be agreed, for example at the European Union level, as these would help Utilities reconsider their existing business model and help defined their future responsibilities and liabilities in distributing and supplying electricity.

5. A commonly agreed legal framework would also facilitate the definition of the value proposition for energy storage which in turn would positively impact on the disposition of private financial means which are key and necessary to achieve the required deployment of energy storage facilities.

6. The aforementioned regulation should seek a twofold objective: (i) clarify and simplify the technical regulations required in order to implement electricity storage facilities; (ii) recognize the economic benefits to be reaped by the electricity system as a result of the implementation of storage facilities, in terms of reducing network access costs or incentives for the use of electricity storage.

III

GOVERNANCE AND INTERNATIONAL COOPERATION

Modern Renewable Energy: Approaching the Tipping Point?

PAUL ISBELL

CAF Energy Fellow, Center for Transatlantic Relations,
Johns Hopkins University, USA

After a pause in the pace of renewable energy development in the northern Atlantic regions of North America and Europe following the 2008-9 financial crisis and global recession, the momentum of modern renewable energy (RE) – as distinguished from 'low carbon' energy[1] -- has picked up again globally, but also across the Atlantic Basin. Not the anti-renewable energy backlash (both in Northern Atlantic energy policy and in the global investment markets) that followed the crash, nor even the great oil price collapse of 2014-15 -- from over 100 dollars a barrel to less than half that today – has managed to halt the growth of modern RE deployment within the Atlantic world. Although the energy plan of president Donald Trump is manifestly pro-fossil fuel and anti-regulation, it will not necessarily represent more than a temporary short-term slowdown in what will likely remain an increasingly intense long-term development of modern REs.

As this chapter intends to demonstrate, a number of key factors have recently shifted their dynamics, while a number of critical protagonists and agents have changed their positions on the relevant global energy maps, such that the arguments of the incumbent energy class – which justify fossil energy subsidization despite the continued structural advantage of the incumbent, while denying the political legitimacy and economic logic of renewable energy support -- are now wearing thin. Recent developments on all four Atlantic continents suggest that modern REs -- primarily solar (photovoltaic, or PV, both utility- and small-scale, along with different forms of concentrated solar power, or CSP) and wind power (both onshore and, increasingly, offshore), but also geothermal power and different forms of bioenergy -- have now positioned the low carbon revolution at a tipping point in the West.

---

[1] For the purposes of this chapter, 'modern renewable energy' is defined to include wind, solar and geothermal power (and, in certain specified instances, it also may include bioenergy). 'Low carbon energy' incorporates 'modern REs' but it also includes nuclear power and conventional 'renewable' energy, like hydroelectric power.

This chapter will bring such long controversial terrain up to date in a brief review of the recent past, the current moment, and some possible futures of the historic transition from a fossil fuel-driven energy economy to a low carbon reality, with a focus on the Atlantic Basin. It will also offer initial reflections on the meaning of a Trump presidency for modern REs. And while such a limited 'chapter' cannot possibly be exhaustive, it hopes be indicative.

1. RECENT EVOLUTION OF RE DEPLOYMENT

If the shale revolution in the US surprised nearly everyone, the intensity and resilience of the rollout of renewable energy capacity over the last ten years has also caught certain quarters off-guard. This remarkable resilience of modern REs in the face of both the shale revolution and the oil price decline has been particularly noteworthy in Asia, but also across most of the Atlantic Basin. Indeed, the IEA has already undershot in its projections for the development of modern REs within the global energy mix on a number occasions in the past – and, as a result, has overstated the future vigor and longevity of fossil fuels, one of the central arguments of the fossil fuel classes.

For example, in 2006 the IEA's World Energy Outlook projection for solar energy generation was for 34 TWh in 2015 and 238 TWh in 2030. However, actual solar rollout has been far more intense: 253 TWh in 2015 (out of a global total of 24,100 TWh, or 1% of the global generation mix). In fact, more than 50 GW of solar power capacity are being added each year to the global energy system.[2] Under-projection characterizes the evolution of wind power, as well: although in 2006 the IEA projected 449 TWh of wind generation in 2015, according to BP wind generated 841 TWh of electricity globally last year.[3]

Investment in Modern REs

Investment in modern REs globally peaked in 2011 at $279bn. With the second phase of the global economic crisis unfolding in Europe, however, and with the wave of consolidation that took place within renewable energy sectors (like bioenergy or solar power), global investment levels fell to a trough in 2013 at $234. Since then, a strong recovery has brought global RE investment levels to a level now just above their previous 2011 peak, at $286bn in 2015.[4] (See Table 1) More than half of this investment in modern REs last year was made in solar PV (US$67bn in rooftop solar PV, US$92bn in utility-scale PV systems, and US$267mn for off-grid applications).[5]

---

[2]   David Hone, "Solar deployment rates," The Energy Collective, August 31, 2016.
[3]   BP Statistical Review of World Energy, June 2016.
[4]   Frankfurt School-UNEP Centre/Bloomberg New Energy Finance, Global Trends in New Energy Investment, 2016.
[5]   IRENA, The Power to Change: Solar and Wind Cost Reduction Potential to 2025, June 2016.

Within the Atlantic Basin, investment levels have now either recovered their pre-crisis peak, or continue to rise again towards it – at least in three out of the four continents of the Basin. In the US, the 2011 peak of $49bn has nearly been regained ($44bn in 2015), while in Latin America and Africa current investment levels now exceed their previous peaks. However, in Europe – once the clear leader in RE investment – levels continue to decline each year, falling from $123bn in 2011 to less than $49bn in 2015. (See Table 1). In the meantime, however, the Asia Pacific region (which includes Oceania), has continue to register rising RE investment levels during each of the last five years.

Table 1. Modern Renewable Energy, Investment, $ billion, 2000-15

$ bn	2010	2011	2012	2013	2014	2015
World	239.19	278.5	257.26	233.99	273.03	286.19 *
Atlantic Basin	171.38	194.44	157.61	120.99	128.19	125.57
US	34.72	49.06	40.65	35.33	37.05	44.1
Brazil	7.24	10.23	7.66	4.41	7.97	7.14
Other Americas	11.98	9.29	10.09	12	13.28	12.83
Africa*	4.06	2.98	10.16	9.27	7.9	12.74
Europe	113.38	122.88	89.05	59.98	61.99	48.76
Great Crescent**	NA	NA	NA	NA	NA	NA
Asia Pacific	67.81	84.06	99.65	113	144.84	160.62
China	39.64	47.44	61.7	62.01	87.78	102.9
India	8.84	12.78	7.78	6.56	8.3	10.16
Other Asian and Oceania	19.33	23.84	30.17	44.43	48.76	47.56

* This 2015 figure was adjusted upward by IRENA to $304 billion at the beginning of 2017.

Note: Data from IRENA, Data and Statistics, Featured Dashboard. Source: Frankfurt School-UNEP Centre/Bloomberg New Energy Finance, *Global Trends in New Energy Investment, 2016*. Note: NA = not available. ** The data from this source groups RE investment in the Middle East -- a negligible figure up to 2015 -- together with that of Africa; however, given that Africa has installed more than three times as much modern RE capacity as the Middle East (7GW vs 1.27GW), we assume that the large majority of the 'Africa' figures represents RE investment in Africa, as opposed to the Middle East. **Investment figures for Eurasia are not reported by this source.

Modern RE rollout

Despite the drop-off in RE *investment* in the Atlantic Basin as a whole (from $194bn in 2011 to $126bn in 2015), modern RE *rollout* (expressed as accumulated installed capacity in GW) has continued rapidly apace. Installed RE capacity increased nearly ten-fold in the Atlantic Basin from 2000 (46 GW) to 2015 (443 GW), but it rose nearly five-fold from 2005 and nearly doubled again over the last five years (from 223 GW in 2010). Since 2005, the RE rollout pace has been the fastest in Africa (536%) and Latin America (482%) – although they have been growing from much smaller bases – and in North America (455%). Europe still leads the Atlantic continents in terms of absolute levels of installed RE capacity (248 GW in 2015, or one-third of the global total), but its growth rate has slowed considerably during the last five years.[6] (See Table 2)

Table 2. Modern Renewable Energy, Electrical Capacity Installed, 2000-15

GW in-stalled	2000	2005	2010	2015	% of total 2015	% growth 2005-15
World	59.8	117.6	305.3	757		
Atlantic Basin	45.75	92.7	223	442.7	58.5%	378%
North America	16.7	23.9	62.5	132.7	17.5%	455%
Latin America	5.5	6.0	14.8	34.9	4.6%	482%
CA & Carib.	1.6	1.8	2.3	4.8	0.6%	167%
S. America	3.9	4.2	12.5	30.1	4.0%	617%
Africa	0.85	1.1	2.1	7.0	0.9%	536%
Europe	22.7	61.7	143.6	248.1	32.8%	302%
Great Cres-cent	1.39	1.54	3.05	8.67	1.1%	463%
Eurasia	1.38	1.48	2.83	7.4	1.0%	400%
Middle East	0.014	0.060	0.221	1.27	0.2%	2017%
Asia Pacific	12.5	23.3	79.2	293.5	38.8%	1160%
Asia	11.5	20.9	74.6	281.5	37.2%	1247%
Oceania	1	2.4	4.6	12	1.6%	400%

Source: Data from IRENA, Data and Statistics, Featured Dashboard.

[6] IRENA, Data and Statistics, Featured Dashboard.

At the global level, in 2000 there were 60 GW of installed capacity in modern REs and 842 GW of installed capacity in low-carbon sources (including modern REs and all hydropower). This rose to 118 GW and 987 GW, respectively, in 2005; to 305 GW and 1,331 GW in 2010; and 757 GW and 1,965 GW by 2015.[7] Nearly two-fifths of all globally installed capacity in modern REs is located in the Asia-Pacific region, where it has grown by a whopping 1160% over the last decade (if from what was originally a much smaller base).

2. FOSSIL FUEL INCUMBENCY

One of the central arguments (and, rhetorically, one of the most effective) long used by the fossil fuel industry and its allies has been to claim that, whatever happens, fossil fuels are here to stay, set to dominate the world's energy mix for decades and decades to come. The claim typically involves invoking the 'business as usual' projections for the global energy scenario, annually developed by the world's most respected national and international energy institutions -- like the International Energy Agency (IEA) or the US's Energy Information Agency (EIA) – and private sector companies (like BP, Exxon and Total), which almost inevitably foresee fossil fuels providing around 80% or so of global energy indefinitely into the future – or at least to 2040. Indeed, according to BP, fossil fuels constituted 86% of the world's primary energy mix in 2015. Furthermore, BP's regularly revised projections of the business-as-usual future currently see this share falling to only 79% by 2035.

From there the argument usually concludes with the derivative claim that any significant attempt to rapidly and deeply displace fossil fuels with renewable energy is not realistically possible, and that undue pressures on fossil fuel companies to reduce their share of GHG emissions are not sensible, or even legitimate, bound only to reduce growth and destroy wealth. It should be obvious, however, that the argument that fossil fuels should continue to dominate the global energy mix over the mid- and long-run future – simply and mainly because they 'inevitably' will – is dangerously tautological, given that such a claim relies upon the assumption that we do not consciously change the trajectory of status quo behavior and dynamics, particularly with respect to fossil fuel incumbency, dominance or centrality.

Yet despite this recent surge in modern RE deployment, fossil fuels remain entrenched, at least for the moment, as the dominant sector in both the global electricity mix and in the broader global primary energy mix (which also incorporates the transportation sector, the last bastion of oil within the global energy economy, and industry, the last bastion of coal, particularly in Asia).

---

[7] IRENA, Data and Statistics, Featured Dashboard.

This continued dominance can be easily grasped from a presentation of the global electricity mix. (See Figures 1 and 2) Approximately two-thirds of both installed capacity and generation globally is fired by fossil fuels, mainly coal and gas but also oil.

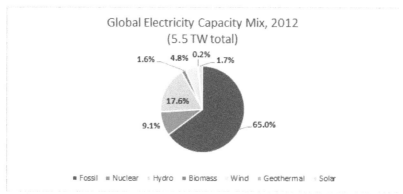

Figure 1. Global Electricity 'Capacity Mix' 2012
Source: EIA, 2016. Note: TW = terrawatts.

Modern REs (wind, solar and geothermal) accounted for only 6.7% of all installed capacity, even after the surge in deployment documented above (and a mere 8.3% if biomass-generated electricity is included in the RE share). Modern RE's share in the global generation mix (3.1%) is even more modest, given the comparatively low capacity factors of 'variable' REs like wind and solar power.

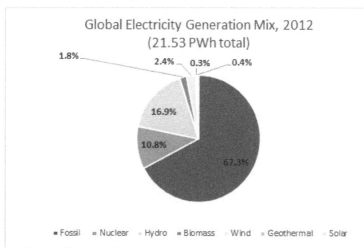

Figure 2. Global Electricity 'Generation Mix' 2012
Source: EIA, 2016. Note: PWh = pentawatt-hour.

Current fossil fuel dominance – and modern RE marginality – is even more starkly revealed by the global final energy consumption mix, which includes the transportation, industry and buildings sectors, in addition to electricity. Modern REs accounted for only 2.7% of all the energy consumed in the world during 2015 (see Figure 3). Fossil fuels contributed nearly 86% of all the final energy consumed.

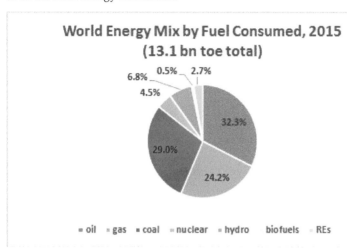

World Energy Mix by Fuel Consumed, 2015 (13.1 bn toe total)

6.8% 0.5% 2.7%
4.5%
32.3%
29.0%
24.2%

■ oil ■ gas ■ coal ■ nuclear ■ hydro biofuels ■ REs

Figure 3. Global Final Energy Consumption Mix, 2015
Source: BP Annual World Energy Statistics, 2016. Note bn toe = billion tons of 'oil equivalent.'

Most current analysis of the evolution and prospects for modern REs focuses on global and national efforts to 'decarbonize' the power sector, where REs have their most direct and obvious applications. According to annual data from the US Energy Information Agency (EIA), as of 2012 the global power sector had a total of 5.55 TW of installed capacity, which generated a total of 21,532 TWh of electricity. This is the 'oil equivalent' of 4.9 billion tons of oil of electricity generated globally in 2012.[8] BP reported 12.52 bn toe of total global energy consumed in 2012. This means that the global electricity sector contributes to only 39% of global energy consumption before accounting for transmission losses, and only 33% if assuming an average 15% transmission loss on average globally.

This has a number of implications. First, efforts to decarbonize the power sector only can reach up to between one-third and two-fifths of the global energy economy. The GHG emissions of the other 60%-70% remain

---

[8] One million tons of oil or oil equivalent produces about 4400 gigawatt-hours (= 4.4 terawatt hours) of electricity in a modern power station.

beyond the reach of renewables servicing the power sector as it now stands. Indeed, BP's projection of the most likely future in 2035 (that is to say, the 'business-as-usual' scenario) still foresees, fossil fuels contributing nearly 80% of the total global final energy mix (see Figure 4). As a result, modern REs are likely to prove capable of incorporating the transportation, industrial and buildings sectors *only through the progressive electrification of these, the largest parts of the energy economy.*

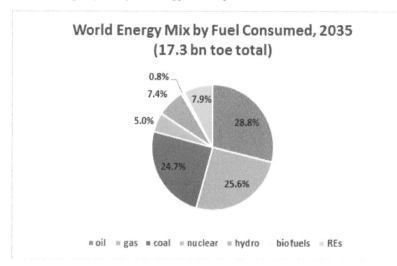

World Energy Mix by Fuel Consumed, 2035 (17.3 bn toe total)

oil ▪ gas ▪ coal ▪ nuclear ▪ hydro biofuels ▪ REs

Figure 4. Global Final Energy Consumption Mix, 2035
Source: BP Annual World Energy Statistics 2016.

Second, not only must RE-generated electricity displace petroleum in the transportation sector across the globe, but in Asia-Pacific, in particular, coal's centrality in the power and industry energy mixes must be broken at a much faster rate than the business as usual attrition projected by BP. Table 3, which breaks down BP's global energy mix projections into the global system's two major geographic components – the Atlantic Basin (Europe, Africa, Latin America and North America) and Asia Pacific (the rest of Eurasia and Oceania except the ex-Soviet/Russian sphere and the Middle, or the 'Great Crescent') – reveals the principal difference in the fossil fuel dominance (and its fading) of these two macroregions. While the Atlantic Basin will remain relatively (and overly) dependent on the hydrocarbons (oil 34% and gas 31%), coal will have been significantly displaced (with only 9% of the mix in 2035). On the other hand, in Asia-Pacific, the region's historic super-dependence on coal will still define the final energy mix, under the current 'business as usual' trajectory, in 2035 (nearly 43%).

Table 3. Current and Projected 'Business as Usual' Global Final Energy Mix, 2015 and 2035

	World		Atlantic Basin		Asia-Pacific	
	2015	2035	2015	2035	2015	2035
Fossil Fuels	**85.5%**	**79.1%**	**84.2%**	**74.2%**	**89.5**	**80.7**
oil	*32.3%*	*28.8%*	*38.1%*	*34.4%*	*27.3%*	*24.7%*
gas	*24.2%*	*25.6%*	*27.1%*	*30.5%*	*11.5%*	*13.1%*
coal	*29%*	*24.7%*	*19%*	*9.3%*	*50.7%*	*42.9%*
Low Carbon	**14.5%**	**21.1%**	**19.6%**	**24.8%**	**10.5**	**19.2**
Nuclear	*4.5%*	*5%*	*7.4%*	*5.6%*	*1.7%*	*4.9%*
Hydropower	*6.8%*	*7.4%*	*7.9%*	*9.2%*	*6.5%*	*6.7%*
Biofuels	*0.5%*	*0.8%*	*0.22%*	*0.28%*	*0.15%*	*0.19%*
Modern REs	*2.7%*	*7.9%*	*4.1%*	*10.7%*	*2.1%*	*7.4%*
Total Energy Consumed (bn toe)	**13.1**	**17.3**	**5.75**	**6.7**	**5.4**	**8.2**

Source: BP Energy Outlook 2016.

3. EXCESSIVE RE COSTS?

Another increasingly weak argument of the fossil fuel apologists is that renewable energies are simply too expensive, that they cannot compete economically with fossil fuels. Ignoring the numerous structural factors favoring fossil fuels – and even more the long-standing tendency of RE costs to decline rapidly with time – this argument is typically then wedded to the first: fossil fuels will and, therefore (!) must remain the mainstay of the energy mix, simply because to promote renewables through active policy intervention would be, from this 'point of view', simply economic suicide.

To begin with, the fossil fuel industry has not only enjoyed the inherent structural economic advantage that comes with position of the dominant incumbent energy source and technology, it has also been able to leverage that position to increase it protection against the emerging economic competition of alternative energy sources. The IEA estimated last year that fossil fuel subsidies came to more than $550bn in 2014.[9] Data from the IMF confirms these levels – some five times higher than the equivalent figure for subsidies

---

[9] Kraemer and Stefes, "The Changing Energy Landscape in the Atlantic Space," in Jordi Bacaria and Laia Tarragona, (eds.), Atlantic Future: Shaping a new hemisphere from the 21st Century Africa, Europe and the Americas, CIDOB Monograph Series, Barcelona, 2016, p. 97.

granted to renewable energies worldwide ($100bn in 2012 and $120bn in 2014).[10] Furthermore, the Fund also has estimated that 'post-tax' subsidies to fossil fuel companies were as high as $1.7tn in 2012[11], and that if all of fossil fuel's 'negative externalities' are taken into account (eg, air pollution) then the overall subsidy to fossil fuel energy globally would top $5tn.[12]

But the most important news in the energy sector has been the dramatic decline of RE costs, despite the recent decline in oil prices, and even in the face of the lopsided public subsidy advantage of fossil fuels. (See Tables 4 and 5) Renewable energy costs have been declining by 15% to 25% each year now for nearly two decades and have now reached, in many parts of the world, the cost parity point with subsidized fossil fuel and nuclear energy, even as RE costs continue to decline.[13] One estimate, from Lazard's, shows that the 'levelized cost of energy' from wind and solar power fell by 61% and 82% respectively over the six years to the end of 2015.[14] The tipping point in the US, for example – when wind and solar power will be "firmly in place as the cheapest kilowatt-hours around" – is now projected to occur over the next five years, by the time the recently renewed renewable energy tax credits are set to expire after 2020.[15]

Table 4. Trends in Global RE Levelised Cost of Electricity 2010-2015 (Ranges and Weighted Averages)

2015 USD/kWh	2010	2015
Hydropower	0.046	0.046
Onshore wind	0.071	0.060
Offshore wind	0.157	0.159
Solar PV	0.285	0.126
Solar thermal	0.331	0.245
Biomass	0.056	0.055
Geothermal	0.071	0.080

Source: IRENA, Data and Statistics, Dashboard, LCOEs 2010-2015
http://resourceirena.irena.org/gateway/dashboard/?topic=3&subTopic=33

[10] International Monetary Fund, Energy Subsidy Reform— Lessons and Implications, 2013 http://www.imf.org/external/np/pp/eng/2013/012813.pdf. (IMF 2013), and Kraemer and Stefes, 2016, p. 98.
[11] IMF, 2013, cited in Kraemer and Stefes, 2016, p. 98.
[12] Coady et al. 2015, cited in Kraemer and Stefes, op. cit.
[13] Kraemer and Stefes, 2016, p. 95, and p. 92.
[14] Lazard's Levelized Cost of Energy Analysis, Version 9.0, November 2015.
[15] Chris Nelder and Mark Silberg, "Congress extends the renewable investment tax credit: What now" greenbiz.com (https://www.greenbiz.com/article/congress-extends-renewable-investment-tax-credit-what-now), December 28. 2015.

The International Renewable Energy Agency (IRENA) foresees these costs continuing to plummet over the next ten years, driven by expanded economies of scale, increasingly competitive supply chains and further technological advances. With the appropriate regulatory and policy frameworks in place, IRENA predicts that the costs for wind power will fall between 25% (onshore) and 35% (offshore) compared to levels in 2015, while those of concentrated solar power (CSP) will drop some 43% and costs of solar PV will collapse by as much as 59% by 2025.[16]

Solar power now looms at the edge of an inflection point. With costs projected to fall another 60% over the coming decade, IRENA sees solar PV alone accounting for as much as 13% of the global generation mix as early as 2030 (up from only 2% in 2016)– *far outpacing BP's business-as-usual scenario which projects only 7.9% of the global primary energy mix to be accounted for by all modern REs even as late as 2035*. Already solar photovoltaic panels constitute the most "widely owned electricity source in the world in terms of number of installations." Rollout is accelerating at a much faster rate than anticipated: solar PV accounted for 20% of all new electrical generation capacity in 2015, according to IRENA, and since 2010 global installed PC capacity has expanded nearly five-fold, from 40 GW to 227 GW.[17] Although annual PV capacity additions would need to more than double in 14 years in order to achieve the 13% share in the electricity mix by 2030 that IRENA projects, it does not seem to be out of reach.

Table 5. Cost reduction potential for solar and wind power, 2015-2025

	Global weighted average data							
	Investment costs (2015 USD/kW)		Percent change	Capacity factor		Percent change[2]	LCOE (2015 USD/kWh)		Percent change
	2015	2025		2015	2025		2015	2025	
Solar PV	1 810	790	-57%	18%	19%	8%	0.13	0.06	-59%
CSP (PTC: parabolic trough collector)	5 550	3 700	-33%	41%	45%	8.4%	0.15 -0.19	0.09 -0.12	-37%
CSP (ST: solar tower)	5 700	3 600	-37%	46%	49%	7.6%	0.15 -0.19	0.08 -0.11	-43%
Onshore wind	1 560	1 370	-12%	27%	30%	11%	0.07	0.05	-26%
Offshore wind	4 650	3 950	-15%	43%	45%	4%	0.18	0.12	-35%

Source: IRENA, The Power to Change: Solar and Wind Cost Reduction Potential to 2025, June 2016

---

[16] IRENA, The Power to Change: Solar and Wind Cost Reduction Potential to 2025, June 2016.
[17] IRENA, Letting in the Light: How solar photovoltaics will revolutionise the electricity system, June 2016.

After all, as IRENA reports: "Solar PV regularly costs just 5 to 10 US cents (USD 0.05-0.10) per kilowatt-hour (kWh) in Europe, China, India, South Africa and the United States." Record low prices were registered in the United Arab Emirates (5.84 cents/kWh), Peru (4.8 cents/kWh) and Mexico (4.8 cents/kWh).[18] Such low solar auction bids bear out and reinforce the strong trend of cost reduction projected by IRENA for solar power in the coming decade.

4. LONGER TERM OUTLOOK

Although in the short run, the outlook for modern REs may remain muddied, or even become volatile, as a result of the election of Donald Trump to the presidency in the US (more on this below), in the long run the only development that could halt the low carbon revolution, and even the decarbonization of the world's power sectors – at least in the Atlantic Basin and Asia-Pacific – would be cheaper than anticipated fossil fuel energy sources, possibly even increasingly subsidized. Yet even this kind of fossil revival is increasingly unlikely.

A new study by Bloomberg New Energy Finance (New Energy Outlook 2016) isolates some of the new aspects of the emerging pathway to the future that BP (and other fossil fuel-focused entities) miss in their projections of the likely business-as-usual future -- particularly the radical fall in RE costs. The BNEF study concludes with this central, synthetic projection:

> "Cheaper coal and cheaper gas will not derail the transformation and decarbonisation of the world's power systems. By 2040, zero-emission energy sources will make up 60% of installed capacity. Wind and solar will account for 64% of the 8.6 TW of new power generating capacity added worldwide over the next 25 years, and for almost 60% of the $11.4 trillion invested."[19]

Of that $11.4 trillion that BNEF projects will be invested in the global electricity sector in the years to 2040, only $1.2 trillion will go into new coal-burning capacity, and only $892 billion into new gas-fired plants. This may surprise many expecting a gas-based fossil renaissance. Meanwhile, $7.8 trillion will be invested in low carbon electricity (or 'green power' in the language of BNEF), with $3.1 trillion going into (both on- and offshore) wind power, $3.4 trillion into utility-scale, rooftop and other small-scale solar power, and $911 billion into hydroelectricity.[20]

---

[18]   Ibid. However, more recent RE auctions in Latin America and the Persian Gulf have even produced prices as low as 3.0 cents/kWh, or lower.
[19]   BNEF New Energy Outlook 2016.
[20]   Ibid.

But for the world to follow a 2ºC-consistent scenario pathway – like the IEA's 450 Scenario, for example -- would require much larger investment sums: an additional $5.3 trillion in 'green power' by 2040 would be needed, according the BNEF, "to prevent CO2 in the atmosphere rising above the Intergovernmental Panel on Climate Change's 'safe' limit of 450 parts per million." Furthermore, a successful 2ºC-consistent pathway may require foregoing much of even the limited fossil fuel investment in the power sector projected by BNEF. In February 2016, a team at Oxford University concluded that to have even a chance of defending the 2-degree guardrail, all power plants built after 2017 would have to be zero carbon.[21] This would leave 'stranded' at least the plans for thousands of coal and gas power plants currently on the boards around the world, given that carbon capture and sequestration technologies are not yet available commercially.[22]

If BNEF's new business-as-usual projection (or 'new status quo pathway') captures more of the realities and potentials of the low carbon revolution than those of the fossil fuel sector (represented here by BP), it does not capture all of the aspects and dynamics of the low carbon revolution that might impose themselves upon the status quo simply through the force of economics. First, BNEF's projections are based upon estimates for future declines in RE costs that are significantly more modest than those projected by IRENA (see above). Whereas IRENA projects that costs will fall between 25% (onshore) and 35% (offshore) for wind power, and between 40% (CSP) and 60% (PV) for solar over the coming decade, BNEF foresees that the levelized cost of electricity (per MWh) for onshore wind will fall by 41%, and for solar PV by 60%, *but only by 2040*.[23]

Although BNEF claims that "these two technologies (will be) the cheapest ways of producing electricity in many countries during the 2020s and in most of the world in the 2030s," low carbon electricity would still only generate 70% of Europe's power in 2040, up from 32% in 2015, and only 44% in the US.[24] But to reach a 2-degree scenario, the penetration of modern REs will have to be even higher. Faster than expected cost declines, like those projected by IRENA, could be responsible for a deeper penetration of modern REs into the global power mix than even that projected by

---

[21] Alexander Pfeiffer, Richard Millar, Cameron Hepburn, Eric Beinhocker, "The '2°C capital stock' for electricity generation: Committed cumulative carbon emissions from the electricity generation sector and the transition to a green economy" *Applied Energy*, available online 24 March 2016, ISSN 0306-2619, http://dx.doi.org/10.1016/j.apenergy.2016.02.093
[22] David Fullbrook, "A turning point looms for electricity and climate" *Energy Post*, August 31, 2016.
[23] BNEF New Energy Outlook 2016.
[24] Ibid.

BNEF.[25] This suggests that declining RE costs could be the crucial variable in nudging the world onto a 2-degree consistent pathway in time to avert the worst damages from climate change.

The second variable that could change the future of modern REs as a share of the global energy mix would be the question of electrification, primarily of the transportation sector, but also potentially of much of the industrial and building sectors. While it would be unrealistic to expect all of the global energy economy to be electrified, even over the long run, in most of the world's megacities and in densely populated regions (where most of the world's population resides) it would be feasible. We could even expect Europe and Latin America to take the lead.

As mentioned above, in 2012 electricity represented some 39% of the global energy consumed -- before approximately 15% transmission losses are assumed worldwide (ie, the 'secondary mix'), and only 33% after (ie, the final consumption mix). By 2015, the share of energy inputs used for global power had increased to 42%, but it was projected by BP to rise to only 45% by 2035, reflecting only minimal electrification of transport by then, as most of this increase is projected to come from countries where much of the population still remains beyond the reach of electricity services.[26]

The BNEF projection, however, does foresee the penetration of electric vehicles (EVs) increasing electricity demand by 8% in 2040, making a claim on an additional 2,701 TWh to be produced by the power sector annually. By that time, according to BNEF, EVs will have expanded 90 times (to some 41mn cars) and account for 35% of new annual light-duty vehicle sales.[27] Yet, while BNEF foresees a much larger share for modern REs by 2040 than that implicit in BP's projection to 2035, in part driven by a faster assumed penetration by EVs into the global vehicle fleet, it still leaves an insufficient share of the global energy mix covered by low carbon energy, particularly modern REs. This is because the BNEF forecast assumes that the bulk of the transportation fuel mix will still be supplied by hydrocarbon-based liquids over the long run.

The BNEF scenario only projects just over 40mn EVs in 2040, when there could be as many as 2.5 billion vehicles operating on the planet (BP projects around 2.3 bn for 2035). In other words, there remains tremendous scope for the electrification of transportation and other sectors to amplify

[25] Interestingly enough, the BNEF outlook does not envision any 'golden age' for gas, or even a significant role as a 'bridge' fuel, except to some extent in North America. The share of gas in the global energy mix is projected to be outstripped by renewable energies in 2027, some 10 years before they are projected to overtake coal.
[26] BP Energy Outlook 2016.
[27] BNEF New Energy Outlook 2016.

the capacity of modern REs to reduce the outstanding GHG emissions gap by more deeply displacing fossil fuels. Indeed, the real bastion of the entrenched market-place advantage of fossil fuel structural incumbency lies in the transportation sector; more rapid expansion of EVs and widespread potential for electrification of the economy is what threatens it the most.

5. PEAK OIL DEMAND

More than any other variable, the penetration rate of electricity into the transport fuel mix will determine the longevity of fossil fuel dominance and the approximate date of the 'end of oil.' A broad and interesting range of projections have recently been made concerning the future evolution of global oil demand. Some oil companies, like BP and Exxon, do not foresee oil demand peaking any time before 2040. BP projects oil demand will rise from 87mbd in 2015 to 100mbd in 2035, while Exxon believes oil demand will grow 20% by 2040.[28]

However, the IEA's 450 scenario (in theory consistent with defending the 2-degree guardrail) requires oil demand to be as low as 80mbd in 2035 and 74mbd in 2040.[29] In addition, two out of the three recent World Energy Council scenarios for 2040 project global oil demand to peak in 2030.[30] But the recent acceleration of the rollout of electric vehicles, together with the slowdown in demand from China and the continued increase in conventional vehicle efficiency are beginning to point to the possible risk of an earlier peak in the global demand for oil than even the WEC has foreseen.

But BNEF has also recently projected a potential crisis in the oil sector as early as 2028, driven by peak oil demand being brought forward by accelerated electrification of transportation, generating a supply glut of some 2mbd – equal to that which provoked the 2014 collapse in oil prices -- and sending hydrocarbons companies into a "death spiral" in the markets. An update by BNEF, along with a similar yet more recent projection made by Fitch, brings this crisis date for oil forward to 2023.[31] Finally, the most telling projection of all has just come from the industry itself – from Shell -- which allows for the possibility of peak oil demand occurring as early as 2021.[32]

[28] Tyler Durden, "Shell Warns that 'Peak Oil Demand' May be Reached in 2021," zerohedge. com, Nov. 6, 2016.
[29] Claudio Aranzadi, "Introduccion" in Energia y Geoestrategia 2016, IEEE-CECME-Enerclub, Madrid, 2016, p. 12.
[30] World Energy Council, World Energy Scenarios 2016.
[31] Joe Romm, "Electric car revolution may drive 'oil investor death spiral," ThinkProgress. org, October 16, 2016.
[32] Durden, ibid.

The upshot is that the current business-as-usual trajectory for global energy – modified recently by the acceleration of EV penetration – will imply the prospect of significant 'stranded assets' in the fossil fuel industries. Recent studies posit that "more than 80% of current coal reserves, half of all gas reserves and a third of oil reserves must remain unburned through at least 2050."[33] Carbon Tracker has estimated that such usuable, 'stranded assets' currently on the books of global energy companies could be worth $2.2 trillion.[34]

Although such an accelerated scenario may seem to reflect the increasingly strong economic in favor of modern REs, it certainly signals a coming struggle for the world's markets, as the hydrocarbons sector is likely to continue vie with the renewable energy sector for regulatory influence and infrastructural lock-in.

6. THE POLICY HORIZON FOR MODERN RES

International Scene

The Paris Climate Accord firmly establishes the international community's goal and universally accepted imperative to limit the future rise in global temperatures to no more than 1.5C-2C above pre-industrial levels. This historic international agreement is an undeniable signal of the inevitable low carbon transition to come: it lays down a clear policy marker for national governments, the energy industry and the investor community and provides for a powerful stimulus for the creation of new clean energy markets.

The agreement establishes the critical framework within which the relevant protagonists – energy and related companies, investors, consumers and policy makers at all levels of jurisdiction – make decisions moving forward. The agreement engages a critical mass of global actors with a different pattern of incentives and therefore a different dynamic than that which has dominated energy markets and policies for the past several decades. It has already been ratified by the required 55% of the parties to the agreement covering at least 55% of global GHG emissions, and would still meet such quotas even should the US 'withdraw,' as the new president has promised. In any event, the design of the Paris accord allows that US presidential executive authority is sufficient to 'ratify' it (as opposed to requiring the ratification of the US senate, as in the case of a

---

[33] Christophe McGlade and Paul Elkins, "The geographical distribution of fossil fuels unused when limiting global warming to 2 °C," *Nature*, January 2015, vol. 517, p. 187.
[34] Barbara Grady, "Stranded assets may add up to $2.2 trillion – blame COP21?" Greenbiz. com, November 24, 2015.

formal binding treaty), and the same is true for a withdrawal or even an eventual re-entry.

Nevertheless, even with perfect compliance with the commitments contained in the 187 INDCs there will remain a significant 'emissions gap' with the levels required to defend the 2-degree guardrail. The five-year reviews to which the parties must submit themselves will help by allowing for the possibly of 'ratcheting up' national commitments, but they will also remain vulnerable to the disruptions caused by possible exogenous shocks along the way.

Massive uncertainties remain, as most national commitments are vulnerable to domestic policy changes. Furthermore, a newly emerging backlash to international climate action is potentially taking shape in the form of ethno-nationalist movements that could capture the governments of many Western countries, at least for some years.

The potential impact of President Trump in the US

The election of Donald Trump in the US presents just the kind of exogenous shock the could symbolically scuttle the Paris agreement and throw more roadblocks in the way of renewable energy in the US, in many ways the global sector's leader. Trump's energy plan during the election campaign was a superficial reproduction of the long-standing Republican party platform which prioritizes domestic fossil fuels under the banner of an 'all of the above' national energy strategy (meaning open, if not necessarily free, competition between all domestic energy sources). He has also pledged to eliminate the EPA and to reverse all of the EPA's action under Obama, along with the rest of Obama's executive orders on energy and climate change. Such pledges also include a repeal of Obama's Clean Power Plan and a 'withdrawal' of the US from the Paris Agreement. Trump's proposed rollback of regulations includes an extensive opening of federal lands (and offshore areas) to more oil and gas drilling, and a more *laissez faire* federal attitude toward 'fracking'. He has also promised to reverse the Obama Administration's rejection of the Keystone XL pipeline. Indeed, Trump has already signed a number of executive orders on energy (one begins the long and complicated process of dismantling the CPP while another has finally cleared the way for the Keystone XL pipeline).

Trump's plans for energy have generally been considered to be beneficial, on balance, for fossil fuels, and negative, or at least potentially problematic, for renewable energy. But Trump has shifted positions on both renewable energy and climate change over the years, so there is little clarity or certainty generated by his stated positions at any particular moment – at least until policy begins to be formulated and implemented.

Nevertheless, the energy and environment team that Trump has begun to appoint includes a number of climate change 'sceptics' and advocates for the oil and gas industries.

On the other hand, energy and climate change do not appear to be high on the list of priorities for Trump's transition team and the first 100 days of the new administration. Far more attention is being given to health care and tax proposals, border issues and 'national security.' Furthermore, there are some reasons to suspect that even an aggressive policy of fossil fuel deregulation by the Trump administration will not necessarily derail the nascent boom in modern REs.

First, coal won't survive on Trump's rhetoric alone, and the new shale gas boom he promises would undercut much of what is left of the sector, and modern REs will take care of the rest through the force of lower costs. Opening up more federal lands to more oil and gas drilling will also change little -- in part because this argument has always been something of a canard, given that oil companies have left undeveloped most of the leases they have long held on the federal lands that are open to fossil fuel activity; and in part also because the oil and gas companies already have an abundance of booked reserves to develop. Low oil and gas prices – and their increasingly muddied future outlook – along with the continued momentum of REs – are the major barrier to more drilling in the US and they may actually present the danger of significant stranded assets.

Trump has revived the prospects for the Keystone XL pipeline – and this will assist with the struggles of the Dakota pipeline, but the overall impact will be minimal beyond some localities and for some companies. Congressional oversight could at least complicate Trump's intention of reversing Obama's executive directives to the EPA, and the Democrats in the Senate retain the capacity to block any legislation, including an elimination of the EPA, by using the 'filibuster' mechanism which requires a supermajority of 60 votes. Furthermore, infrastructure proposals, in general, continued to face the same stock 'fiscal' opposition as always from the Republican leaders of Congress. Indeed, the most direct damage Trump is unleashing is budgetary -- his new budget outline proposes a 31% budget cut for the EPA, for example, and another 28% cut for the Department of State.

While none of the above will help the deployment of modern REs, such actions, effective or not, may not have much direct impact. Much more important to the short and mid-term future of renewable energy development in the US are the investment and production tax credits for REs which were recently reinstated by the US congress. If Trump or the

Congress were to rescind these tax credits (which are the principal support for renewable energy at the national federal level in the US), the short-term outlook would be negatively affected. The last time the Production Tax Credit (which provides a wind farm with a tax credit of 2.3 cents per kilowatt-hour of electricity produced during the first 10 years of production for a new project) expired in 2012, new wind power projects dropped by 92% the following year, although they rebounded once the credit was renewed.[35] The Investment Tax Credit, for its part, provides a 30% tax credit to individual households or commercial solar plants against the cost of installing a new renewable energy project.

However, many 'red states' in the Midwest, Prairie and Western states are heavily invested in wind power and stand to gain if they are not rescinded, and vice versa. For example, while Texas is the largest fossil fuel producing state, it is also the leader in wind power. Renewables also generate jobs and other co-benefits, which accrue not only on the coasts but also across various US heartlands. Already 600,000 jobs have been created in the wind and solar sectors (equal to what critics of NAFTA says were the lost as a result of that trade deal). Although there are 3.6 million employed in the US fossil fuel industries, these sectors also contribute three-quarters of the US energy mix; but they will continue to lose share in the future. In any event, there is evidence that modern REs are more intensive in both skilled and unskilled labor than any of the fossil fuels.

Although it is true that US public opinion is increasingly polarized on climate change, more and more Americans favor renewable energy, in any case. In a recent Pew poll in the US in October, 2016, 89% wanted more solar installations and 83% wanted more wind.[36] In a March 2016 Gallup poll, 73% of Americans claimed they preferred more alternative energy to more oil and gas, including a majority (51%) of self-defined Republicans.[37]

Finally, over 28 states and many cities have put into place renewable energy mandates and climate change legislation which have already begun to reorient markets. Not only will energy policy continued to be made closer to the ground in the states, but this reality nullifies much of the potential of a Trump presidency to stop, let alone roll back, the ongoing investment in the deployment of renewables.

---

[35] Maggie Koerth-Baker, "It's Hard To Tell Whether Trump Supports Renewable Energy — And That May Not Matter Much" FiveThirtyEight.com, Nov 14, 2016.
[36] PEW Research Center, The Politics of Climate, October 4, 2016. http://www.pewinternet.org/2016/10/04/the-politics-of-climate/
[37] Koerth-Baker, op. cit.

7. TENTATIVE CONCLUSIONS

The American hydrocarbons revival of recent years – driven by the shale revolution – now faces the combined headwinds of the depressed prices that the surge in US production in part generated and the flattening demand that is structurally built into the future. Easier access to resources on federal lands and less government interference in pipelines will not materially alter the long-term outlook for fossil fuels. Ending the Clean Power plan will not save coal, and it will not stop modern REs. Withdrawing from the Paris agreement will not create an American energy renaissance out of the shale revolution – although it might undermine American leadership in the low carbon revolution, given that the Paris accord generates the parameters for global markets to be created in precisely the modern RE goods and services that US companies excel in. Eliminating the current RE tax credits, which already are set to expire in 2020, would pose a barrier to RE development in the US, at least in the short-run; but it will not stop their development globally. And domestic politics could save the US renewable energy tax credits in the end.

Although there are a number of other factors beyond the scope of this overview which could hinder the development of modern REs in the future, pushing back the tipping point between fossil and RE dominance some years into the future, and perhaps even placing the 2-degree climate goal out of reach, the essential pre-requisites for a low carbon, RE-based future – competitive and falling costs and successful early deployment -- have now been demonstrated. Developments on these fronts suggest that with somewhat more policy guidance modern REs are capable of, even in the face of a Trump presidency, making the key contribution to the world's avoidance of the worst catastrophes of fossil fuel-induced climate change.

8. REFERENCES

Aranzadi, Claudio. "Introduccion" in Energia y Geoestrategia 2016, IEEE-CECME-Enerclub, Madrid, 2016.

Bloomberg New Energy Finance (BNEF), *New Energy Outlook 2016*. https://www.bloomberg.com/company/new-energy-outlook/#form

BP Statistical Review of World Energy, June 2016.

BP Energy Outlook 2016.

Durden, Tyler. "Shell Warns that 'Peak Oil Demand' May be Reached in 2021," zerohedge.com, Nov. 6, 2016.

Energy Information Agency, International Data, 2016.

Fullbrook, David. "A turning point looms for electricity and climate" Energy Post, August 31, 2016.

Frankfurt School-UNEP Centre/Bloomberg New Energy Finance, *Global Trends in New Energy Investment*, 2016.

Grady, Barbara. "Stranded assets may add up to $2.2 trillion – blame COP21?" Greenbiz.com, November 24, 2015.

Hone, David. "Solar deployment rates," The Energy Collective, August 31, 2016. http://www.theenergycollective.com/davidhone/2386926/solar-deployment-rates

IRENA, Data and Statistics, Featured Dashboard, http://resourceirena.irena.org/gateway/dashboard/

IRENA, The Power to Change: Solar and Wind Cost Reduction Potential to 2025, June 2016

IRENA, Letting in the Light: How solar photovoltaics will revolutionise the electricity system, June 2016

Isbell, Paul. "Atlantic Energy and the Changing Global Energy Flow Map" Atlantic Future Scientific Paper, 2014, 17   http://www.atlanticfuture.eu/files/338-ATLANTIC%20FUTURE_17_Energy.pdf

Isbell, Paul. "Shale gas, offshore y geopolitica: el potencial de la Cuenca Atlantica," Integracion y Comercio, numero 39, INTAL-BID, Buenos Aires, 2015.

Isbell, Paul. "Regionalism and Interregionalism in Latin America: The Beginning or the End of Latin America's 'Continental Integration'?" Atlantic Future Scientific Paper, European Commission, 2015.

Isbell, Paul. "The Dynamics and Paradoxes of the Atlantic Energy Renaissance," in Paul Isbell and Eloy Alvarez Pelegry, eds, *The Future of*

Energy in the Atlantic Basin, Center for Transatlantic Relations, Johns Hopkins University SAIS and Orkestra (Basque Institute for Competitiveness), Washington, DC and Bilbao, 2015.

Kraemer, R. Andreas and Christoph H. Stefes, "The Changing Energy Landscape in the Atlantic Space," in Jordi Bacaria and Laia Tarragona, (eds.), Atlantic Future: Shaping a new hemisphere from the 21st Century Africa, Europe and the Americas, CIDOB Monograph Series, Barcelona, 2016.

Koerth-Baker, Maggie. "It's Hard to Tell Whether Trump Supports Renewable Energy — And That May Not Matter Much" FiveThirtyEight. com, Nov 14, 2016.

Lazard's Levelized Cost of Energy Analysis, Version 9.0, November 2015.

Lovins, Amory. The Troubled Oil Business: Hitting peak oil will come faster than any of us think. But don't blame dwindling supply – it's all about disappearing demand. July 28, 2015. (online) https://medium.com/@amorylovins/the-troubled-oil-business-21ad430eff10

McGlade, Christophe and Paul Elkins, "The geographical distribution of fossil fuels unused when limiting global warming to 2 °C," *Nature*, vol. 517, January 2015.

Nelder, Chris and Mark Silberg, "Congress extends the renewable investment tax credit: What now" greenbiz.com (https://www.greenbiz.com/article/congress-extends-renewable-investment-tax-credit-what-now), December 28. 2015.

Olabe, Antxon and Mikel González-Eguino, Teresa Ribera, "El Acuerdo de Paris y el fin de la era del carbon," Real Instituto Elcano, Working Paper 12/2016, 28/7/2016.

PEW Research Center, The Politics of Climate, October 4, 2016. http://www.pewinternet.org/2016/10/04/the-politics-of-climate/

Pfeiffer, Alexander and Richard Millar, Cameron Hepburn, Eric Beinhocker, "The '2°C capital stock' for electricity generation: Committed cumulative carbon emissions from the electricity generation sector and the transition to a green economy," *Applied Energy*, Available online 24 March 2016, ISSN 0306-2619, http://dx.doi.org/10.1016/j.apenergy.2016.02.093.

Romm, Joe. "Electric car revolution may drive 'oil investor death spiral," *ThinkProgress.org*, October 16, 2016.

World Energy Council, World Energy Scenarios 2016.

The relevance of the Energy Charter to develop renewable energies in Latin America

MARGARITA NIEVES ZÁRATE*

1. INTRODUCTION

The energy sector is shifting from a national to a global industry due to international issues related to energy trade, investments, transit and climate change, which are becoming increasingly important. In order to strengthen the global response to the threat of climate change and aiming to improve energy security, it is necessary to mobilise energy investments worldwide. At the same time, this energy transition demands not just technology developments, but also a legal framework to the international level where the energy markets operate. Emerging regions such as Latin America are called to play an important role in this new era in order to contribute to sustainable development and each country has undertaken measures to foster renewable energies, including Chile, Colombia and Guatemala. The Energy Charter Treaty, of which these three countries are observers, is a unique instrument under international law to foster investments, trade, transit, cooperation and energy efficiency with a great potential to further promote sustainable energy at global level and to strengthen global energy security by extending the application of its legal framework to an increasing number of countries. This article will help to understand the interactions between the Energy Charter Process and Latin America, as well as the relevance of the ECT to promote renewable energy sources worldwide.

2. NEW TRENDS IN THE GLOBAL ENERGY SECTOR

There are three emerging trends in the global energy sector: energy decarbonisation, demand response encouraged by technology and the Energy Charter Treaty.[1]

* Margarita Nieves Zárate, LLM in Energy regulation, Legal Expert at the Colombian Hydrocarbons Agency and researcher. The findings, interpretations and conclusions expressed in this article are those of the author and do not reflect the positions of the institution.

This article will address two of these trends: the development of renewable energies as a way to contribute to energy decarbonisation and the Energy Charter Process, an important instrument to foster investments, trade, transit, cooperation and energy efficiency worldwide.

The decarbonisation of the energy sector means reducing its carbon intensity. That is, reducing the greenhouse emissions per unit of energy produced. This is one of the commitments adopted in 2015 by 195[2] countries in the Paris Agreement COP-21, which agreed a long term goal of holding the increase in the global average temperature to well below 2°C above pre-industrial levels and pursuing efforts to limit the temperature increase to 1.5°C.

One of the ways to achieve these goals is to increase the share of low-carbon energy sources like renewables, in the global energy matrix. Renewable energy sources include technologies such as wind, solar, biofuels, biomass, geothermal, hydropower and tidal. What unifies these varied technologies is that they are not based upon finite resources; they are widely distributed; they do not add, at least in theory, to carbon, and thus have a much more restricted carbon foot print.[3]

Likewise, renewable energy is usually exploited in a decentralized way in small installations. Conventional energy, on the contrary, tends to be used in big, centralized power stations.[4]

As they are not concentrated in any region, the development of renewable energy sources are also a mechanism to foster energy security in countries highly dependent on imported fossil fuels. In the energy transition era, the Churchill's famous dictum about supply –"variety and variety alone"- still resounds powerfully.[5]

The implementation of alternative energies challenge the traditional market structures in terms of operation and competition. The case of the European Union (EU) and the electricity market is illustrative: *"(…) the use of renewable energy leads to the development of a more decentralized energy*

---

[1] López-Ibor, Vicente in "International Energy Charter addressed at XI. ASIER Conference in Argentina". Energy Charter. Brussels, 2016. http://www.energy charter.org/media/news/article/international-energy-charter-addressed-at-xi-asier-conference-in-argentina/?tx_news_pi1%5Bcontroller%5D=News&tx_news_pi1%5Baction%5D=detail&cHash=fbac5cba5a8cd49b6e49a5fb7d381c0a
[2] Number of countries taken from: http://newsroom.unfccc.int/unfccc-newsroom/finale-cop21/
[3] Yerguin, Daniel. "The Quest: energy, security, and the remaking of the modern world". The Penguin Press. USA. 2011, p. 525.
[4] Maxian, Tim. "EU Renewable Electricity Law and Policy". Cambridge Studies in European Law and Policy. Cambridge. United Kingdom. 2015, p. 3
[5] Yerguin, Daniel. Ob. Cit., p. 716.

system and creates local employment throughout the Union. (…) the promotion of renewable electricity has increased competition in electricity markets. Owners of renewable power plants tend to be new entrants into the electricity market, rather than the incumbent operators. As a result, market power of incumbent operators, which due to their former monopoly often dominated markets, has reduced significantly in some Member States."[6]

The COP-21 is only one of the multiple examples which demonstrates how the energy sector is developing from a national to a global industry due to the increasing importance of international issues related to energy trade, investments, transit and climate change. In order to strengthen the global response to the threat of climate change and aiming to improve energy security, it is necessary to mobilise energy investments worldwide. At the same time, this energy transition demands not just technology developments, but also a legal framework to the international level where the energy markets operate.

At an international level, this policy was adopted in the 90s among Western European and Eurasian countries through the Energy Charter Treaty (ECT), a unique multilateral, legally binding investment protection framework for the energy sector.[7] Nowadays, the ECT covers countries from the Atlantic to the Pacific, from Europe to Japan, being signed or acceded by fifty-two states, the European Union and the European Atomic Energy Community (EURATOM).

The ECT provides a multilateral framework for long-term cooperation in the energy field that is unique under international law. It is designed to promote energy security through the operation of more open and competitive energy markets, while respecting the principles of sustainable development and sovereignty over energy resources. The Treaty was signed in December 1994 and entered into legal force in April 1998. The ECT incorporates the main rules of the World Trade Organisation (WTO) with respect to trade in goods in the energy sector, as a particular sector of the economy. The provisions of the Treaty and its Protocols cover energy trade, competition, transit, transfer of technology, environment, access to capital, investment promotion and protection, energy efficiency and focus on four broad areas:[8]

---

[6] Maxian, Tim. Op. Cit., p. 3.
[7] Rusnák, Urban. "Modernisation of the Energy Charter". 2013. Available at: http://eng.globalaffairs.ru/number/Modernization-of-the-Energy-Charter-16294
[8] This description is taken from http://www.energycharter.org/process/energy-charter-treaty-1994/energy-charter-treaty/ Last accessed December 30, 2016.

- The protection of foreign investments, based on the extension of national treatment, or most-favoured nation treatment (whichever is more favourable) and protection against key non-commercial risks;

- Non-discriminatory conditions for trade in energy materials, products and energy-related equipment based on WTO rules, and provisions to ensure reliable cross-border energy transit flows through pipelines, grids and other means of transportation;

- The resolution of disputes between participating states, and -in the case of investments- between investors and host states;

- The promotion of energy efficiency, and attempts to minimise the environmental impact of energy production and use.

Member countries of the ECT also found in energy integration and cooperation a foremost way to attract investments in energy infrastructure, create economies of scale, increase energy security through the use of geographic and seasonal complementarities, diversify the energy mix, expand trade markets, promote energy efficiency and reduce environmental and infrastructure costs.

In May 2015, the Energy Charter process was modernised through the International Energy Charter (IEC), a declaration of political intention towards a new age of global energy cooperation. The IEC has been adopted by 83 countries from all continents, including the USA, China, the UK and Niger. From Latin America, so far Colombia, Chile and Guatemala have signed the IEC. IEC signatories confirm that cooperation is necessary in the field of efficient use of energy, development of renewable energy sources and energy-related environmental protection.

As it was set by the members of the Energy Charter Conference in the *"Tokyo Declaration"* in 2016 in Japan: *"(…) the ECT has the great potential to further contribute to promoting sustainable energy at global level and to strengthening global energy security by extending the application of its legal framework to an increasing number of countries (…)"*.[9]

3. RENEWABLES AND THE ENERGY CHARTER

Investments in renewable energies share most of the characteristics of those in conventional energies: projects are highly strategic, capital-intensive,

[9] ENERGY CHARTER CONFERENCE. "Tokyo Declaration on the Energy Charter" 26 November 2016. Available at: http://www.energycharter.org/fileadmin/DocumentsMedia/CCDECS/2016/CCDEC201631.pdf.

require complex technology, there is a global competition, and the risks have to be assessed over the long-term.

In 1994, when the Energy Charter Treaty was adopted, unconventional renewable technologies such as solar and wind existed, but without any penetration in the energy markets. However, the treaty was conceived technologically neutral and its provisions promote sustainable development, environmental protection and energy efficiency. An example of these rules is Article 19, which sets that Contracting parties shall have particular regard to improving energy efficiency, to developing and using renewable energy sources, to promoting the use of cleaner fuels and to employing technologies and technological means that reduce pollution. The Energy Charter Protocol on Energy Efficiency and Related Environmental Aspects, which entered into force at the same time as the Energy Charter Treaty (1998), also endorses these principles.

The Energy Charter Treaty benefits investments in traditional energy sources as well as in renewables, promoting the rule of law, the access to capital, investment protection, stability and transparency of the investment climate between contracting parties.

Furthermore, the broad scope of the ECT has been tested during the last lustrum by investor claims against European states such as Spain, Italy, Czech Republic and Bulgaria requiring protection to their investments in renewable energy sources, invoking ECT provisions.

These claims are mainly for *"breach of the fair and equitable treatment standard and for conduct amounting to expropriation. These are amongst the many broad protections provided to foreign investors in the energy sector under the ECT."*[10]

Comparing the conventional versus renewable energy cases, 48 out of a total of 99 ECT claims registered to date, now relate to renewable energy sector investments (26 out of 33 in 2015-2016).[11]

Additionally, the IEC enshrines the use of new and renewable energies and clean technologies, energy efficiency and environmental protection by means of:[12]

---

[10] Grace, Stephanie. "The Energy Charter Treaty: new energy, new era". September 2, 2016. In Thomson Reuters. Arbitration Blog. At: http://arbitrationblog.practicallaw.com/the-energy-charter-treaty-new-energy-new-era/
[11] Ibídem.
[12] International Energy Charter. Title I, numeral 3.

- Creating mechanisms and conditions for using energy as economically and efficiently as possible, including, as appropriate, regulatory and market based instruments;

- Promotion of a sustainable energy mix designed to minimise negative environmental consequences in a cost-effective way through:

  i. Market-oriented energy prices which more fully reflect environmental costs and benefits;

  ii. Efficient and coordinated policy measures related to energy;

  iii. Use of renewable energy sources and clean technologies, including clean fossil fuel technologies;

- Sharing of best practices on clean energy development and investment;

- Promotion and use of low emission technologies.

4. LATIN AMERICA AND THE ENERGY CHARTER PROCESS

Latin America and the Caribbean is a region rich in energy resources: it has the second oil reserves after the Middle East[13], the second[14] hydropower generation worldwide[15] with a further unexploited potential of 430GW[16] of unexploited hydropower potential and a large potential for unconventional renewable energies. The share of renewable energy sources in total final energy consumption is one of the highest in the world, reaching 27% in 2013, compared to a global average of 18%. The region has seen energy demand increase by a third in a decade,[17] and primary energy demand is expected to rise by more than 60% between 2012 and 2040.[18]The region achieved around 96% electricity access, leaving about 30 million people who do not have electricity. Regarding economic performance, in 2015 Latin America attracted 9% of world FDI inflows and 2% of FDI outflows.

---

[13]   [9] British Petroleum. "BP Statistical Review of World Energy". London. June 2016, p. 6.
[14]   After East Asia and Pacific.
[15]   International Hydropower Association. "Hydro Power Status Report". London. 2016, p. 29.
[16]   Ibid, p. 40.
[17]   Ibídem.
[18]   Röhrkasten, Sybille. "Regional energy integration: the global energy governance and the Latin American Scenario" in Konrad-Adenauer-Stifgtung. Regional Energy Integration. 2015, p. 29. Data based on IEA (2014: 678).

It means a decrease respect to the year 2015, when the region attracted 13% of FDI inflows.[19]

To attain its goals in the energy sector, Latin America faces three main challenges: a) growing energy demand, b) need of investments in energy projects, and c) regional and international integration.

Each country has adopted reforms to foster investments in the energy field with different scopes, and some milestone cases are Chile in 1982 and recently Mexico in 2014.

Regarding renewable energy, a marked feature of Latin America's electricity mix is the large share of hydropower. Conversely, unconventional energy sources such as solar and wind are still incipient. For Latin America it is necessary to diversify, considering its growing demand and dependence on hydro sources for electricity generation which are highly vulnerable to climate change. There are still isolated areas where conventional energy sources would be expensive and inefficient. There are several options to promote diversification, which include unconventional renewable sources and energy integration.

The region is looking towards unconventional energy sources, the challenge is to make unconventional energies cost efficient adopting mature technology and delivering appropriate investments signals. Each country has undertaken measures to foster renewable energies. In 2015, Brazil, Mexico and Chile ranked in the list of the top 10 largest renewable energy markets globally.[20]

At the same time, Latin America has experimented multiple initiatives of subregional economic integration: the Andean Community (CAN), Caribbean Community (Caricom), Southern Common Market (Mercosur), Central American Integration System (SICA), Union of South American Nations (Unasur) and Pacific Alliance. The region, however, has not adopted a multilateral agreement for the energy sector. Only Central America has embraced a specific treaty to develop its electricity market.

According to the World Bank's report, Global Economic Prospects 2016, in Latin America:[21] *"Despite a multitude of regional trade agreements,*

---

[19]   UNCTAD. Ob. Cit. p. 36.

[20]   International Renewable Energy Agency (IRENA). "Renewable Energy Market Analysis. Latin America". Abu Dhabi. 2016, p. 10. http://www.irena.org/DocumentDownloads/ Publications/IRENA_Market_Analysis_Latin_America_2016.pdf

[21]   WORLD BANK. "Global Economic Prospects, 2016". Washington. Enero. 2016., p. 112. Accessed Februrary, 2016: http://pubdocs.worldbank.org/en/842861463605615468/Global-Economic-Prospects-June-2016-Divergences-and-risks.pdf

economic linkages within the region [Latin America and Caribbean region] tend to be limited and largely confined to sub-regions."

The existing fragmented landscape in Latin America could benefit from the Energy Charter Treaty, a comprehensive policy and multilateral agreement aiming to maximise energy resources, attract investments and even promote the intraregional flow of capital. This would facilitate rules for energy trade, investments, transit, integration and legal harmonization, which has been a barrier to develop, for instance, interconnection projects.

Among other benefits, increased levels of integration can allow for better incorporation of variable renewables into power systems while ensuring economies of scale for larger projects.[22]

Spain, the UK, Belgium, France, Japan, the Netherlands and Germany are some top 10 investor economies in the region[23] which are full members of the ECT and leaders in renewables energies in the world. Therefore, the adoption of the ECT may be also an opportunity for Latin American countries to re-assess their energy FDI strategies and increase energy cooperation.

From Latin America, so far Colombia, Chile and Guatemala have signed the IEC, taking a step towards global energy integration and bearing in mind the relevance of renewable sources in order to satisfy their energy needs. These three countries have other aspects in common: great potential for renewable energy sources, the implementation of measures in their energy sector aiming to foster private investment and have signed the Paris Agreement –COP-21.

The following paragraphs describe measures and efforts made by Chile, Colombia and Guatemala, the Latin American countries observers to the Energy Charter Conference, in order to deploy renewable energy sources, attract investments to this sector and develop their "green energy law".

4.1 Chile

The main source of primary energy production in Chile is oil (32,9%), followed by coal (24,4%), firewood and biomass (23,7%) and hydroelectricity (6,4%). 95% of oil is imported.[24] In 2014 the electricity matrix relied on fossil fuels: coal (41%) and natural gas (11%), followed by hydroelectricity power

---

[22] IRENA "Renewable Energy Market Analysis. Latin America". Op. Cit., p. 146.
[23] UNCTAD. "World Investment Report". Geneva. 2016, p. 51. http://unctad.org/en/PublicationsLibrary/wir2016_en.pdf
[24] Ministry of Energy. "Energía 2050. Política Energética de Chile". Santiago de Chile. 2015, p. 20. At http://www.minenergia.cl/archivos_bajar/LIBRO-ENERGIA-2050-WEB.pdf

(34%), biomass (4%), wind (2%), solar (1%) and other sources (7%).[25] In 2015 Chile's power *sector* had 20.375 MW of installed capacity.[26] The principal renewable source of energy is hydroelectricity, while unconventional renewables such as solar, wind, biomass and small hydro have increased their share in installed capacity from 286MW in 2005 to 2,269 MW in 2015, representing 11.41% of total installed electricity capacity. [27]

Chile is one of the main importers of energy resources in South America including natural gas, oil and coal. Additionally, in 2016 Chile began to export electricity and natural gas to Argentina.[28] For this reason, renewable energies are called to play a noteworthy role aiming to diversify its electricity mix, carrying the country to undertake policies and enact laws and regulations to achieve this goal.

The legal framework to promote renewable energy sources is made up by Law 20257 enacted in 2007 which sets an initial quota of 5% renewable electricity in 2014 to be increased in 0.5% yearly until 2024. The quota applies to all electricity sales and has a non compliance penalty. In 2013 Law 20/25 increased the quota to 5% in 2013 with yearly increments of 1% until reaching 12% in 2020. Since 2005, Law 20018 introduced a regulatory instrument, non discriminatory auctions, requiring distribution companies to source power for regulated markets through this mechanism (including renewables) and allows renewable energy producers to sign long term power purchase agreements with distribution companies.[29] In 2013 Law 20/25 also brought in a new public auction system. In 2012 Law 20251 introduced a net metering scheme, grid access measures for renewable energies were implemented in 2004 by Law 19940. There are no fiscal incentives for renewable electricity in Chile, though a carbon tax was introduced in September 2014 (Law 20780 tax reform).[30]

In December 2015 Chile enacted Decree 148 which sets up its long term energy policy until the year 2050, founded in four pillars: security and quality of supply, energy to boost development, environmentally friendly energy, efficiency and energy education. Regarding renewable energy sources, this policy establishes a target to generate 60% of

---

[25]   Ibid., p. 22.
[26]   Ibídem.
[27]   Ibid., p. 24.
[28]   See "Chile to begin gas exports to Argentina this week". May 10, 2016. http://www. reuters.com/article/chile-argentina-gas-idUSL5N1877JD and "Argentina to buy gas, electricity from Chile". January 30, 2016. http://www.buenosairesherald.com/article/207792/ argentina-to-buy-gas-electricity-from-chile-
[29]   IRENA (2015). "*Renewable Energy Policy Brief: Chile*". ©IRENA, Abu Dhabi, p. 3. at http:// www.energynet.co.uk/webfm_send/1191
[30]   Ibídem.

electricity from renewable sources by 2035 and 70% by 2050; become an exporter of technology and services for solar industry in 2035;[31] decrease Greenhouse Gas Emissions levels in 30% by 2030 with respect to 2007 levels according with its Intended Nationally Determined Contribution and Paris commitments, and promote higher standards of green energy in transportation introducing 50% of low Greenhouse emissions fuels by 2035 and 60% by 2050.

The long term energy policy, also encourages interconnections to the Andean Electricity Interconnection System (SINEA) and Mercosur countries.

In 2015, Chile along with Mexico joined the list of the top 10 largest renewable energy markets globally.[32] In 2015, Chile added over 400 MW of solar PV for the second consecutive year, while 110 MW of solar Concentrated Solar Power (CSP) is under construction (the first SP project in Latin America).[33]

4.2 Colombia

In Colombia, 93% of primary energy production is made up of fossil fuels (coal, oil and natural gas), 4% is from hydro sources and 3% from biomass and residues. 78% of primary energy resources consumed are fossil fuels and 22% are renewable resources.[34] At the end of 2015 the installed capacity in the National Interconnected System was 16.436 MW[35] and 98% of the population has access to electricity.

Hydroelectric power generation represents 70% of the electricity matrix, followed by thermal energy with 29% and unconventional renewable energy at 0,68% (biomass 0.57% and wind 0.11%). There is still the potential for 56 GW of hydroelectric resources to be developed in Colombia,[36] being the second country in South America after Brazil in potential hydro resources.

In Colombia small hydroelectric (<10 MW), wind, solar, biomass, geothermal and tidal energy are considered unconventional renewable resources. Unconventional renewable energies are emerging in the country.

---

[31] Ministry of Energy. "Energía 2050. Política Energética de Chile". Santiago. Op. Cit., p. 69.

[32] IRENA. "Renewable Energy Market Analysis. Latin America". Op. Cit., p. 10.

[33] Ibid, p. 53.

[34] Mining and Energy Planning Unit. (UPME). "Integración de las Energías Renovables No Convencionales en Colombia." Bogota. 2015, p. 27.

[35] UPME. "Informe Mensual de Variables de Generación y del Mercado Eléctrico Colombiano Diciembre de 2015." Bogota. 2016.

[36] UPME. "Plan de Expansión de Referencia Generación - Transmisión 2015-2029."Bogota. 2016.

There is a solar irradiation average of 194 W/m^2 over the territory, local winds with average speed of 9 m/s (up to 80 metres in the Department of La Guajira) and energy potential around 450.000 TJ per year in biomass residues.[37] The potential of wind power is estimated to be around 49.5 GW and geothermal about 1 -2 GW.

The 'Indicative Plan 2010-2015 PROURE' established targets for unconventional renewable energies in the National Interconnected System. The target for 2015 was an increase of renewable energies participation in the energy matrix by 3.5%, and 6.5% for 2020.

Aiming to boost unconventional renewable energies, the National Development Plan NDP Law (2014-2018) establishes the following policy measures: encourage electricity generation based on unconventional renewables energies; foster energy efficiency; increase the use of biofuels; increase unconventional renewable energies installed capacity from 9.893 MW in 2013 to 11.113 MW in 2018; raise unconventional renewable energies installed capacity in non-interconnected zones from 2,8 MW in 2013 to 9 MW in 2018 and set up a strategy of low carbon development, including goals to reduce greenhouse gas emissions.[38]

The National Development Plan NDP includes as one of the main objectives in the electricity sector to advance in the regional electric integration, developing projects as the Interconnection Colombia–Panama and the Andean Electrical Interconnection System (SINEA) among Columbia, Ecuador, Peru and Chile.

For the transport sector, policy focuses on biofuels with blending mandates (implemented in 2005) which have been progressively set since 2001 through Law 693 and fiscal incentives introduced by Law 939 of 2004. These measures have positioned Colombia as one of the top 10 countries for biofuel production, and the third in Latin America after Brazil and Argentina.[39]

The legislation, as well as the government, have identified that the most feasible way to incorporate renewable energies is in non-interconnected zones, in order to provide electricity by replacing diesel power generation.

[37] UPME, 2015. Ob. Cit.

[38] Nieves, Margarita and Hernández, Augusto. "Colombia Energy Investment Report". Energy Charter Secretariat. Brussels. 2016, p. 34. At http://www.energycharter.org/fileadmin/ DocumentsMedia/Other_Publications/20160729-Colombia_Energy_Investment_Report.pdf

[39] World Economic Forum. (2015, November 17). "Environment: World Economic Forum". Retrieved from World Economic Forum Web site: https://www.weforum.org/ agenda/2015/11/these-countries-produce

-the-most-biofuels/

In 2014 the Colombian Congress enacted Law 1715 to promote unconventional renewable energies within the national energy system and encourage energy efficiency, seeking to support sustainable economic development, reduce greenhouse gas emissions and enhance the reliability of the energy supply. In the electric sector, fiscal incentives are the prevalent policy mechanism for promoting unconventional renewable energy. The main measures introduced by this law include: i) access of renewable self-generators to the transmission and distribution grid to deliver their surplus; ii) development and use of distributed energy resources; iii) the creation of the Unconventional Energy and Efficient Energy Management Fund (FENOGE) to finance renewable energy projects; and iv) fiscal incentives such as: a) reduction of up to 50% in income tax on investments in renewable power generation; b) accelerated depreciation of assets; c) value-added-tax exemption on pre-investments and investments in goods and services; and d) import tariffs exemption on pre-investments and investments in raw materials, machinery and equipment for the development of unconventional renewable projects. For the moment, the regulation has not implemented feed in tariff mechanisms, nor auctions.[40]

By means of Law 629 of 2000 Colombia approved the Kyoto Protocol, which aims to reduce greenhouse gas emissions, fostering energy efficiency in each sector of the economy, among other policies. In 2001 the Congress enacted Law 697 to promote energy efficiency as well as unconventional energy resources, seeking to guarantee energy supply and economic competitiveness, to guard rights of the consumers, and to achieve sustainable development.

The Energy Efficiency Law and its secondary regulations provide the legal basis and measures to promote and support energy efficiency improvements.[41]

4.3 Guatemala

Guatemala has the largest electricity installed generation capacity in Central America and a potential on renewable energy sources estimated at 6.000 MW of hydroelectricity, 1.000 MW of geothermal energy, 280 MW of wind energy and 5.3 kWh/km^2 per day of solar energy.[42]

In 2015, 58% of electricity generation in the country relied on renewable sources of energy.[43] Firewood still represents the main source of primary

[40] Nieves, Margarita and Hernández, Augusto. Ob. Cit., p. 60.
[41] Ibídem.
[42] Ministry of Mines and Energy of Guatemala. "Energy Policy 2013-2027". Guatemala. 2013, p. 15, at http://www.mem.gob.gt/wp-content/uploads/2013/02/PE2013-2027.pdf
[43] Ministry of Mines and Energy of Guatemala. "Revista Mensual de Estadísticas del

energy[44] and over two-thirds of households depend on traditional firewood for cooking,[45] which means that renewable energies are expected to play an important role in order to improve the quality of lives for Guatemalan people. The country is a net importer of oil products[46] and has introduced measures aiming to depend less on imports, replace firewood in 25% of households and change its energy matrix boosting renewable energy sources.

The Central American country has created fiscal incentives to foster renewable energy sources through the "Incentives Law for Renewable Energy Projects" Decree 52-2003 and its regulation in 2005. These incentives consist of value-added tax (VAT) exemptions, import and export fiscal benefits, income tax exemptions, among others. The country also implemented renewable energy auctions, biofuel mandates aiming to diversify its transport fuel mix, enacted a Climate Change Law in 2013 and is working on the implementation of an energy efficiency law.

These pro-renewable energy measures were strengthened in 2013, when Guatemala adopted a new energy policy for the period 2013-2027, which embraces sustainable development as its cornerstone. In terms of renewable energies, it has set up a goal of increasing electricity generation from renewable energies from 65% in 2012 to 80% in 2027, promote investments in new 500MW of renewable electricity generation, increase electricity access from 85% in 2012 to 95% in 2027 and enshrines clear goals in energy efficiency for households and industrial sectors.[47]

Aiming to improve trade and attract global investments Guatemala has signed 18 bilateral investment treaties. Guatemala is a country member of the Central American Electricity Market Treaty, which allows electricity trade through the Central American Electrical Interconnection System (SIEPAC), the first subregional grid in Latin America which interconnects six countries: Guatemala, El Salvador, Honduras, Nicaragua, Costa Rica and Panama, which has been in full operation since 2014.

As has been expressed, Chile, Colombia and Guatemala enshrine within their energy policies the deployment of renewable energy sources and energy integration as some of their main objectives in order to achieve

Ministerio de Minas y Energía". Guatemala. 2016, p.6. At http://www.mem.gob.gt/estadisticas/

[44] Ministry of Mines and Energy of Guatemala. "Energy Policy 2013-2027". Ob. Cit., p. 21,

[45] International Renewable Energy Agency (IRENA). "Renewable Energy Market Analysis. Latin America". Ob. Cit., p. 58.

[46] Ministry of Mines and Energy of Guatemala. "Revista Mensual de Estadísticas del Ministerio de Minas y Energía". Ob. Cit., p.13.

[47] Ministry of Mines and Energy of Guatemala. "Energy Policy 2013-2027". Ob. Cit., p. 38.

national goals and recognizing their relevance for Latin America. They are involved in projects such as SINEA and MER and have interest in becoming energy resources exporters or strengthen their exports. The energy charter process can further strengthen and support these aims and policies, improving investment climate, energy cooperation and transference of technology.

5. CONCLUSION

To foster renewable energy it is essential to link more private investment and remove market and technological barriers. The development of unconventional renewable energies also needs to be carefully considered in light of comparative cost, grid access and dispatch. Latin America faces growing challenges, which require more investments in the energy sector and more international cooperation. The Energy Charter Process is a mature legal framework for global energy cooperation, which could further integrate the Latin American economy to the global energy markets, contribute to the improvement of the investment climate and encourage investments in renewable energy sources.

6. BIBLIOGRAPHY

British Petroleum. "BP Statistical Review of World Energy". London. June 2016.

Grace, Stephanie. "The Energy Charter Treaty: new energy, new era". September 2, 2016. In Thomson Reuters. Arbitration Blog. At: http://arbitrationblog.practicallaw.com/the-energy-charter-treaty-new-energy-new-era/

International Energy Charter. "International Energy Charter addressed at XI. ASIER Conference in Argentina". Brussels, December, 2016. http://www.energycharter.org/media/news/article/international-energy-charter-addressed-at-xi-asier-conference-in-argentina/?tx_news_pi1%5Bcontroller%5D=News&tx_news_pi1%5Baction%5D=detail&cHash=fbac-5cba5a8cd49b6e49a5fb7d381c0a

International Hydropower Association. "Hydro Power Status Report". London. 2016.

International Renewable Energy Agency (IRENA). "Renewable Energy Market Analysis. Latin America". Abu Dhabi. 2016, at http://www.irena.org/DocumentDownloads/Publications/IRENA_Market_Analysis_Latin_America_2016.pdf

IRENA (2015). "Renewable Energy Policy Brief: Chile". ©IRENA, Abu Dhabi, p. 3. at http://www.energynet.co.uk/webfm_send/1191

Konrad-Adenauer-Stifgtung. Regional Energy Integration. Brasilia. 2015. CITY.

Maxian, Tim. "EU Renewable Electricity Law and Policy". Cambridge Studies in European Law and Policy. Cambridge. United Kingdom. 2015, 272. P

Mining and Energy Planning Unit. (UPME). "Integración de las Energías Renovables No Convencionales en Colombia." Bogotá. 2015, p. 27.

Ministry of Energy. "Energía 2050. Política Energética de Chile". Santiago de Chile. 2015, At http://www.minenergia.cl/archivos_bajar/ LIBRO-ENERGIA-2050-WEB.pdf 157 P. Ministry of Mines and Energy of Guatemala. "Energy Policy 2013-2027". Guatemala. 2013, p. 15, at http:// www.mem.gob.gt/wp-content/uploads/2013/02/PE2013-2027.pdf

Ministry of Mines and Energy of Guatemala. "Revista Mensual de Estadísticas del Ministerio de Minas y Energía". Guatemala. 2016, p.6. At http://www.mem.gob.gt/estadisticas/

Nieves, Margarita and Hernández, Augusto. "Colombia Energy Investment Report". Energy Charter Secretariat. Brussels. 2016, p. 34. At http:// www.energycharter.org/fileadmin/DocumentsMedia/Other_Publications/20160729-Colombia_Energy_Investment_Report.pdf

Rusnák, Urban. "Modernisation of the Energy Charter". 2013. Available: http://eng.globalaffairs.ru/number/Modernization-of-the-Energy-Charter-16294

UNCTAD. "World Investment Report". Geneva. 2016. P. http://unctad. org/en/PublicationsLibrary/wir2016_en.pdf UPME. "Informe Mensual de Variables de Generación y del Mercado Eléctrico Colombiano Diciembre de 2015." Bogota. 2016.

UPME. "Plan de Expansión de Referencia Generación - Transmisión 2015-2029." Bogota. 2016.

Yerguin, Daniel. "The Quest: energy, sescurity, and the remaking of the modern world". The Penguin Press. USA. 2011. 803 p.Wood Mackenzie. "Southern Cone's Gas Sector Will Need Significant Investment & Multi-Lateral Approach". 2015. https://www.jsg.utexas.edu/lacp/2015/11/ southern-cones-gas-sector-will-need-significant-investment-multi-lateral-approach/29.

World Economic Forum. (2015, November 17). "Environment: World Economic Forum". Retrieved from World Economic Forum Web site: https://www.weforum.org/agenda/2015/11/these-countries-produce-the-most-biofuels/

7=17: Universal access with renewable energy as leverage to help attain all SDGs

CARLOS SALLÉ *

Director of Energy Policies and Climate Change
Iberdrola S.A., Spain

1. INTRODUCTION

There have been several major changes in World's Governance in recent months, with important implications for the renewables sector. The approval of the Social Agenda in September 2015, defined by the 17 Sustainable Development Goals (SDGs), and all the momentum achieved by the Paris Agreement in December 2015 for an ambitious process to tackle climate change have led to a critical change of mind among stakeholders from the stance of just a few months before.

Using the fight against climate change as an example (Paris Agreement and SDG 13), governments from almost the whole world have undertaken a commitment, which is supported by religions, NGOs, business sector, capital markets, etc. This increases the pressure to reach the different goals, mainly based on the decarbonisation of the economy. Renewables are essential in this framework.

SDG 7 establishes the goal of ensuring access to modern forms of energy to those that are deprived of access and also the need to increase the production of renewable energy. The 1.2 billion people without access to electricity are entitled to a decent supply to enable their development. Lack of access to modern

---

* This article was completed in July 2016.

forms of energy not only prevents many people from enjoying decent and fair human development; it also hinders them in their attempts to overcome all the problems caused by poverty: hunger, health issues, lack of education, perpetuation of gender-based discrimination against women, environmental damage, migration, etc.

The increase in the demand originated by this service should not be based on the current energy model, which is dependent on fossil fuels and wastefulness in demand. This is where the connection between universal access and combating climate change arises or, in other words, between SDG 7 mentioned above and SDG 13, which focuses on confronting climate change. If decent universal access is provided using energy models that are similar to those in the developed countries, the pressure of that increasing energy demand will be enormous on climate change. Therefore, this universal access must be provided on the basis of sustainable models: renewables and energy efficiency.

This article analyses several initiatives that are geared towards achieving universal access and explains with a certain degree of detail how SDG 7 impacts on the rest of the SDGs.

We will also be examining the need to take steps to align, on the one hand, those stakeholders that are reluctant to allow the participation of the private sector in solving the problems addressed in the Agenda for Sustainable Development (the 17 Sustainable Development Goals), and on the other hand, those inside the companies that believe that solving these problems does not create incentives to invest in the base of the pyramid. The solution for this lack of harmony requires that mutual trust be built up, which is one of the reasons for including SDG 17: to create public-private partnerships.

In that sense, we will explain the importance of business getting involved in effectively achieving the sustainable development goals and how helping to address social issues is also beneficial for companies. We will be introducing the concept of "SDG actors" (employees, investors and clients that support the SDGs) that help "SDG companies" to turn social return into real benefits, so as to change the idea that supporting the agenda for sustainable development reduces the profitability of these companies.

Finally, we will be introducing the steps defined by the UN Global Compact to be taken by any SDG advocate (citizen, company, Administration, country) in order to confirm their commitments with the SDGs: education, focus, defining goals and reporting on progress.

As we will explain in this article, renewables projects have a crucial role to play in achieving the SDGs.

2. NEED FOR UNIVERSAL ACCESS TO SUSTAINABLE ENERGY TO ENSURE THE WELLBEING OF THE POPULATION AND THE PLANET

Our current model of energy consumption (transport, electricity, gas, building…) and the productive instruments that supply it are unsustainable for the balance of the planet.

The demand for energy worldwide is growing, particularly in the developing countries. As can be seen in Figure 1, in the central scenario (called "New Policies Scenario") of the International Energy Agency's *World Energy Outlook* (WEO)[1], the global demand for energy will increase by 32% from 2013 to 2040, with all of the net growth coming from non-OECD countries. The demand from the OECD countries will be 3% lower (more than twice as low as that of the non-OECD countries in absolute terms).

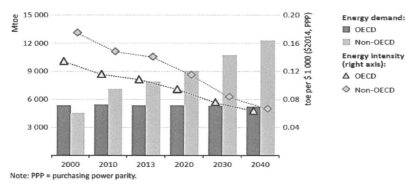

Note: PPP = purchasing power parity.

Figure 1. - Demand for primary energy and energy intensity of GDP in the New Policies Scenario

Source: (International Energy Agency (IEA), 2015)

Studies conducted by the IEA in 2014 show that, driven by technology cost reductions and policy support, renewable energy technologies have become the second-largest source of electricity (behind coal), accounting for 85% of the increase in total generation compared to 2013 levels. This continuous increase will lead renewables to overtake coal as the largest source of power generation by the early-2030s, assuming more than half of global growth over the period analysed.

Despite these efforts to decarbonise the world's energy system, this central scenario managed by IEA also forecasts a future dominated by

[1]   (International Energy Agency (IEA), 2015)

fossil fuels (accounting for a 75% share in the world's demand for primary energy, not too much less than the 81% recorded in 2013). Hence, it is crucial to promote alternative scenarios in order to heavily decarbonise the world economy without hampering the opportunities of developing countries to maintain their growth path.

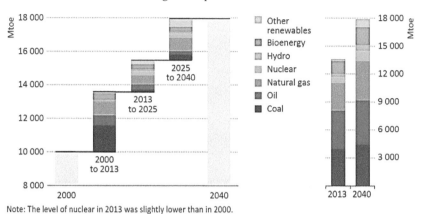

Note: The level of nuclear in 2013 was slightly lower than in 2000.

Figure 2. – Demand for primary energy by fuel in the New Policies Scenario

Source: (International Energy Agency (IEA), 2015)

In 2013, approximately 17% of the world's population, around 1.2 billion people[2], did not have access to electricity. 95% of these people live in developing countries in Sub-Saharan Africa and Asia (mainly in rural areas - around 80% of the total worldwide). Although the most recent estimate reflects the continuous improvements achieved (84 million people fewer than in the previous year), it still represents a major challenge.

More than 2.7 billion people (38% of the world's population) relied on traditional biomass for cooking and heating in 2013 due to the lack of cooking facilities meeting minimum health and safety standards. This represents an increase of around 40 million since the previous year.

This improvement in access to modern energy (essentially in access to electricity) was achieved thanks to the important quantity of resources that have been allocated to addressing this challenge. According to the World Energy Outlook 2015, the investment allocated to achieving universal

[2] These figures match the SE4All data for 2012 presented in the report (International Energy Agency (IEA) and World Bank, 2015), where the number of people without access to electricity was estimated to amount to 1.1 billion, and the number of people without access to clean cooking and heating facilities was estimated to be 2.9 billion

access to modern energy and clean cooking facilities is estimated at $13.1 billion, which comes from different financial sources.

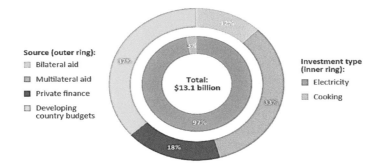

Source (outer ring):
▨ Bilateral aid
▣ Multilateral aid
■ Private finance
▢ Developing
   country budgets

Total:
$13.1 billion

**Investment type
(inner ring):**
▨ Electricity
▨ Cooking

Figure 3. – Investment in access to energy worldwide, by type and source, 2013

Source: (International Energy Agency (IEA), 2015)

Nevertheless, this is not enough and much more work needs to be done. Proof of this can be seen in the fact that IEA, in its central scenario[3], considers that in 2040 there will still be important world regions where over 25% of the population will not have access to electricity (as may be seen in Figure 4), such as in Sub-Saharan Africa, along with all of the problems this lack of access implies. The figures are even worse if we analyse the numbers that will still be using traditional stoves for cooking and heating purposes.

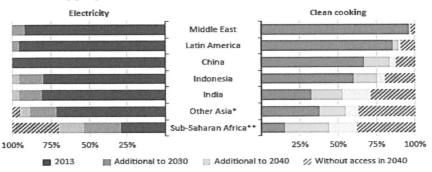

* Includes rest of developing Asia. ** Excludes South Africa.

Figure 4. - Share of the population with access to electricity and clean cooking facilities by region in the New Policies Scenario

Source: (International Energy Agency (IEA), 2015)

---

[3] (International Energy Agency (IEA), 2015)

This lack of access to modern forms of energy not only prevents many people from enjoying decent and fair human development; it also hinders them in their attempts to overcome all the problems caused by poverty: hunger, health issues, lack of education, perpetuation of gender-based discrimination against women, environmental damages, migration, etc.

These 1.2 billion people without access to electricity are entitled to be given access to a decent supply in order to enable their development. The increase in demand generated by this service should not be based on the current energy model, which is dependent on fossil fuels and wastefulness in demand.

The way the different forecasted scenarios used by different institutions, like the IEA, contemplate universal access for the 1.2 billion people is "stingy", in the sense that "access" is considered to be only having a couple of light bulbs and a plug for charging a few items (for example: mobile telephones). The energy demand that this access would generate is small, in individual terms, although it rises depending on the number of connections. However, what would happen if we took solving the so-called "ambition gap" into consideration? In other words, if we were to make an effort so that this access to electricity could be more than just those light bulbs and plugs and approach more "decent" levels of electrification, which can help improve the financial and social development of those people a little more?

This is where the connection between universal access and combating climate change arises, or, in other words, between SDG 7 mentioned above and SDG 13, which focuses on combating climate change. If decent universal access is provided using energy models that are similar to those in the developed countries, the pressure of this increase in energy demand will be enormous on climate change. Therefore, this universal access must be provided on the basis of sustainable models: renewables and energy efficiency....which, incidentally, are also included as targets in SDG 7

3. SUSTAINABLE DEVELOPMENT GOAL 7: UNIVERSAL ACCESS TO SUSTAINABLE ENERGY AS LEVERAGE FOR ACHIEVING ECONOMIC GROWTH AND HELPING ATTAIN THE REST OF THE SUSTAINABLE DEVELOPMENT GOALS.

3.1 Tools: (SDG 7 + SE4All) + (SDG13 + Paris Agreement) + Reduction in Costs of Renewable Technologies

Access to energy is vital to enable humans to attain a decent level of development. However, the right to energy was not specifically included among the Human Rights, and neither was it included among the 8

Millennium Goals, despite it being subsequently accepted that such access is essential if those Goals are to be achieved.

In the Millennium Declaration proclaimed by the world leaders in 2000, a set of goals was adopted to fight against the huge challenges the world is facing. Although progress has been made in recent years, a considerable percentage of the world's population lacks access to basic services and there is still a lot of work to be done in reducing extreme poverty, ending hunger, improving health, promoting gender equality, ensuring environmental sustainability or access to drinking water and sanitation facilities.

The *Sustainable Energy for All* (SE4All) project launched in September 2011 by the United Nations was the first initiative implemented to leverage the role of energy in overcoming the global challenges facing humankind.

The SE4All initiative tackles a dual challenge at global level: reducing the carbon intensity of energy while at the same time making it available to everyone on the planet.

This challenge is addressed via three goals:

- Ensuring universal access to modern energy services;

- Doubling the global rate of improvement in energy efficiency; and

- Doubling the share of renewable energy in the global energy mix

In this regard, and taking over the baton from the Millennium Goals, the United Nations established the Sustainable Development Goals (SDGs) in 2015. These include a specific target for universal access to modern, reliable, affordable and sustainable energy by 2030. With this target, United Nations acknowledges the importance of energy and its role in reaching the aforementioned goals.

As has already been mentioned, achieving this goal is a major challenge, because there are still more than 1.2 billion people without access to electricity and 2.7 billion people that rely on the traditional use of solid biomass for cooking and heating. Bearing this in mind and in an attempt to address these issues, SDG 7 has established two lines of work:

a)   By 2030, enhance international cooperation to facilitate access to clean energy research and technology, including renewable energy, energy efficiency and advanced and cleaner fossil-fuel technology, and promote investment in energy infrastructure and clean energy technology, and

b)   By 2030, expand infrastructure and upgrade technology for supplying modern and sustainable energy services for all in developing countries, in particular least developed countries, small island developing States, and land-locked developing countries, in accordance with their respective programs of support.

These lines of work are translated into three different targets:

1.   By 2030, ensure universal access to affordable, reliable and modern energy services;

2.   By 2030, increase substantially the share of renewable energy in the global energy mix;

3.   By 2030, double the global rate of improvement in energy efficiency.

As may be seen, these targets are fully aligned with the SE4All goals and have the same time frame for attainment.

The IEA also recognises renewable energy and energy efficiency as the key mechanisms that will allow us to trace a path to a sustainable future that is consistent with the 2°C target.

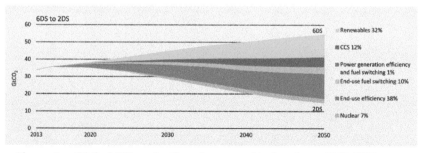

Figure 5. – Global CO_2 reductions by area of technology, 2013-2050

Source: (International Energy Agency (IEA), 2016)

260

People in developing countries require energy, not only to meet their current energy needs but also to gain access to new appliances that can help improve their standard of living. However, these improvements in quality of life should not be synonymous with environmental degradation. That is why we cannot rely on fossil fuels in meeting these new energy needs.

Fortunately, something has changed for the better in recent months. Not only did the UN approve the Agenda for Sustainable Development in September 2015, as mentioned previously, with its 17 Sustainable Development Goals and the inclusion of the 7th Goal, but also a very important agreement on combating climate change was achieved in Paris by almost 200 countries. Besides many important aspects linked to a common goal, the Paris Agreement sets out a global agenda to avoid dangerous climate change by introducing a long term goal of keeping the increase in the global mean temperature to well below 2°C above pre-industrial levels, leaving the door open to raising this target to 1.5°C. It also provides several mechanisms focusing on adaptation, mitigation, reporting, etc., which are supported by the nationally determined contributions of all the signatory countries and there is a commitment to creating a Green Fund that is to be allocated at least US$100 billion/year from 2020 onwards. This is very relevant and it should be set up on an urgent basis because apart from being necessary in order to provide energy for their economic development, receiving this finance/technology transfer will help developing countries to transition towards a low-carbon economy. It will also mean they will be able to avoid what is referred to as the "lock-in" effect, i.e. investing in technologies based on fossil fuels because of their availability at local level and lower cost than renewable energy options.

There is more good news, which allows to leverage the effects of the Green Fund, and help avoid the "lock-in" effect: the declining technology costs in recent years/months have undoubtedly helped boost the increase in the rollout of renewable energies, making it easier to attain the targets defined by SDG7 and SE4All. As may be seen in Figure 6[4], solar photovoltaic technology has experienced a rapid decline in costs since 2010.

---

[4] (Bloomberg New Energy Finance, 2016a)

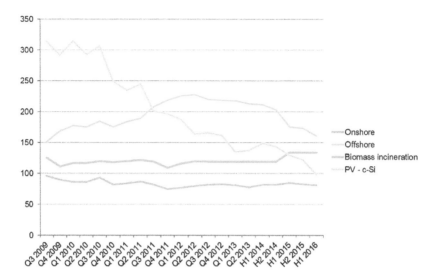

Figure 6. – Levelized cost of electricity from biomass, wind, solar 2009 to H1 2016, $/MWh

Source: (Bloomberg New Energy Finance, 2016a)

To cite another source, according to a recent report by IRENA, the cost of solar photovoltaic electricity decreased by 58% between 2010 and 2015 and it will continue to fall by a further 59% between now and 2025. This trend is also evident with other renewable energy sources, such as onshore and offshore wind farms, with drops of around 26% and 35%, respectively.

This is good news for SDG7 and SDG 13 and, as we will see later on, for the other SDGs as well!

If the long-term goal of the Paris Agreement (holding the increase in growth to well below 2º C) is to come true, additional investments will be needed. According to Bloomberg New Energy Finance analysis[5], the global investment in green power would have to increase by around US$7.8 trillion and be complemented by an additional US$5.3 trillion investment in zero-carbon power plants by 2040 (these figures do not include other investments needed to adapt and mitigate the effects of climate change in sectors other than energy). Meeting the SE4All targets implies a much more ambitious scenario than just accomplishing the 2ºC target and therefore the level of investment has to be far higher than the aforementioned figures. To cite yet another information source, according to the IRENA REmaps

[5]   (Bloomberg New Energy Finance, 2016b)

report[6], investment in renewable power generation capacity needs to be scaled up until it accounts for a level of US\$634 billion per year[7] for the period 2016-2030 (approximately US\$9.5 trillion in green technology alone with a period ten years shorter).

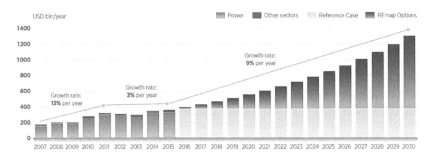

Figure 7. – Links between renewable energies and SDGs

Source: (IRENA, 2016)

3.2 The "special mathematics": 7=17

All of the SDGs are interconnected. I will now go on to talk about the effect of universal access to electricity included in SDG 7 on the rest of the SDGs. I tend to alter the mathematical rationale, introducing a sort of "license" that, I hope, my teachers will forgive me for… "7=17".

The interplay between energy and priority areas of development such as water, poverty alleviation, hunger, health, and gender should not be overlooked. In fact, it is crucial for meeting the goals of the SE4All initiative, which suggests that various opportunities can arise from wider cross-sector perspectives and more holistic decision-making in energy.

As Ms. Rachel Kyte[8] remarked in her intervention at the UN Sustainable Development Summit on September 25, 2015 *"without sustainable energy we cannot realize the full ambition of many other goals. This is about a woman being able to give birth safely, knowing that the lights won't go out. It's about a small farmer being able to use an irrigation pump. It's about children being able to do their homework, graduate and contribute more to their communities. And it's about fighting climate change that threatens to wipe out these gains"*.

---

[6] (IRENA, 2016). Report designed to set a path for aligning SE4All targets with the2°C target.
[7] The total investment in renewables will amount to \$770 billion per year, with over 80% coming from the power sector.
[8] She is currently Chief Executive Officer of SE4All and Special Representative of the UN Secretary-General, and formerly Vice-President of the World Bank Group and Special Envoy for Climate Change.

Let's do an exercise then, with results supported by surveys conducted in the years after the arrival of electricity in long term projects, such as the "*Luz Para Todos*" program in Brazil: let's look at what happens when electricity arrives in a village and enables, for example, the installation of lamps in public zones, hydro pumps, refrigerators, electric stoves, etc.

1. Women and children, who are the ones entrusted with the task of collecting water or wood, no longer need to go on such long journeys.

2. Children have more time to devote to their education (SDG 4): the time they no longer need to spend carrying water and wood, and the time at night when they can study by lamplight. The use of computers and the access to internet that are enabled with the arrival of electricity enhance the quality of education. A higher level of education is a bonus for many aspects of their lives in the future: it allows knowledge to be exchanged and for new technologies to be used, so it creates more business opportunities in the future. For example, surveys conducted after the Brazilian "*Luz para Todos*" program reveal that 61% of people studied at night after their daily work.

3. The arrival of electricity improves security (which links up with SDG 16). Not having to go far from the village to collect wood and water increases the security of those that are entrusted with these tasks (mainly children and women). It has also been demonstrated that the fact of having lighting at home and in the public areas in the village has a dissuasive effect on crime levels...

4. Having electricity in the village improves health (SDG 3) and water quality and sanitation (SDG 6) in many ways:

    • The reduction of biomass (wood) use for lighting and cooking avoids accidents at home caused by fire and reduces mortality from household pollution (we have to bear in mind that 4 million people around the world die prematurely from illnesses caused by the use of traditional stoves).

    • Having refrigerators allows to extend the length of time that food may be conserved and keep stocks of vaccines and medicines.

    • Water obtained using pumps requires less handling in the carrying process. It can also be treated with chemicals and filtered to improve water quality. Treatment networks for wastewaters can also be set up to improve sanitation. Apart from that, the availability of enough water allows to implement cleaner habits (showers, cleaning food, etc.).

5. Access to electricity supports women's empowerment (SDG 5): The time women do not need to devote to long journeys to collect water and wood can be used to enhance their education (see Figure 8. below, which is based on surveys conducted in the Brazilian *"Luz Para Todos"* project). It can also be used to start a business or be devoted to a job. Improved security levels thanks to lighting also benefits women widely.

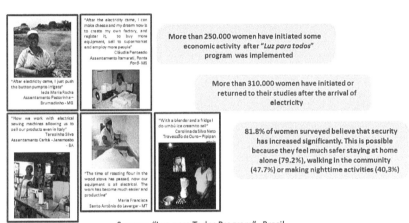

Source: "Luz para Todos Program". Brazil

Figure 8. - Examples *of* how the Brazilian *"Luz para Todos"* programme affected gender equality

6. Electricity enables economic development (SDGs 8&9). It creates new business possibilities. Electricity allows people to use specific tools or machinery that can be used to create manufactured products or services. It also extends the length of time that food can be kept in refrigerators. New electrical appliances (stoves, refrigerators, lamps, TVs, phones, computers, pumps...) create new specialised shops where they can be purchased and this creates jobs. Health centres also can be opened to meet new needs, etc. Performing maintenance on these new devices also creates the need for expert technicians (new jobs), which feeds into a virtuous circle.

The use of pumps means that the volume of water available to the community also allows for the development of industrial processes such as vegetable-cleaning or to supply the water needed for farms.

These new business opportunities allow to create trade activities between other rural areas.

An important collateral effect of access to electricity is that it allows for universal access to telephony and internet, with all the relevant effects that these two services have on all the SDGs.

In the surveys conducted in the Brazilian *"Luz para Todos"* project, there is proof of the effect that the arrival of electricity had on economic development:

i. 40% people improved their jobs:

ii. 93% of beneficiaries experienced an increase in their standard of living

iii. 82% enhanced their homes by gaining better access to services like the internet and new appliances for both domestic and industrial use.

7. When we take electricity to a town, we help attain SDG 10, because we end what is referred to as "double discrimination" compared to other citizens, which is defined as follows:

   (a) Lack of access to electricity, with all the implications this entails in terms of asymmetries in possibilities for growth...

   (b) ...and the consequent lack of access to the subsidies on electricity use that are received by other citizens in areas that do have an electricity supply.

8. The positive effect that access to electricity brings avoids rural flight and migration (which helps attain SDGs 10, 11 & 16, for instance). Economic growth roots citizens to territories and, in extreme cases, prevents mass-scale migration to cities, which in turn prevents social unrest that can turn into military conflicts, with additional migratory processes, as can be seen with the current refugee crisis in Syria (which, it must be said, has been identified in some studies as having initially been caused by climate change itself).

9. Access to electricity, if achieved through the generation of renewable energy (in both off-grid and on-grid solutions) helps to mitigate the effects of climate change and local pollution (SDGs 13, 14, 15). First of all, because of the switch in fuel when stopping the use of fossil fuels like kerosene or biomass (and avoiding the lock-in investment problem when new energy could come from new

plants powered by fossil fuels). Secondly, because using less wood/ biomass reduces deforestation, with the positive effects this has on climate change and also on reducing local pollution. All of these elements have indirect effects that help reduce ocean acidification (SDG 14).

10. Responsible consumption (SDG 12) is intrinsic to universal access to electricity. When people do not have any electricity at all, they place more value on it, and because starting from scratch means that the resource is very scarce, efficiency is part of the DNA of universal access projects.

11. It is obvious that all the developments described in the above paragraphs help attain the main SDGs: to end poverty (SDG 1) and to end hunger (SDG 2).

12. Moreover, if we accept that increasing access to 1.2 billion people is not a challenge that could be undertaken only by philanthropy or social action, or by public actors acting on their own, new business models and new forms of collaboration among different stakeholders are needed, through what are called PPPs (Public-Private Partnerships). This is where the connection arises between SDG 7 and the last SDG: No. 17.

Figures 9 and 10 below include some references that back up this interconnection that has been explained in the previous paragraphs, albeit with a little less passion!

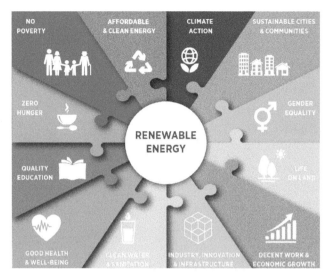

Figure 9. – Links between renewable energies and SDGs

Source: (IRENA, 2015)

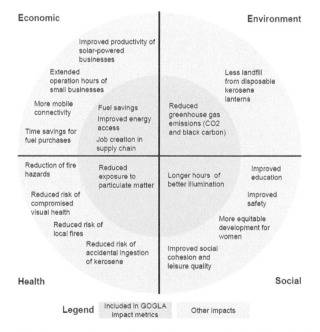

Figure 10. – First- and second-order impacts of off-grid solar lighting

Source: (Bloomberg New Energy Finance, 2016c)

Figure 10 reflects the first- and second-order impacts derived from the arrival of electricity in communities not connected to the grid. As we can see, these impacts go far beyond providing access to electricity; they imply a brand new set of opportunities to which the population would never have had access without the role of electricity as a catalyst.

4. KEY ELEMENTS IN UNIVERSAL ACCESS AND COMBATING CLIMATE CHANGE WITH ELECTRICITY PROJECTS: THE "SDG ACTORS"

4.1 Shared Value and business involvement in addressing the problems affecting humanity

Relatively small projects may be carried out by combining social action, official development aid funds and private or corporate philanthropy. However, providing 1.2 billion people with access to electricity and combating climate change with new technologies on a mass-scale is a challenge that cannot be addressed with those limited means. Massive economic resources are required to tackle this target. Therefore, it is important to search for scalable and stable solutions that can be sustained over time. Business models are required at what is referred to as the base of the pyramid (essentially isolated rural areas in developing countries) so as to attract investments to generate profits and, therefore, new resources that can be used for new investments, establishing a "virtuous circle" as described in a previous section of this article.

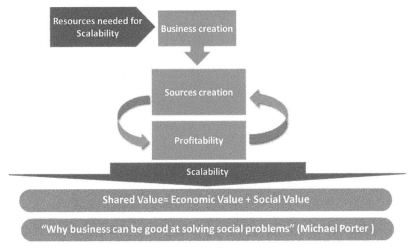

Figure 11. – The role of private enterprise in scalability

Source: (Sallé Alonso, 2015)

According to Michael Porter, this amount of resources can only be generated by creating specific businesses at the "bottom of the pyramid"[9], which are founded on profitability and not on social action or philanthropy. Bottom of the pyramid businesses, protected by sustainable frameworks defined by the public sector, will encourage private companies to contribute, maximising what is referred to as "shared value"[10].

The contribution of the private sector is crucial to the successful development of scaled solutions because the private sector has elements that enhance the viability of the projects:

- Technical expertise to implement projects (human resources, technical equipment, etc.);

- Corporate culture based on efficient resource management;

- Financial weight that enables them to obtain considerable resources for investment purposes;

- Incentives that enhance innovation in the technical and business areas;

- The ability to create added value by generating products and services and by minimising costs;

- Experience that gives a clear advantage in allocating risk management, which is vital in the process of obtaining capital on the financial markets to make the investments required by major electrification projects.

Even where internal social action is concerned, private companies are able to mobilise groups of volunteers (both working members of staff and retiree) who can put the value of their corporate expertise at the service of electrification projects in a supportive capacity.

Therefore, business involvement is important for tackling the big problems facing humanity.

4.2 Social involvement is good business (SDG-actors and social return)

Solving human problems is also important for businesses. Some people have the feeling – even inside companies – that investing in projects at the base of the pyramid is not worthwhile from the financial point of view and that it does not provide "actual EBITDA or profits". This is a huge mistake!

---

[9] (Porter, 2013)
[10] The sum of the economic value provided by the projects and the social value that is given to society

If nearly 200 countries, with the support of civil society, NGOs, multilateral actors (United Nations, World Bank...), the business community, etc. have approved the Agenda for Sustainable Development. Administrations in the various countries will develop legal frameworks and incentives to achieve their compromises (for instance, in the Paris Agreement). The pressure on companies that is exerted on an indirect basis by society/general public will come from four "SDG-actors", all of whom are stakeholders in companies:

- "SDG-employees": "Salary is not everything". People will be happy and proud to work in a company that backs and helps to fulfil the social agenda. They can focus their sensitivity to social support on projects run inside rather than outside the company, which, if properly defined, will be geared towards electricity skills, so as to maximise how this support is shared. This situation enhances the sense of belonging, which helps retain talent. Having happy and motivated employees improves productivity.

- "SDG-clients": "The price is not everything". People are appreciative of companies that are identified as SDG-advocates and will tend to buy their products, even if they are a little bit more expensive than the ones offered by non-SDG advocate competitors.

- "SDG-Administrations": "Having good relations with SDG-companies". Public Administration does not just consist of members of the public that are SDG advocates. As an institution, it is also an advocate in its own right, because it is one of the signatories of the United Nations Agenda for Sustainable Development and one of the 196 countries that signed the Paris Agreement. Therefore, it will have a better understanding of proposals coming from a SDG-advocate company. The lower pressure and fewer complaints it will receive from the general public regarding these SDG-advocate companies are not insignificant.

- "SDG-investors": "Higher dividends are not everything". Investors and capital markets are part and parcel of companies. They interpret the decisions made by Governments worldwide regarding the Agenda for Sustainable Development and combating climate change. In recent months, a lot of decisions coming from the capital markets increased the amount of pressure concerning the targets set out in the Paris Agreement, altering the relative risk premium between investment (or divestment) in companies with fossil fuel assets (which increase their risk premium) and those with a decarbonisation strategy for investing in renewables or divesting in CO2 emitting facilities that will see a reduction in their relative risk premium. Some examples: Moody's and Standard and Poor's announcing that they will include in their rating processes whether or not companies are aligned with the Paris Agreement; the biggest funds in the world are pulling out of companies that do not have de-carbonisation strategies and investing their money in companies that have strategies on mitigation and adaptation to climate change; the Rockefeller Foundation withdrawing its investments in new coal mining; the Governor of the Bank of England and the European Systemic Risk Board at the European Central Bank alerting against the potential risk of stranded assets for companies that fail to fulfil decarbonisation strategies, etc.). Therefore, SDG-advocate companies will attract more capital than their non-SDG advocate peers.

Hence, those that say the social return created by SDG-advocate companies does not provide actual EBITDA/ profits have not understood the world in which we are living. The virtuous circle is evident: not only do SDG-advocate companies feel better about helping to solve human problems but also this is good for all of their stakeholders.

4.3 The importance of public-private partnerships: SDG 17

As the main conclusion to the abovementioned points, we have to take steps to align, on the same side, those that are reluctant about the participation of the private sector in solving the problems presented in the Agenda for Sustainable Development (the 17 Sustainable Development Goals), and, on the other side, those that think that solving these problems does not create incentives for investing at the base of the pyramid. The solution to this lack of harmony is the creation of mutual trust, which is one of the reasons for including SDG 17: to create public-private partnerships.

4.4 The steps to be taken by SDG-advocates

Members of the public, Administrations, NGOs, Universities, Companies and Countries have to create a pathway for establishing their respective commitments to the SDGs. The Global Compact, a UN initiative, has defined four steps to be taken by all SDG-advocates:

a)   To acquire knowledge about the SDGs.

b)   Without setting any of them aside, to select the SDGs on which the person, company, Administration or country will be focusing.

c)   To present public commitments regarding the SDGs that have been selected for focused support.

d) To inform on a regular basis about the level of progress made with the commitments.

Following these principles, I will use as an example the way that my company, Iberdrola, is approaching the Agenda for Sustainable Development. Fortunately, many other interesting initiatives have been launched worldwide focusing on all of the SDGs. With all the humility that comes with acknowledging that there is still a long way to go, we have focused mainly on two SDGs, without neglecting the others, for which we have also adopted commitments):

a) SDG 13 (combating climate change), for which we have already officially presented the commitments to reduce our CO_2 intensity by 2020 (30% reduction compared to 2007 level)), by 2030 (50% reduction), and by 2050 (to be carbon- neutral). Iberdrola currently has an installed capacity of 25,000 MW in renewable energy technologies. It is a global leader in wind power production and has announced significant investments in these technologies, including offshore wind power facilities, in its strategic plan.

b) SDG 7 (universal access to modern forms of energy): apart from continuing investing in renewable energies, which is also part of SDG7, we presented a commitment of *bringing electricity to 4,000,000 people without access to this source of energy in emerging and developing countries by the year 2020*. This commitment was presented during the second edition of the United Nations Sustainable Energy for All (SE4ALL) Forum.

In order to implement this commitment, we developed a specialised line of action, called *"Electricity for All"*[11], which brings together all of the initiatives linked to universal access to electricity through an integral approach based on three pillars:

- To continue with its philanthropic and social action (through our team of volunteers and collaboration on NGO projects) through specific projects. Iberdrola has implemented initiatives such as the construction and commissioning of a solar farm in the village of Nyumbani in Kenya with the *Energy Without Borders* NGO (http://energiasinfronteras.org/es/proyectos), studies for the electrification of the refugee camps in Ethiopia with UNHCR, Philips, the Spanish Agency for International Development Cooperation (AECID), Acciona and an initiative

---

[11] http://www.iberdrola.es/reputacion-sostenibilidad/principales-iniciativas-indices/inicia-tivas/entorno-social/programa-electricidad-todos/

to provide electricity to a school in Rwanda in collaboration with MIT.

- To participate in projects launched by governments in the countries where Iberdrola has operations. Among others, this includes its participation in the ambitious Brazilian *"Luz para Todos"* programme, the largest universal access programme in the world, through which Iberdrola has provided access to electricity to over 2 million people in its distribution area.

- To participate in innovative business initiatives (aimed at the base of the pyramid) that demonstrate scalability and sustainability over time. For instance, Iberdrola has invested in the company *SunFunder* with a view to funding off-grid solar projects in emerging countries via its *Iberdrola Ventures-Perseo* corporate venture capital scheme.

5. CONCLUSIONS

- Access to modern forms of energy, as stated in SDG 7, is critical for enabling decent growth for a significant part of humanity. It also helps attain the other goals that make up the Agenda for Sustainable Development.

- Growth in demand has to be supported by sustainable consumption and productive models, in order to preserve the health of the planet. This is why SDG 7 also establishes goals for efficiency in consumption and investment in renewables.

- The solutions for the problems of humanity, such as the ones described in the Agenda for Sustainable Development, will not come only from philanthropy or social action, but from setting up scalable and sustainable business models at the base of the pyramid. This calls for mutual trust among stakeholders and tools such as public-private partnerships

- "SDG-advocate companies" are essential actors in fulfilling the Agenda for Sustainable Development.

- "SDG-advocate actors" (employees, clients and investors) will put pressure on companies to support the Agenda for Sustainable Development, punishing those that are not aligned with it (for instance in combating climate change) and rewarding companies that are SDG-advocates.

6. ACKNOWLEDGMENTS

The author would like to thank Antonio Erias Rodriguez and Miguel Ángel Rodríguez for their collaboration in drafting this article.

7. BIBLIOGRAPHY

Bloomberg New Energy Finance Off-grid solar market trends [Report]. - London : BNEF, 2016c.

Bloomberg New Energy Finance H1 2016 Global biomass market outlook. - London : BNEF, June 2016a.

Bloomberg New Energy Finance New Energy Outlook 2016 [Report]. - London : BNEF, 2016b.

International Energy Agency (IEA) and World Bank Sustainable Energy for All 2015—Progress Toward Sustainable Energy [Report]. - Wahsington DC : World Bank, 2015.

International Energy Agency (IEA) Energy Technology Perspectives [Book]. - Paris : OECD/IEA, 2016.

International Energy Agency (IEA) World Energy Outlook 2015 [Book]. - Paris : IEA/OECD, 2015.

IRENA REmap: Roadmap for a Renewable Energy Future, 2016 Edition [Report]. - Abu Dhabi : International Renewable Energy Agency (IRENA), 2016.

IRENA REthinking Energy: Renewable Energy and Climate Change [Report]. - Abu Dhabi : International Renewable Energy Agency (IRENA), 2015.

Porter M. Why business can be good at solving social problems [Video]. - Edinburgo : TEDTalks, 2013.

Sallé Alonso Carlos Universal access to electricity and its role n the fight against poverty [Book Section] // Energy and Geostrategy 2015 / book auth. Studies Spanish Institute for Strategic. - Madrid : Ministry of Defense, 2015.

AFTERWORD
The Tangled Webs of Energy Transition

LUIS FRANCISCO MARTÍNEZ MONTES[1]

1. A TANGLED WEB

As the previous contributions to this book demonstrate, over the past few decades, the transition towards a sustainable model of development respectful with the environment has gradually made its way to the forefront of the international agenda. During this period, most major governments, international organizations, members of an enlarging and active international civil society and quite a few major corporations have devoted considerable efforts to devise and implement strategies and policies aimed at coping with, *inter alia*, the social, economic and security implications of climate change and the dawn of a new global economic regime increasingly based on renewable sources of energy. At the multilateral level, these efforts have produced such remarkable, albeit far from perfect, outcomes as the 2030 Agenda and its 17 Sustainable Development Goals (SDGs) adopted in September 2015 and the Paris Agreement on Climate Change, adopted in December of the same year, both under the auspices and umbrella of the United Nations. The European Union, the US, the G77 +China and other actors have played a major role in the negotiations leading to those agreements that now are the basis of a multilateral framework for change. Most essays in this book deal with the repercussions of this process as different regional and national actors, as well as diverse industries and markets, try to strike a more balanced relationship between energy use and environmental sustainability. At this point, it is important to underline that those different initiatives at the national, regional and sectorial levels are now supposed to fit into a global architecture of governance aimed at implementing the SDGs and the Paris Agreement. This global architecture concerns all members of the international community for, as stated in paragraph 5 of the Declaration at the forefront of the 2030 Agenda:

> *"This is an Agenda of unprecedented scope and significance. It is accepted by all countries and is applicable to all, taking into account different*

---

[1] Spanish diplomat. The author contributes to this volume in his personal capacity.

national realities, capacities and levels of development and respecting national policies and priorities. These are universal goals and targets, which involve the entire world, developed and developing countries alike. They are integrated and indivisible and balance the three dimensions of sustainable development"[2].

But we should not come to the conclusion that this emerging multilateral network of norms and commitments is the whole picture. It rather constitutes one side of the story, the one driven by cooperation. We must not forget, though, that the other side is still driven by geopolitical and economic competition. Willingly or not, States and other actors are bound together in this sustainable agenda because they face similar threats and challenges posed by climate change and diminishing non- renewable energy resources; but many of them are also motivated by the opportunities offered by renewable sources of energy and their related technologies when it comes to obtaining advantages over their competitors and rivals. In an era of globalization, cooperation and geopolitical competition are intertwined in a manner that is difficult to be unbound, even for analytical purposes. Playing at the same time the cards of energy security – i.e. by using energy as a geopolitical tool- and environmental and economic sustainability is a new normal. For instance, since 2014, the US and the EU were busy imposing sanctions on Russian fossil-oriented firms because of Moscow's actions in Crimea and Eastern Ukraine while their respective official delegations were negotiating COPS 21 and the 2030 Agenda and jointly steering the direction of the global energy sector towards a low-carbon future, at least on paper. Other major oil and gas producing countries were also actively trying to influence those multilateral negotiations - and ultimately adopting their outcome- while shoring up their positions in the same fossil fuels markets that are supposedly marked for downgrading in the not so distant future[3]. We should not be surprised by this apparent duplicity. We live, after all, in a world made up of tangled webs weaved not by Shakespearian witches but by human agency. The domains of energy security and environmental sustainability are no exception: everyone is hedging their bets. While the new framework of governance that emerged in 2015 sets up the stage for collaborative endeavors aimed at achieving the SDGs and reducing carbon emissions, it will continue to co-exist with the highly competitive game of energy geopolitics for the foreseeable future. In fact, renewable sources of energy are liable to be subject to a similar interplay of cooperation and competition as it is currently being the case with fossil fuels. Actually, the

---

[2] Paragraph 5 of the Declaration in Transforming Our World: The 2030 Agenda for Sustainable Development. Accessible in https://sustainabledevelopment.un.org/post2015/transformingourworld

[3] See Pascual, Carlos, *The New Geopolitics of Energy*, published by Columbia/SIPA, September 2015.

geopolitics of renewable energy is bound to be even more complicated as these sources are more widely distributed than oil and gas. Therefore, the current configuration of the carbon- based energy markets along well-known supply, transit and demand countries will most probably be turned upside-down. Old and new players will be able to position themselves along all the value chain as, simultaneously, producers, consumers and distributors of solar, wind, tidal or biomass sources of energy. Besides, since electricity is the main carrier of primary renewable sources of energy, access to and control of the electricity grids, both at the local, national and regional levels, will be of the essence. As it will be equally important to master the storage capacity to face potential shortages or irregularities in the flow of, say, solar or wind energy supplies, particularly at times of peak-demand[4]. Concomitantly, let us not forget that many technologies currently instrumental both for the production and storage of renewables are dependent upon rare earth elements like the neodymium used in wind turbines or the lithium found in electric car batteries. Now, it happens that most of those rare earth materials are more concentrated in a handful of locations than fossil fuels ever were. In fact, it is estimated that 95% of those strategic elements are currently produced in just one country, China, therefore giving Beijing the upper hand in this strategic market for the time being. As a reminder, in September, 2010 China stopped the flow of rare earth materials to Japan as a punitive sanction when Japan detained a Chinese fisherman in waters disputed by both countries[5].

Thus, a reasonable assumption based on the above considerations is that the energy transition whose birth pains we are witnessing is not going to do away with old-fashioned power politics over the control of energy resources, technologies and markets, be them renewable or not. Beneath the emerging multilateral framework facilitating the transition to a more cooperative energy and climate regime, a Great Game for Renewable Resources and Technologies is already in the making. It is a new Great Game involving a relatively different set of actors playing over a novel chessboard but, unfortunately, there is a high risk that those very same actors will end up inheriting entrenched patterns of behavior from the old, though still ongoing competition for the control of limited fossil fuels.

2. A COGNITIVE TRANSITION

For this behavior to change and thus for avoiding that a world of low (or no) carbon energy would end up resembling its unsustainable predecessor, something else must change. A cognitive transition is as

---

[4]   See Paltsev, Sergey, *The Complicated Geopolitics of Renewable Energy,* Bulletin of the Atomic Scientists, Vol.72. Iss. 6, 2016.
[5]   See Minter, Adam, *The Geopolitics of 17 Very Obscure Minerals,* Bloomberg View, January 12, 2015.

essential as the energy transition now underway. Ultimately, we will need to dispense with the prevalent fragmented and competitive approach to the complex interplay between energy, security and the environment and start adopting a more comprehensive and evolutionary attitude to these interrelated topics. Instead of being based on geopolitical premises, a new global strategy for energy security and environmental sustainability underpinning the 2030 Agenda and the Paris Agreement could import some of its basic tenets from the field of "Planetary Ecology". In fact, some proponents of this emerging and promising field of study are already building a process- based methodology derived from the understanding of the Earth as a single system where energy flows and social evolution, together with the environment, are addressed as co-evolving, mutually reinforcing (instead of mutually disruptive) factors in the equation for maintaining and improving the conditions for life and human progress in our shared planet[6].

This process- based approach is based on the following sequence as known in energetics and ecology studies (see Box1):

Box 1

A Neutral, Process-based Approach to Energy, Evolution and the Environment:

Energy from the environment (specially renewable energy) ▶ when properly captured and transformed creates and maintains order and increases the mass and complexity of living organisms (including human communities) ▶ Energy waste produced in the previous process get backs into the environment ▶ Part of the waste is dissipated as entropy while another part is recycled and fed back into the process either naturally or by using human- made clean technologies ▶ the outcome when all things being equal is as follows: energy keeps on flowing, the environment is sustained and organismic and social evolution continues its path.

As king Solomon said, "*Nihil novo sub sole*": there is nothing new under the sun. For most of human history politically organized communities have mastered increasing amounts and flows of energy in order to built and manage larger and more complex societies and productive systems within an evolving environment. This pattern seems to be a consequence of a well- known biological law formulated in 1925 by Alfred Lotka: the law of

---

[6] Wilkinson, David M., *Fundamental Processes in Ecology. An Earth Systems approach.* Oxford University Press, New York. 2006.

maximum energy[7]. This law stipulates that evolution tends to increase the total mass and complexity of a living system and therefore the amount of energy consumed by the whole of the organic world. As Vaclav Smil puts it, *"human dependence on ever higher energy flows can be seen as an inevitable continuation of organismic evolution"* [8] following Lotka's Law.

Unfortunately, during the Geopolitical Era in which we are still immersed, the interrelationship between energy, security and the environment has been mostly considered as a competitive game. Within the conventional geopolitical paradigm (see Box 2) the more energy a particular polity would consume, the less would be available for other communities and the most damaging the consequences for the environment would be. Security-wise, the increasing competition for limited and even declining energy resources would increase the likelihood of inter-state and intra-state conflicts. Thus, the compound effect of an ever expanding and usually inefficient use of energy and the shock caused by wars and other human-made catastrophes has provoked major environmental degradation to the extent that entire civilizations have collapsed in the past as a result[9].

Box 2

The Geopolitical Paradigm

Limited energy from the environment ▶ is competitively captured and consumed by a restricted number of organisms (including human societies) to the detriment of the rest ▶ Energy is mostly used in an inefficient way, improperly recycled and released back into the environment as polluting waste ▶ Energy stocks decline and the environment irremediably suffers▶ Living organisms (including human societies) increase their strife for survival in a world of diminishing resources ▶ the outcome (s) all things being equal can be either a) consumption of energy is drastically reduced or halted. As a result, organismic and social evolution stops and/or regresses as the only way for the environment (and for usable energy stocks) to recover; or b) the competition for limited energy continues unabated, conflict prevails and the environment is irremediably damaged leading to a final catastrophic event.

---

[7]   Lotka, Alfred J. "Contribution to the Energetics of Evolution". Proceedings of the National Academy of Science, nº 8, 1922. Pags. 147-155.
[8]   Smil, Vaclav, *Energy in World History*. Westwiew Press, Colorado. 1994.
[9]   Pointing, Clive, *A New Green History of the World. The Environment and the Collapse of Great Civilizations*. Vintage Books, London. 2007.

The task that we have ahead of us is transitioning from Box 2 to Box 1. As said, in doing so, we will have to overcome the negative mood currently prevailing in most academic and political discourses when it comes to linking our increasing energy consumption and energy dependency –be it from traditional or renewable sources- with more geopolitical competition, decreasing security as well as with inevitable environmental degradation in a seemingly unbreakable vicious circle.

Part of the explanation for the prevailing negativity is due to the tendency to over- emphasize the security dimension as a kind of zero-sum game when dealing both with energy issues – thus we constantly talk about "energy security" in a tone reminiscent of the "scramble for resources" of past centuries- and the environment. As a result there is an unremitting trend towards an excessive "securitization" of energy and environmental matters with evident policy planning and implementing reverberations. Just a cursory glance at the flurry of national energy and environmental security strategies being adopted around the world can give us an idea of the kind of mentality still prevailing in this transitional era[10]. There is no serious regional or global player lacking one or several of those strategies whose contradictory goals and means, if acted upon at the same time, could lead us to a total conflagration. In a nutshell, if for instance, as it is actually the case, the European Union deems it vital to reduce its energy dependency from Russia while Russia considers access to European Union markets as instrumental for its growth and survival as a great power or, if say, several countries strife to preserve the Arctic as a natural sanctuary where energy exploitation is forbidden whilst others are launching a "race for the resources of the Arctic" taken advantage of the former´s "ingenuity", then we are bound for serious trouble. In fact, these conflicting national and regional strategies are unfolding while its main protagonists are allegedly devoted to achieving the lofty goals contemplated in the 2030 and Paris Agendas. Something, apparently, does not match here. We need to avoid that the contradiction between an emerging global governance framework for sustainability and the ongoing deployment of national and regional energy security and environmental strategies widens and deepens. What is required is a comprehensive and shared energy and environmental security strategy that bridges that gap. This is the task we have ahead of us and should be the topic for an urgent discussion among national strategists and decision makers, stakeholders in the global architecture for sustainability and the members of the scientific community involved in developing a holistic view of human and planetary

---

[10] See Kalicki, Jan H. (editor), *Energy and Security: Strategies for a World in Transition.* Edited by Woodrow Wilson Center Press / Johns Hopkins University Press; second edition (October 1, 2013).

evolution, the uses of energy and the preservation of our precious and fragile environment.